Free Speech in Indonesia

This book discusses the practice of free speech and its limitations – defamation and hate speech – in the context of Indonesia.

Focusing on several legislations, mainly in the Indonesian Criminal Code (KUHP) and the Information and Electronic Transaction Law (The ITE Law), the analysis centers on defamation and hate speech and how public interest defense is implemented in such limitations. The book discusses free speech in Indonesia through historical context and legal framework, both national and international. Detailed analyses of laws and case studies are provided, and the author examines key judicial decisions in defamation and hate speech cases that occurred in offline and online realms. The book demonstrates that Indonesia has ratified international human rights frameworks but that democracy in Indonesia has been declining in recent years, particularly due to the restrictions on free speech imposed by laws, which has resulted in a significant increase in cases involving free speech limitations.

Offering a much-needed analysis of free speech and its implementation in Indonesia, this book will be of interest to academics studying Southeast Asia, Indonesia, Human Rights, Media Law, and Law in Asia.

Eka Nugraha Putra is a Research Fellow at the Centre for Trusted Internet Community – National University of Singapore. His research includes criminal law, cyber law, media law, human rights, and free speech.

Routledge Contemporary Southeast Asia Series

The aim of this series is to publish original, high-quality work by both new and established scholars on all aspects of Southeast Asia.

Planning Indonesia's New Capital City
Behind Nusantara
Delik Hudalah

The Literature of Brunei
History, Culture, and Challenges
Edited by Ooi Keat Gin and Kathrina Mohd Daud

War Memorialization and Nation-Building in Twentieth-Century Southeast Asia
John Lee Candelaria

The Urban Vernacular in Southeast Asia
Settlement as Serendipity
Edited by Nor Zalina Harun and Shireen Jahn Kassim

Material Cultures in Southeast Asia
Objects in Context
Edited by Sabine Chaouche

Digital Diplomacy in Indonesia's Foreign Policy
Albert Triwibowo

Free Speech in Indonesia
Legal Issues and Public Interest Litigation
Eka Nugraha Putra

For more information about this series, please visit: www.routledge.com/Routledge-Contemporary-Southeast-Asia-Series/book-series/RCSEA

Free Speech in Indonesia

Legal Issues and Public Interest Litigation

Eka Nugraha Putra

Routledge
Taylor & Francis Group
LONDON AND NEW YORK

First published 2025
by Routledge
4 Park Square, Milton Park, Abingdon, Oxon OX14 4RN

and by Routledge
605 Third Avenue, New York, NY 10158

Routledge is an imprint of the Taylor & Francis Group, an informa business

British Library Cataloguing-in-Publication Data
A catalogue record for this book is available from the British Library

Library of Congress Cataloging-in-Publication Data
Names: Putra, Eka Nugraha, author.
Title: Free speech in Indonesia : legal issues and public interest litigation / Eka Nugraha Putra.
Description: Abingdon, Oxon [UK] ; New York, NY : Routledge, 2025. | Series: Routledge contemporary Southeast Asia series | Includes bibliographical references and index.
Identifiers: LCCN 2025001762 (print) | LCCN 2025001763 (ebook) | ISBN 9781032661483 (hardback) | ISBN 9781032661490 (paperback) | ISBN 9781032661544 (ebook)
Subjects: LCSH: Freedom of speech--Indonesia.
Classification: LCC KNW2474 .P88 2025 (print) | LCC KNW2474 (ebook) | DDC 342.59808/53--dc23/eng/20250118
LC record available at https://lccn.loc.gov/2025001762
LC ebook record available at https://lccn.loc.gov/2025001763

ISBN: 978-1-032-66148-3 (hbk)
ISBN: 978-1-032-66149-0 (pbk)
ISBN: 978-1-032-66154-4 (ebk)

DOI: 10.4324/9781032661544

Typeset in Times New Roman
by SPi Technologies India Pvt Ltd (Straive)

To my mother, my mother, my mother.
For all the love and inspiration for being consistent and resolute.

Contents

Tables

Table of Cases

Table of Legislations

International

Indonesia

Foreword

The question of what speech can legitimately be prohibited in a democratic society is as much a political as a legal question. For countries in transition, this has always been a particular challenge – balancing aspirations for freedom and openness against the need to maintain order and stability. Now that digital communication transcends national boundaries and the public sphere is increasingly mediated through electronic platforms, the legal frameworks governing freedom of expression in one country must also situate themselves in a global context.

Indonesia offers a fascinating case study for these tensions: decades into a democratic transition that began with the fall of President Suharto in 1998 and the rise of *Reformasi*, it now rides a technology wave with a highly connected and digitally savvy population. Eka Nugraha Putra's *Free Speech in Indonesia: Legal Issues and Public Interest Litigation* provides a close study of the evolving legal approach to free speech in Indonesia, also offering larger lessons about how such issues may not reflect an inexorable path to openness and freedom.

Indonesia's diversity also makes it a compelling case study in the interplay between legal frameworks, societal values, and the evolving concept of free expression. Historical legacies, conflicting statutes, and the tension between safeguarding public order and protecting individual rights create a complex legal landscape. The book seeks to offer clarity in unpacking these complexities.

The book methodically analyses free speech in Indonesia through historical, domestic, and international lenses. The author's examination of the legal framework – from the Indonesian Criminal Code (KUHP) and its recently amended provisions to the Information and Electronic Transactions (ITE) Law – provides readers with a granular understanding of how statutory limitations on free speech, such as defamation and hate speech laws, have evolved and are applied. Furthermore, the integration of international human rights norms, particularly through the lens of the International Covenant on Civil and Political Rights (ICCPR), allows for a nuanced critique of Indonesia's compliance with global standards.

The public interest defense provides a foil for examining limit cases that have tested Indonesia's courts as they work through cases in online and offline contexts. This jurisprudence must navigate local sensibilities as well as global norms and practices.

Structured as a textbook, *Free Speech in Indonesia* will be an essential resource for law students and professionals seeking to deepen their understanding of free speech issues in Indonesia. Yet, the book's relevance extends beyond academia. Policymakers, activists, and legal practitioners will find in its pages a critical resource for advocating reforms and fostering a more balanced approach to freedom of expression in Indonesia.

As the book's conclusion suggests, robust protection of free speech is not only a legal imperative but also a societal one. For Indonesia, the question is how to protect freedoms while addressing legitimate concerns about public order and harms. For the wider global community, this book offers lessons in how to navigate these tensions within diverse and dynamic societies.

Simon Chesterman, David Marshall Professor of Law, National University of Singapore

Acknowledgement

First and foremost, I am grateful for the gift of knowledge from Allah the Almighty, who led me to this incredible journey. Under Allah's blessing, I wish that this small contribution is beneficial to everyone who reads this book.

Some parts of this book are taken from my dissertation when I was an SJD student at Indiana University-Maurer School of Law in the United States. Therefore, I extend my gratitude to my dissertation supervisors, Austen Parrish and Gabrielle Goodwin, for their guidance and discussion during my research and writing, which was insightful and encouraged me to write this book. My deepest thanks also extend to Anthony Fargo and Joseph Tomain for their input and feedback during the early stages of my research.

I would also like to thank my friends, colleagues, and fellow SJD students for all the fruitful discussions and friendships; I learned a lot from them and am proud to become a larger community and global scholar. My doctoral study would also not have been possible without the support of my "new family" at the Graduate Legal Studies of Indiana University-Maurer School of Law. Therefore, I sincerely thank Lesley Davis, Will Schaad, Elizabeth Ryba, and Kaiya Grundmann, who made me feel at home far away from home.

The research journey of this book would become feasible with the generosity of Fulbright, which, through their funding, allowed me to pursue my degree and research the dissertation that was developed into this book. I would also like to express my gratitude for the generosity of AIFIS (American Institute for Indonesian Studies) for the support through the AIFIS-Luce Fellowship during the research of the book's theme.

While the main book's theme is about Indonesia, the writing process was a global journey. I want to thank you for the support of colleagues at the University Merdeka Malang, Indonesia, particularly Supriyadi and Setiyono, two former Deans during my tenure at the Faculty of Law, University Merdeka Malang, whose support has been invaluable throughout my academic career. I also had a great opportunity to work at Jindal Global Law School – O.P. Jindal Global University, which has greatly opened new opportunities and insights for me as an academic. I want to thank Akmal Handi Ansari Nasution, Dennis Agelebe, Nurhasanah Sudarshan, R. Sudarshan, Nizamuddin Ahmad Siddiqui, and also all my colleagues at the Centre for Human Rights Studies.

The writing of this book was concluded at the National University of Singapore, where I found another great place that offers a diverse and positive work culture. My involvement in the Digital Information Resilience project at the Centre for Trusted Internet and Community is significantly broadening my knowledge and perspective about research. In particular, I would like to thank Simon Chesterman for his support and especially for his generosity in writing the foreword of this book. Finally, I would like to thank Yustika Sari for the editing assistance with the early draft of the book.

On a personal note, I completed this book because of the love provided by my nurturing family. I want to thank my mother, and my father, for teaching me about hard work and diligence to complete the book. My sister, for the joy and laughter every time we meet. I and Z, thank you for your unwavering support and for providing a space where I feel loved and safe.

Glossary

Defamation Law offense which is an expression that is harmful to a person's reputation.

Dewan Perwakilan Rakyat The Indonesian Representative Council which serves as a legislative body, and its members are elected through a National Election every 5 years.

Hate Speech Law offense which is an expression that uses pejorative language and is discriminative to particular groups, usually related to identity factors such as religion, ethnicity, and nationality.

The ITE Law The Information Electronic and Transaction Law.

KUHP The Indonesian Criminal Code, stands for *Kitab-Undang-Undang Hukum Pidana.*

Mahkamah Agung The Indonesian Supreme Court, the highest judicial body in the Indonesian legal system, which can re-examine criminal and civil law cases as the final court of a case appeal.

Mahkamah Konstitusi The Indonesian Constitutional Court, the highest judicial body in the Indonesian legal system, but its main function is to review the constitutionality and dispute settlement of state power institutions and the result of the Indonesian regional and national elections.

Kementerian Komunikasi dan Informatika The Indonesian Ministry of Communication and Information, a government authority, was established in 2014 under the first term of President Joko Widodo. The Ministry's main task is in the sector of communication, information, and internet. Since October 2024, under the new administration of President Prabowo Subianto, the Ministry's nomenclature was changed to the Ministry of Communication and Digital.

Komisi Nasional Hak Asasi Manusia The National Human Rights Commission, which has the main task of promotion and protection of human rights.

Komisi Pemberantasan Korupsi The Indonesian Commission of Corruption Eradication, which has the main function of the prevention of corruption as well as corruption case investigation.

Komisi Pemilihan Umum The National Election Commission is an Indonesian government agency that organizes regional elections (for Mayor, Regent, and Governor) and national elections in Indonesia (for President and Vice President and parliament members).

Majelis Permusyawaratan Rakyat The Indonesian Consultative Assembly, a legislative body which is higher than *Dewan Perwakilan Rakyat*, and has constitutional powers such as the amendment of the Indonesian constitution and the impeachment of the President and Vice President.

Memorie van Toelichting The Elucidation Section of Legislation that was used during the Netherlands' colonization of Indonesia.

Normalisasi Kehidupan Kampus/Badan Koordinasi Kemahasiswaan A policy that was enforced from 1977 to 1978 during the regime of President Suharto to prevent political expression within student organizations and activisms.

Opportunity Principle An authority by a public prosecutor to indict or not indict the defendant in a criminal case due to the reason of public interest.

Orde Baru The political period which was popularly used during the 32 years of President Suharto's administration.

Orde Reformasi The political reformation that occurred in 1998 marked the civil society movement against the dictatorship of President Suharto, in which the President decided to step down from the Presidency.

POLRI *Kepolisian Republik Indonesia* or the Indonesian Police Force.

Reglement op de Rechterlijke Organisatie Regulation on the judicial system that was implemented during the colonization of Indonesia by the Netherlands.

Perppu The abbreviation for *Peraturan Pemerintah Pengganti Undang-Undang* which means a regulation in lieu of an Act that is usually passed by the President in an urgent matter.

Surat Izin Usaha Penerbitan Pers The permit required by the Ministry of Information (the former name of Ministry of Communication and Information) for any press company to run their businesses.

Surat Keputusan Bersama Joint Decree by several government agencies or government authorities.

Three-Step Test A principle to assess whether any free speech limitations are proper according to the international human rights framework, using the indicators of legality, legitimacy, and necessity.

Wetboek van Koephandel The Dutch Commercial Code, was implemented during the colonization of Indonesia.

Wetboek van Strafrecht The Dutch Criminal Code, which was implemented since the colonization of Indonesia. After the independence of Indonesia in 1945, it was translated to Indonesian as KUHP until 2026, when it is going to be replaced by the new and original Criminal Code by the Indonesian government.

WvS voor Europeanen The Dutch Criminal Code for Europeans.

WvS voor Inlander The Dutch Criminal Code for Indigenous and Far East.

1 Introduction

1.1 Definition of Free Speech

Commonly seen as a cornerstone of fundamental human rights, free speech has a long history as an essential element of democracy. Etymologically, the Greek language has three separate terms referring to freedom of speech: *eleutheros legein, isegoria*, and *parrhesia*[1]. Of these, it is the term *parrhesia* that specifically captures the essence of freedom, while the other two emphasize equality[2].

By the end of the fifth century B.C., *parrhesia* allowed for open discussion and criticism of the government by various people in Greece, which helped democracy to flourish. The right to express oneself was viewed as inseparable from the essence of democracy. The importance of free speech was reflected in citizens' participation in government, as well as their rights to vote, assemble, and associate. In their view, free speech needed to be protected and provided for people to ensure that people could fully exercise the latter rights[3].

Pharessia was also a method commonly employed by Socrates, a Greek philosopher. While *isegoria* refers to a more civic manner of speech, *pharessia* is characterized by its bold and candid form. In conversations, Socrates would often dismantle his conversation partner's arguments down to their core. Ironically, *pharessia*, as the practice of "speaking freely and boldly" was not always aligned with the state's vision of governance. Socrates' method was quite controversial. He was charged with "impiety" for his teachings, which did not acknowledge the state-sanctioned Gods, and with "corrupting the youths" through his influence on young people. Socrates was ultimately put on trial and sentenced to death by poison for his "crimes." He is recorded as the first martyr for free speech in history[4].

Even though free speech has been recognized since Ancient Greece as the right to speak freely, it was not until 1948 that free speech was formally acknowledged as one of the human rights. This recognition came with the adoption of the Universal Declaration of Human Rights (UDHR) by the United Nations General Assembly. Article 19 of the UDHR states the following:

DOI: 10.4324/9781032661544-1

> Everyone has the right to freedom of opinion and expression; this right includes freedom to hold opinions without interference and to seek, receive and impart information and ideas through any media and regardless of frontiers.

The UDHR may not be legally binding on states, but its recognition of free speech demonstrates that free speech is widely recognized as a human right with legal force in customary international law[5]. A more robust recognition of free speech as a human right was established in 1966 with the adoption of the International Covenant on Civil and Political Rights (ICCPR). As an international treaty, the ICCPR imposes legal obligations on states to adhere to the classic tripartite framework of human rights: Respect, protect, and fulfil[6].

Article 19 of the ICCPR states protection of freedom of expression without interference, but with some specific limitations. Which means that the ICCPR's provision offers more robust protection for free speech but does not make it absolute. The minimum standard set by the treaty aims to ensure vital protection of free speech that state parties should not abuse. Article 19, Section 3, allows restrictions on free speech when expressions harm the rights or reputations of others (e.g., defamation, hate speech), threaten national security and public order (e.g., terrorism, riots), or jeopardize public health or morals (e.g., obscenity). However, these restrictions must meet a three-part test: They must be provided by law, serve a legitimate aim, and be necessary in a democratic society.

As an international human rights treaty, the ICCPR must be ratified by countries that choose to be bound by it. Once a state ratifies the treaty, it is obligated to comply with its provisions and adopt them into its domestic law. As of 2022, 173 States have ratified the ICCPR.

The existence of the ICCPR underscores the importance of free speech for the international community. Even though each state can regulate free speech through its domestic laws, a minimum standard agreed upon globally is necessary. In addition, even in states that are not democratic, free speech should be justified.

Many scholars have justified the importance of free speech. Douglas Fraleigh and Joseph Tuman pose four key reasons for freedom of speech protection: (1) it is vital to our system of self-government, (2) it facilitates the discovery of the truth, (3) it promotes individual dignity and self-worth, and (4) any regime for speech control would be unworkable and deleterious[7].

The justification for self-government is in line with the concept of democracy, where people hold the ultimate control over the government. This forms the basis for the first reason to protect freedom of speech. Therefore, the flow of information and people's right to access it should not be barred by law. As Alexander Meiklejohn notes[8], democracy cannot be achieved if there is a power that manipulates information and oppresses criticism. He illustrates this with the concept of a town hall meeting, where community members gather to discuss public interests, and everyone who attends has an equal right to express their thoughts and opinions[9].

Equality means that there should be no barriers to the expression of ideas. If an expression is offensive, it should be countered by another expression, rather than through state intervention via criminal law. Equality among members of society also indicates that they hold the ultimate power to decide their own fate. For this to occur, citizens should have equal access to information and the freedom to express their ideas.

John Stuart Mill developed one of the classic theories of free speech. As a philosopher, Mill is well-known for his notion of utilitarianism, which argues that human beings always seek and evaluate actions based on their potential consequences or benefits. Mill emphasizes that pleasure and freedom from pain are the only things desirable as ultimate goals for each individual's actions[10].

Regarding free speech, Mill's work entitled *On Liberty* posits that pain can result from suppressing expressions related to historical, scientific, theological, philosophical, political, and moral topics[11]. However, Feinberg's analysis suggests that the expression of opinions can also potentially harm others, such as through defamation and sedition[12]. Defamation involves an expression that attacks another individual's reputation, including that of public officials, while sedition refers to conduct or speech that potentially incites attacks against the authority of a state.

Therefore, the potential to harm others sets the limits of free speech. When one person's exercise of freedom conflicts with another person's right to avoid harm, it helps define the boundaries of free speech. In this regard, there is a substantial difference between conventional public spheres and the internet, as the internet is largely controlled by private parties[13]. These private internet companies act as online intermediaries, which can intervene to address any online harassment by revoking a user's anonymity or removing abusive speech that violates community guidelines[14].

If the goal of protecting freedom of speech is to discover the truth, the question arises whether communicating that truth to a community is worth potentially harming an individual. This debate would not exist if there were a clear scope on the limits of free speech.

The third justification for free speech, according to Fraleigh and Tuman, is to promote individual dignity and self-worth. As previously mentioned, free speech ensures that everyone has equal rights, particularly in articulating and expressing their thoughts. This freedom allows ideas and information to flow freely. If individual equality is compared to a town meeting, the flow of ideas within a community is often referred to as the "marketplace of ideas" metaphor. With the advances in technology, such as the internet, today's marketplace of ideas has become very crowded, and the exchanges of ideas now include a much greater variety.

The current developments in society and technology present significant challenges, sparking debates on how to properly regulate speech. While strict speech controls may seem to conflict with Fraleigh and Tuman's fourth justification – that strict speech controls would be ineffective and harmful to society – some form of regulation is still necessary. The goal should be to distinguish between true and false information and between better and worse opinions, without relying on coercive government power[15]. By making these distinctions, citizens, as the rulers of a state, can essentially provide political decision-making for their community[16].

One way to distinguish between true and false information is to consume information from credible media, and in a broader context, from the press. Therefore, freedom of the media is essential, as reflected in Article 19 of the ICCPR, which includes two key dimensions: (1) the right to impart information and opinions, and (2) the right to seek and receive information[17]. The first dimension is what underpins press freedom. However, in the digital age, the internet has created a lot of opportunities for anyone to impart information. As a result, the press, including both professional journalists and ordinary citizens, has the same right to seek and impart information to the public. Nevertheless, press independence may be undermined when disseminating correct and accurate information to the public, as the essential value of information dissemination is transparency. Transparency is required in government-citizen relations, as it leads to accountability and other good governance principles while ensuring that citizens' rights are not violated.

1.2 Overview of Free Speech in Indonesia

According to Article 1 of the 1945 Indonesian Constitution, Indonesia is a democratic country based on people's sovereignty, with governance by the Indonesian People's Consultative Assembly (*Majelis Permusyawaratan Rakyat-MPR*). The principle of democracy is important as it allows people to self-govern, which means that people can exercise their rights and obligations in society without unnecessary interventions, including from the government. The government's role is to facilitate citizens in exercising their rights. Free speech protection is a crucial aspect of self-governance and is closely connected with democracy. The more ideas and opinions are expressed, the more people are exposed to diverse ways of managing their lives in society. Free speech ensures that both citizens and the government have equal rights to express themselves because it is a fundamental element of democracy[18].

Unfortunately, this is not always the case in Indonesia. For example, during the COVID-19 outbreak, the detention of individuals criticizing the government's COVID-19 mitigation reflects how Indonesia's law curtailing free speech can lead to a flawed democracy[19].

Indonesia has been independent from colonization and a free country since 1945, but significant political changes were not achieved until the political reforms in the late 1990s. During the 1998 reformation, the legal system underwent significant changes as the House of Representatives revised many critical statutory provisions and enacted new ones[20].

Free speech in Indonesia is regulated under the 1945 Indonesian Constitution, the 1998 Freedom to Expressing Opinion in Public Spaces Law, the Human Rights Law Number 39 of 1999, the Criminal Code, and the 2008,

2016, and 2024 Information and Electronic Transaction (ITE) Laws. While all these laws regulate free speech in Indonesia, the first three bills provide a general framework. Most free speech cases in Indonesia stem from violations of the Criminal Code and the ITE Laws, which are the main focus of this book.

Free speech is protected under Article 28 and Article 28 Section E of the Indonesian Constitution. The first provision outlines the general dimensions of free speech, including the rights to assembly, association, and expression through spoken and written forms. Meanwhile, the latter provision, enacted through an amendment in 2000, further emphasizes the protection of free speech. However, the Constitution does not specify the scope of unprotected speech or outline any restrictions that can be enforced to limit free speech.

The 1998 Freedom to Expressing Opinion in Public Spaces Law was passed after Indonesia's political reformation in 1998. The 1998 Reformation Order marked a historic turning point for Indonesians, ending 32 years of the authoritarian regime under Suharto's presidency. Even though this 1998 Act builds on the free speech protection in the 1945 Constitution and offers a broader framework for free speech, it primarily regulates limited aspects of free speech, such as the procedure for getting a permit to protest in a public space. The Act is more of an administrative guideline that the public could refer to during the various protests that emerged during the 1998 political reformation. The provision regarding punishment is not about free speech limitation, but about the unpermitted rallies that can be dispersed by authorities, as well as criminal offenses for obstructing permitted protests in public spaces by other parties[21].

Another law passed after the 1998 political reformation is the Human Rights Law Number 39 of 1999. This law provides more specific free speech dimensions, including the right to seek and impart information (Article 14), the right to disseminate opinion through various platforms (Article 23), the right to peacefully assemble and associate (Article 24), and the right to protest in public spaces (Article 25). While the Law does not provide specific sanctions for violations of these Articles, it facilitates the establishment of the Indonesian Human Rights Commission.

The Criminal Code was officially passed as a foundational criminal legislation in 1946. Because the Criminal Code is a takeover bill from the Dutch Criminal Code, which was used during the colonial period, numerous attempts to amend it have been made since the 1960s.

Many attempts to amend the Criminal Code have sparked controversies. The latest attempt in 2019 included a provision related to defamation toward the President, which was eventually revoked following a 2006 Indonesian Constitutional Court decision[22]. This provision was repealed because of its chilling effect on free speech. Unfortunately, the 2019 draft of the Criminal Code, which was previously rejected by the public, has resurfaced. Even though the Indonesian Council of Representatives (*Dewan Perwakilan Rakyat-DPR*) drafted a new amendment in July 2022, the latest draft does not include significant changes that adequately acknowledge public input. The Indonesian government has finally passed the new Criminal Code Act, but it will not be officially enforced until 2026, three years after its enactment[23].

The new Criminal Code will be enforced in 2026, meaning the 1946 Criminal Code remains in effect until then. This existing Code consists of criminal provisions toward free speech limitations such as defamation (Articles 310 and 311), hate speech (Article 157), and pornography (Article 282). Meanwhile, several changes in the 2023 Criminal Code include the addition of criminal offenses such as hoax dissemination (Article 263), blasphemy (Article 304), and defamation against the government (Article 240).

The current legislation in Indonesia governing the Internet is the ITE Law. Following Indonesia's recent political reforms, the debate over how far content and expression on the internet should be regulated is also driven by Indonesian internet users. Social media has changed the way people express their opinions. One notable change is how people are now able to engage in conversations with others worldwide. Additionally, information technology and social media facilitate the broad and easy dissemination of information. In cases of defamation, the more widespread the expressions, the greater the potential harm. Therefore, the law should keep pace with these developments, even amending laws to prevent further harm[24]. This harm is particularly likely to occur due to the widespread and easy dissemination of false information through the internet. This is exactly what has happened in the Indonesian context. A side effect of social media is the increase in allegedly defamatory online speech, which has consequently led to an increased risk of criminal prosecutions.

However, the laws in Indonesia are either obsolete or inadequate in protecting free speech. The ITE Law, for example, includes several forms of online speech that are punishable under criminal provisions, including defamation, hate speech, pornography, and threats[25]. All provisions related to online expressions under the ITE Law are ambiguous and fail to provide sufficient details on how they should be enforced[26].

The Information and Electronic Transaction Law Number 11 of 2008 (the ITE Law 2008) was partially revised by the Amendment of the Information and Electronic Transaction Law Number 19 of 2016 (the ITE Law 2016), but it did not revoke the earlier Law. Both acts are valid laws, and Indonesian legal enforcers should consider them together. The 2016 Law updated the definition of defamation and provided more detailed explanations of several acts that are regulated in the provisions. Ultimately, with the two acts, online defamation is regulated by both criminal and civil law, which means that it can be addressed in both areas.

The first amendment of the ITE Law did provide some changes, but the law still poses problems in criminalizing expression. For example, it only reduced the prison term for online criminal defamation from 6 years to 4 years under Article 27 Section 3.

In February 2021, during a meeting with police and military officials, President Joko Widodo (Jokowi) stated that the ITE Law should be amended, emphasizing that several articles with multiple interpretations should be revoked[27]. However, in June of the same year, instead of a proper amendment, a joint decree by the Ministry of Communication and Informatics, the Indonesian Police Chief, and the Indonesian Supreme Court was passed under the title "Guidelines of Implementation on Provisions of ITE Law" (the Joint Decree ITE Law). The joint decree was intended to serve as a guideline, especially for police and prosecutors investigating criminal cases under the ITE Law[28].

Despite some progress, such as emphasizing that research reports and insults should not be investigated as criminal offenses under Article 27 Section 3, the joint decree still fails to provide clarity on how the guidelines apply to private information that may contain defamatory expressions, such as text messages or e-mails. This is important because one of the main elements of defamation under the provision is that it must be made known to the public[29]. Moreover, the joint decree is not legally binding, as it is not a judicial product but simply serves to guide investigators.

The ITE Law was officially amended by the government in December 2023. However, the amendment process was mostly not open to the public, and the revised law still does not fully align with human rights principles. For example, the online hate speech provision in Article 28 Section 2 does not comply with the ICCPR and the Rabat Plan of Action[30].

The Indonesian government eventually passed the second amendment to the ITE Law through Law Number 1 of 2024. This amendment resulted from a lengthy process to revise the draconian law that civil society organizations had been advocating for over the years[31]. The second amendment aims to introduce several changes, including a reformulation of the criminal provisions for online defamation and online hate speech in Articles 27A and 28, respectively.

Given the issues with the current laws, it is essential to explicitly regulate public interest. Although the Indonesian Constitution suggests that limitations should be provided, such limitations are lacking. Therefore, the derivative legislation does not establish a clear minimum standard regarding the scope of protected and unprotected expressions.

The concept of public interest as a defense for free speech is recognized under international human rights frameworks and is included in Indonesia's Criminal Procedure Code. However, its implementation is rare and limited to specific criminal offenses. Furthermore, Indonesia, which follows a civil law system, relies primarily on legislation as its primary source of legal authority, unlike common law countries that depend on jurisprudence, where recent court decisions can amend a judicial decision regarding free speech. Therefore, there is both a challenge and an opportunity to amend the current free speech protections scattered across various laws, mainly to provide a clear definition of public interest and the scope of protected speech. In addition, Indonesia has ratified the ICCPR, which sets up the minimum guidelines for free speech limitations, including considerations of public interest. This principle provides the "margin of appreciation" recognized in international law[32].

1.3 Purpose of the Book

The main reason for writing this book is to significantly contribute to the discourse on free speech in Indonesia, addressing the lack of scholarly books on this topic in both English and Indonesian. While scholarship on free speech is more commonly found in broader Southeast Asian contexts, such as civil society or human rights, Indonesian scholarship mainly focuses on free speech limitations such as defamation and hate speech, regulated as the criminalization of online expressions in the ITE Law. However, cases involving free speech limitations have significantly increased in recent years, indicating a decline in Indonesian democracy. Therefore, a comprehensive written publication is needed to analyze and discuss free speech discourse as a whole.

Due to the lack of scholarship on free speech as a distinct discourse in Indonesia, this book aims to encourage a more focused discussion on the topic, especially in the context of defending the public interest. This writing coincides with the Indonesian government's plans to draft a second amendment to the ITE Law through the Ministry of Communication and Information. The Law, enacted in 2008 and amended in 2016 and 2024, has not significantly contributed to the reduction of criminal offenses regarding online expressions. Furthermore, the Joint Decree of ITE Law Guidelines for the law enforcers in 2021, which was intended to provide a more apparent implementation for police, prosecutors, and judges to apply the ITE Law, has proven ineffective. This is because the ITE Joint Decree is not a legal product and is, therefore, not legally binding.

This book offers an alternative approach to free speech and the defense of public interest. The ideas presented in this book are based on research, but any feedback is welcome. The aim of this book is to encourage a deeper and more focused discussion on free speech. As the famous metaphor goes, this book is one of the many ideas in the "marketplace of ideas."

Notes

1 Chris Berg, *In Defense of Freedom of Speech; From Ancient Greece to Andrew Bolt*, 8 (2012).
2 Chris Berg, *In Defense of Freedom of Speech; From Ancient Greece to Andrew Bolt.*
3 Emily Howie, 2018, *Protecting the Human Right to Freedom of Expression in International Law*, 13, doi https://doi.org/10.1080/17549507.2018.1392612.
4 Jacob Mchangama, *Free Speech: A Global History from Socrates to Social Media*, 23 (2022).
5 Centre for Law and Democracy, Briefing Note Series Freedom of Expression, 2 (2014).
6 Frederic Megret, Nature of Obligations, in 98 *International Human Rights Law 3rd Edition*, (Daniel Moeckli ed., et., al., 2017).
7 Douglas M. Fraleigh and Joseph S. Tuman, *Freedom of Speech in the Marketplace of Ideas*, 6 (1997).
8 Alexander Meiklejohn, *Free Speech, and Its Relation to Self-Government*, 22 (2012).
9 Alexander Meiklejohn, *Free Speech, and Its Relation to Self-Government*, 22 (2012).
10 John Stuart Mill, *Utilitarianism*, 7 (1979).
11 John Stuart Mill, *Utilitarianism*, 15.

12 Joel Feinberg, *Limits to the Free Expression of Opinion*, *in* Philosophy of Law: Joel Feinberg and Jules Coleman, 306 (1999).

13 Danielle K. Citron and Neil M. Richards, *Four Principles for Digital Expression (You Won't Believe #3!)*, 95, Wash. U. L. Rev. 1353, 1361 (2018).

14 Danielle Keats Citron, 2014, *Free Speech Does Not Protect Cyberharassment*, The New York Times (September 4, 2021) https://www.nytimes.com/roomfordebate/2014/08/19/the-war-against-online-trolls/free-speech-does-not-protect-cyberharassment.

15 Eugene Volokh, 2011, *In Defense of the Marketplace of Ideas / Search for Truth as a Theory of Free Speech Protection*, Virginia Law Review Vol. 97:3, 596.

16 Thomas I. Emerson, *The System of Freedom of Expression*, 6 (1970).

17 Kathryn Roberts, Freedom of Expression Includes a Free Internet, in *Net Neutrality*, Kathryn Roberts (Ed.), 63 (2019).

18 Arnold H. Loewy, 1993, *Freedom of Speech as a Product of Democracy*, University of Richmond Law Review, Volume 27 Issue 3, 428.

19 Fadhilah Fitri Primandari, 2020, *Indonesia's Democracy Is Flawed, But Do Enough People Care?* The Interpreter (June 8, 2022), https://www.lowyinstitute.org/the-interpreter/indonesia-s-democracy-flawed-do-enough-people-care.

20 Widodo Ekatjahjana, Kai Hauerstain and Daniel Heilman, 2017, *Regulatory Reform in Indonesia: A Legal Perspective*, 5, https://southeastasia.hss.de/download/publications/1_-_Regulatory_Reform_in_Indonesia_-A_Legal_Perspective.pdf.

21 Indonesian Act, 1998, art. 15 and 18, (Indonesia), Freedom to Expressing Opinion in Public Spaces Act (Indon.).

22 Reza Gunadha, 2019, *ICJR Kritik RUU KUHP yang tetap atur Pasal Penghinaan Presiden* [*ICJR Criticisize the Criminal Code Draft which still regulates the Article on Insulting the Presiden*t], suara.com (March 22, 2021) https://www.suara.com/news/2019/08/29/220052/icjr-kritik-ruu-kuhp-yang-tetap-atur-pasal-penghinaan-presiden?page=all.

23 Audrey Santoso, 2023, *KUHP Baru diteken Jokowi Resmi jadi UU, Berlaku 3 Tahun Lagi [The New Criminal Code has Officially Signed as a Law, Implemented in 3 Years]*, detik.com (Jan. 19, 2023) https://news.detik.com/berita/d-6495179/kuhp-baru-diteken-jokowi-resmi-jadi-uu-berlaku-3-tahun-lagi.

24 Mark Tushnet, 2020, *The Kids Are All Right: The Law of Free Expression and New Information Technologies*, Harvard Public Law Working Paper No. 21-09, 17.

25 Indonesian Act, 2016, art. 27, 28 and 29 (Indonesia), Information and Electronic Transaction Act (Indon.).

26 Titik Puji Rahayu, 2021, *The Uncertain Future of Online Free Speech in Indonesia*, The East Asia Forum (April 22, 2021) https://www.eastasiaforum.org/2021/04/02/the-uncertain-future-of-online-free-speech-in-indonesia/.

27 Nur Azizah, 2021, *President Jokowi Considering the to Revise ITE Law*, medcom.id (February 27, 2021) ihttps://www.medcom.id/english/national/9K5565aK-president-jokowi-considering-to-revise-ite-law.

28 Kominfo, 2021, *SKB Pedoman Implementasi UU ITE ditandatangani, Menko Polhukam berharap beri Perlindungan pada Masyarakat [Joint Decree on Guidelines for Implementation of ITE Law Signed, Coordinating Minister for Political, Legal and Security Affairs Hopes to Provide Protection to the Society]*. Kominfo.go.id (March 23, 2023) https://www.kominfo.go.id/content/detail/35229/skb-pedoman-implementasi-uu-ite-ditandatangani-menko-polhukam-berharap-beri-perlindungan-pada-masyarakat/0/berita.

29 Eka Nugraha Putra, 2021, *SKB UU ITE bawa Kemajuan, tapi Revisi tetap Mutlak dilakukan karena masih banyak Kelemahan* [*Joint Decree on ITE Law Brings Progress, but Revision is Still Absolutely Necessary Because There Are Still Many Weaknesses*], The Conversation Indonesia (August 12, 2022) https://theconversation.com/skb-uu-ite-bawa-kemajuan-tapi-revisi-tetap-mutlak-dilakukan-karena-masih-banyak-kelemahan-163499.

30 ICJR, 2023, *Catatan Singkat Draft Revisi Kedua UU ITE: Substansi Revisi Ke-2 UU ITE Alami beberapa Perubahan namun masih Menyisakan Perdebatan [Brief Notes on the Draft of the Second Revision of the ITE Law: The Substance of the Second Revision of the ITE Law Has Several Changes but Still Leaves Debate]*, icjr.or.id (September 11, 2023) https://icjr.or.id/catatan-singkat-draft-revisi-kedua-uu-ite-substansi-revisi-ke-2-uu-ite-alami-beberapa-perubahan-namun-masih-menyisakan-perdebatan/.
31 Nina A. Loasana, 2023, *Civil Groups Urge Broader ITE Law Revision from Lawmakers to Protect Free Speech*, The Jakarta Post (April 30, 2023) https://www.thejakartapost.com/indonesia/2023/03/29/civil-groups-urge-broader-ite-law-revision-from-lawmakers-to-protect-free-speech.html.
32 Frederic Megret, Nature of Obligations, 99.

Bibliography

Books

Meiklejohn, Alexander, *Free Speech and Its Relation to Self-Government* (Lawbook Exchange, New York, 2012).
Chris Berg, *In Defense of Freedom of Speech; From Ancient Greece to Andrew Bolt* (Institute of Public Affairs, Melbourne, 2012).
Douglas M. Fraleigh and Joseph S. Tuman, *Freedom of Speech in the Marketplace of Ideas* (St. Martin's Press, Boston, 1997).
Frederic Megret, Nature of Obligations, in *International Human Rights Law* 3rd Edition, (Daniel Moeckli ed., et. al., Oxford University Press, Oxford, 2017).
Jacob Mchangama, *Free Speech: A Global History from Socrates to Social Media* (Basic Books, New York, 2022).
Joel Feinberg, *Limits to the Free Expression of Opinion, in Philosophy of Law: Joel Feinberg and Jules Coleman (Eds)* (Wadsworth Thomson Learning, Belmont, 1999).
John Stuart Mill, *Utilitarianism* (Hacket Publishing Company, Indianapolis, 1979).
Kathryn Roberts, Freedom of Expression Includes a Free Internet, in *Net Neutrality*, Kathryn Roberts (Ed.) (Greenhaven Publishing, New York, 2019).
Thomas I. Emerson, *The System of Freedom of Expression* (Random House Publisher, New York, 1970).

Journals

Arnold H. Loewy, 1993, Freedom of Speech as a Product of Democracy, *University of Richmond Law Review*, Volume 27 Issue 3, 428.
Danielle K. Citron and Neil M. Richards, Four Principles for Digital Expression (You Won't Believe #3!), 95 Wash. *U. L. Rev*. 1353–1361 (2018).
Emily Howie, 2018, Protecting the Human Right to Freedom of Expression in International Law, *International Journal of Speech-Language Pathology*, doi: https://doi.org/10.1080/17549507.2018.1392612.
Eugene Volokh, 2011, In Defense of the Marketplace of Ideas / Search for Truth as a Theory of Free Speech Protection, *Virginia Law Review* Vol. 97:3.
Mark Tushnet, 2020, *T*he Kids Are All Right: The Law of Free Expression and New Information Technologies, *Harvard Public Law*, Working Paper No. 21–109.

Indonesian Legislations

Indonesian Act, 1998, art. 15 and 18, (Indonesia), Freedom to Expressing Opinion in Public Spaces Act Number 9 (Indon.).
Indonesian Act, 2016, art. 27, 28 and 29 (Indonesia), Information and Electronic Transaction Act Number 19 (Indon.).

Reports

Centre for Law and Democracy, Briefing Note Series Freedom of Expression (2014).

Internet

Audrey Santoso, 2023, KUHP Baru diteken Jokowi Resmi jadi UU, Berlaku 3 Tahun Lagi [The New Criminal Code has Officially Signed as a Law, Implemented in 3 Years], *detik.com* (Jan. 19, 2023) https://news.detik.com/berita/d-6495179/kuhp-baru-diteken-jokowi-resmi-jadi-uu-berlaku-3-tahun-lagi.

Danielle Keats Citron, 2014, Free Speech Does Not Protect Cyberharassment, The New York Times (September 4, 2021) https://www.nytimes.com/roomfordebate/2014/08/19/the-war-against-online-trolls/free-speech-does-not-protect-cyberharassment.

Eka Nugraha Putra, 2021, SKB UU ITE bawa Kemajuan, tapi Revisi tetap Mutlak dilakukan karena masih banyak Kelemahan [Joint Decree on ITE Law Brings Progress, but Revision is Still Absolutely Necessary Because There Are Still Many Weaknesses], The Conversation Indonesia (August 12, 2022) https://theconversation.com/skb-uu-ite-bawa-kemajuan-tapi-revisi-tetap-mutlak-dilakukan-karena-masih-banyak-kelemahan-163499

Fadhilah Fitri Primandari, 2020, Indonesia's Democracy Is Flawed, But Do Enough People Care? The Interpreter (June 8, 2022), https://www.lowyinstitute.org/the-interpreter/indonesia-s-democracy-flawed-do-enough-people-care.

ICJR, 2023, Catatan Singkat Draft Revisi Kedua UU ITE: Substansi Revisi Ke-2 UU ITE Alami beberapa Perubahan namun masih Menyisakan Perdebatan [Brief Notes on the Draft of the Second Revision of the ITE Law: The Substance of the Second Revision of the ITE Law Has Several Changes but Still Leaves Debate], icjr.or.id (September 11, 2023) https://icjr.or.id/catatan-singkat-draft-revisi-kedua-uu-ite-substansi-revisi-ke-2-uu-ite-alami-beberapa-perubahan-namun-masih-menyisakan-perdebatan/.

Kominfo, 2021, SKB Pedoman Implementasi UU ITE ditandatangani, Menko Polhukam berharap beri Perlindungan pada Masyarakat [Joint Decree on Guidelines for Implementation of ITE Law Signed, Coordinating Minister for Political, Legal and Security Affairs Hopes to Provide Protection to the Society]. *Kominfo.go.id* (March 23, 2023) https://www.kominfo.go.id/content/detail/35229/skb-pedoman-implementasi-uu-ite-ditandatangani-menko-polhukam-berharap-beri-perlindungan-pada-masyarakat/0/berita.

Nina A. Loasana, 2023, Civil Groups Urge Broader ITE Law Revision from Lawmakers to Protect Free Speech, The Jakarta Post (April 30, 2023) https://www.thejakartapost.com/indonesia/2023/03/29/civil-groups-urge-broader-ite-law-revision-from-lawmakers-to-protect-free-speech.html.

Nur Azizah, 2021, President Jokowi Considering the to Revise ITE Law, *medcom.id* (February 27, 2021) ihttps://www.medcom.id/english/national/9K5565aK-president-jokowi-considering-to-revise-ite-law.

Reza Gunadha, 2019, ICJR Kritik RUU KUHP yang tetap atur Pasal Penghinaan Presiden [ICJR Criticisize the Criminal Code Draft which still regulates the Article on Insulting the President], *suara.com* (March 22, 2021) https://www.suara.com/news/2019/08/29/220052/icjr-kritik-ruu-kuhp-yang-tetap-atur-pasal-penghinaan-presiden?page=all.

Titik Puji Rahayu, 2021, The Uncertain Future of Online Free Speech in Indonesia, The East Asia Forum (April 22, 2021) https://www.eastasiaforum.org/2021/04/02/the-uncertain-future-of-online-free-speech-in-indonesia/.

Widodo Ekatjahjana, Kai Hauerstain and Daniel Heilman, 2017, Regulatory Reform in Indonesia: A Legal Perspective, 5, https://southeastasia.hss.de/download/publications/1_-_Regulatory_Reform_in_Indonesia_-A_Legal_Perspective.pdf.

2 Historical Context of Free Speech in Indonesia

2.1 Pre-Independence Era

Historically, Indonesia was colonized by the Netherlands and Japan, and information on free speech during these periods is limited. As was common in colonized countries, many of the people's rights were either unfulfilled or taken away.

In response to the limited resources discussing free speech in particular, the focus can be slightly shifted to laws that were enforced during the colonial era, particularly under the Dutch colonial era, given the most prolonged invasion of Indonesia for 350 years. Despite the debatable timeline, as the name "Indonesia" had not yet been established, colonialization was more fragmented, with various kingdoms ruling over their respective provinces in different regions.

During Dutch colonization, at least two pieces of legislation were classified as "Basic Law," namely, *Burgerlijk Wetboek* (BW) and *Wetboek van Strafrecht* (WvS). BW is the Civil Law Code, while WvS is the Criminal Code. BW was originally a Civil Code of the Netherlands, but it was enforced in Indonesia during the colonial period when the region was known as the Dutch-East Indies (*Hindia-Belanda*). This territory, which was a nationalized trading post of the Dutch-East India Company, served as a hub for trade activities in Asia and initiated the Netherlands' colonization.

BW became Indonesia's Civil Code through a codification that outlined the laws to be enforced in the country. Other codified rules included *Reglement op de Rechterlijke Organisatie* (Regulations on the Judicial System) and *Wetboek van Koephandel* (Commercial Code), among others. BW focused on private law provisions, making it a Civil Code, because its provisions covered private law aspects such as natural persons, patrimony, and property law. However, in 1962, the Indonesian Supreme Court issued a Decree which stated that BW was no longer relevant to Indonesia as an independent country. The decree also noted that several provisions of BW were no longer valid as law, such as Article 284 Section 3 (Child recognition outside of marriage) and 1579 (Leasing agreement).

DOI: 10.4324/9781032661544-2

WvS, on the other hand, is a Criminal Code that was also enforced during Dutch colonization. Interestingly, when the Netherlands' constitution changed due to the shift from a monarchy to a parliamentary system, this change affected not only the Netherlands but also the Dutch-East Indies. Since 1918, WvS applied to two groups: *WvS voor Europeanen* for Europeans *and WvS voor Inlander* for indigenous people.

Several provisions regarding free speech are found in WvS. For example, Articles 186 and 187 of *WvS voor Europeanen* addressed defamation against state leaders (*aan gelstede machten*) and government institutions (*openbare lichament*). WvS also includes a specific explanatory section called the Elucidation Note or *Memorie van Toelichting* (MvT). In relation to Articles 186 and 187 of *WvS voor Europeanen*, MvT discusses two main issues: an accusation expressed through spoken or written form against various groups, such as supporters of liberal ideology and employer–employee relationships[1].

The second issue addressed in MvT on Articles 186 and 187 of *WvS voor Europeanen* is whether a legal entity, such as a corporation, company, or organization, can be defamed. MvT suggests that the defamation provisions were overly broad to be classified as a criminal offense and that the provisions are more appropriately enforced to defamation against individuals. Furthermore, WvS does not recognize a legal entity as a subject of law, a principle that ironically remained in place until the amendment of the Indonesian Criminal Code in 2023.

However, MvT on Articles 186 and 187 of *WvS voor Europeanen* does not address whether defamation provisions, particularly criminal defamation, violate free speech. This lack of explanation may be understandable, as the provisions were part of the Criminal Code enforced by the colonizers.

2.2 Post-Independence Era

After gaining independence on 17 August 1945, the Indonesian government started to address various aspects of state organization, including human rights. The initial step was drafting the Constitution. Article 1 Section 2 of the Indonesian Constitution 1945 clearly states that Indonesia is a democratic country. It states that the sovereignty lies in the hands of the people and is exercised through the Indonesian People's Consultative Assembly (*Majelis Permusyawaratan Rakyat*).

Initially, human rights were addressed in six Articles of the 1945 Indonesian Constitution, decades before the Constitution's first amendment in 2000. One aspect of human rights, namely, freedom of speech, is protected under Article 28 of the 1945 Indonesian Constitution. This article states:

> "Freedom to associate and gather, expressing ideas by spoken or written and so forth are regulated by laws."

Article 28 clearly outlines the need for legal regulations to protect expression and the various ways to channel it. It establishes that any limitations on freedom of expression should be prescribed by law. Furthermore, Article 28 F of the 1945 Indonesian Constitution states:

> "Everyone has the right to communicate and gather information to develop himself or herself and the society, also has the right to search, obtain, possess, save, articulate and disseminate information through any media available."

The Article provides a broad interpretation of free expression, including the right to access and share information. Historically, the freedom to associate and assemble in Indonesian practice has been considered part of the freedom of expression. In the past, the opportunity to gather and engage in a dialogue of opposing views with the government was forbidden, and those involved could be prosecuted for treason. Therefore, defining the right to gather and associate in Indonesia's constitution is as crucial as protecting freedom of expression itself.

One of the critical moments of free speech after independence occurred in 1965. The primary situation was not free speech per se but rather stemmed from an alleged treason by the Indonesian Communism Party (*Partai Komunis Indonesia*-PKI) on the night of 30 September 1965. The accusation against the party was affected by the public fear of its ideology and by concerns within the international community regarding the Cold War[2].

The tense political situation leading up to 1966, a year before President Sukarno's presidency was taken over by Suharto, affected the government's actions. It shaped how the government responded to the two competing ideologies of realist pluralism – one rooted in colonization and the other in unification[3].

One of the Indonesian government's reactions to the politically tense situation was the issuance of Law Number 1/PNPS/1965 on Freedom of Religion. This Presidential Decree was intended to serve as a cornerstone for religious tolerance. However, decades after the law was enacted, various abuses arose due to the vague definition of blasphemy. Furthermore, the provisions of the 1965 law were later used as the basis for Article 156a of the Indonesian Criminal Code about blasphemy, which regulates expressions of hostility and defamation against religion, particularly in cases where individuals are accused of no longer practicing a religion[4].

Many provisions in the Indonesian Criminal Code are problematic. In addition to the blasphemy provisions, defamation provisions also serve the interests of authorities. Criticisms are primarily due to the vagueness of the defamation provisions. For example, there is no clear distinction between defamation and a legitimate political opinion about the President's action[5].

After becoming President, Suharto's authoritarian regime exacerbated the issues with the already problematic and obsolete Criminal Code. One dimension of free expression that Suharto's government interfered with was the freedom to seek information. Suharto's policy involved censoring and banning several books for various reasons, such as criticism of the failure of his presidency and content related to the teachings of Marxism, Leninism, and Communism[6].

The book-banning policy was an action that complied with a Presidential Decree in 1963 (Law Number 11/PNPS/1963 on Subversive Activities). The Decree was issued during Sukarno's presidency, but Suharto took further action. The Decree was eventually declared unconstitutional through Law Number 26 of 1999, a year after the Reformation Order. Suharto's regime banned books and enforced several policies that curbed free speech. Through the Press Act of 1966, 70 newspapers were prohibited from being published and circulated[7].

The government repealed provisions that required special permits to establish a press company (*Surat Izin Usaha Penerbitan Pers*-SIUPP), which was enforced from 1984 to 1998 under the Decree of the Indonesian Minister of Information. This permit system faced criticism because it limited the freedom of the press and was used to censor media that opposed the government's view. *Tempo* was one of the media outlets that faced the government's censorship under the 1982 Press Law. In Tempo's case, the magazine was even shut down twice, in 1982 and 1994, under the New Order regime[8]. Both closures were attributed to alleged violations of journalism ethics codes.

The new Press Law eventually replaced the obsolete 1982 Press Law in 1999, a year after the political reformation. The 1999 law, still regarded as robust legislation, consists of several provisions aimed at addressing free press issues, emphasizing that the law should not be used to criminalize the press. For instance, the right of clarification under the Press Law is one of its most important provisions. It allows anyone who believes they have been defamed to publish a clarification or response. This mechanism is intended to protect a person's reputation by clarifying the issue through the same media outlet where it was originally published.

However, the "right of clarification" is rarely used in the Indonesian legal system. Instead, most people directly report defamation to the police, asserting that it violates Indonesia's criminal law[9]. While the Press Law was designed as a specific law to govern the press (*lex specialis*), it has not been applied to alleged defamation, which is more often prosecuted as a crime under the Indonesian Criminal Code (*lex generalis*).

Another example is the ban on college students associating with and joining organizations through Normalization of College Life/Body of College Students Coordination (*Normalisasi Kehidupan Kampus/Badan Koordinasi Kemahasiswaan*-NKK/BKK). This policy dismissed most of the college student organizations and reformed them into a single organization called *Resimen Mahasiswa* (Menwa), which was organized with military principles. Menwa was also formed to monitor student activism.

Many Indonesians, particularly legal scholars, recognized the chilling effect on free speech caused by the problematic Criminal Code. In 1963, during the First National Seminar on the Criminal Code, discussions began about drafting a new Criminal Code, considering that the existing one was a "legacy" from

Dutch colonization. Despite long-term efforts to amend it, the Criminal Code has not been completed. The obsolete Criminal Code remains the foundational criminal legislation in Indonesia's legal system, and even the Reformation Order, which marked a new regime, could not facilitate its revision.

2.3 Reformation Order and the Rise of Democratic Institutions

Indonesian society has finally been able to enjoy the right to create and express their ideas freely since 1998. Political speech has become easier to express in public across various platforms, as promised by the government. However, obstacles to free speech still exist in Indonesia.

After three decades under Suharto's authoritarian regime, one of the key obstacles that Indonesian society faces is waiting for the government to fulfil its promise of democracy and free speech. The 1998 political reform was still hampered by certain criminal provisions limiting freedom of speech, which clearly contradicts the 1945 Indonesian Constitution, whose ultimate goal is to protect free speech through its provisions.

Reforms in various aspects, primarily in political and legal aspects, catapulted Indonesia toward a new age, commonly called *Orde Reformasi* (Reformation Order). At the beginning of this new age, many believed that Indonesia would respect human rights more consistently and that the new government would be more committed to democratic principles than the previous ruling government before the Reformation Order.

One example is the 1998 political reformation, which introduced regional autonomy in Indonesia in 2001. Local governments were granted more power to regulate issues within their regions. Local authorities (municipal and district) gained the ability to pass more local sharia-based laws (*peraturan daerah* or *perda*), allowing them to introduce additional laws against prostitution, pornography, alcohol, and gambling[10], as these issues violate Islamic law, which is predominantly practiced by Indonesians. However, these laws aimed at regulating moral issues began to clash with artistic expression and were even sometimes applied excessively. The central government was unable to take definitive action to address the excessive number of laws and regulations that had been passed. Many of these local laws even reflected a similar spirit to that of "*Orde Baru*," or Decentralized Authoritarianism[11].

Despite the new laws intended to protect free speech and guarantee democracy, Indonesia still struggles to establish a fully free and democratic society. The promise of the Reformation Order for human rights protection has not yet been fully achieved. The reforms did not dismantle the existing oligarchic system, suggesting that the 1998 Reformation Order may have been merely a brief period of euphoria[12].

Article 28F was introduced as part of the Fourth Amendment to the UUD 1945, followed by legal reform in Indonesia. The Indonesian Council of

Representatives (*Dewan Perwakilan Rakyat-DPR*) passed the Human Rights Law Number 39 of 1999, which includes specific guarantees for free expression, as stated in Article 14 Sections 1 and 2, as well as Article 23 Section 2. A year earlier, the Freedom of Expression in Public Space Law Number 9 of 1998 was officially enacted. This law consists of a set of regulations governing the expression of ideas and opinions in demonstrations and protests, mainly when these actions are carried out in public spaces[13].

Article 9 of the Freedom of Expression in Public Space Law Number 9 of 1998 regulates four types of expression in public spaces: protests or demonstrations, convoys, general meetings, and free pulpits. The remainder of the Law mainly addresses how to prepare proper and appropriate expressions in public spaces[14].

The last chapter of the Law regulates sanctions for violators, which are primarily administrative in nature. However, Article 18 specifies criminal sanctions for those who use violence, as it states that threats of violence hinder a citizen's right to express an opinion in public spaces. While this provision aims to contribute to the protection of the right to free speech, ironically, this fundamental right has been violated numerous times in Indonesia, even by the government.

According to Freedom House – an organization that conducts research and advocacy on democracy, political rights, and human rights – Indonesia has made significant progress toward democracy since the fall of the Suharto regime in 1998, marking a substantial political reform[15]. Political rights are indeed protected and well-enforced, with General Election legislation providing opportunities for Indonesians to cast their votes. The latest democratic process in the form of the election was displayed in the National Election in April 2019. The results were released a month later, yet differing political views have sparked conflict and, at times, chaos. Unfortunately, law enforcement has responded with harsh measures to cope with this aspect of free expression[16].

Law enforcement's attempts to limit free expression through harsh measures have been apparent in Indonesian politics. Since the 2014 National Election, Indonesians have been polarized into supporters of the two presidential candidates: Joko Widodo, more popularly known as Jokowi, and Prabowo Subianto. The political battle between these candidates highlighted the Islamic and pluralist values espoused by each candidate's supporters. When the two candidates competed again in the 2019 National Election, the political polarization intensified.

Jokowi won in 2014 and ran for a second term in the 2019 National Election. Toward the end of the election process, while the Indonesian National Election Commission (*Komisi Pemilihan Umum*-KPU) was still counting all the votes, protests, both offline and online, emerged from Prabowo's supporters in many cities in Indonesia. These protests asserted that fraud had occurred during the

National Election. Unfortunately, a pattern[17] seems to have emerged, where internet content creators who slandered Jokowi as the current President were charged with various criminal acts, such as spreading hoaxes, defamation, hate speech, and even treason.

One of the treason cases raised questions. During one of the protests[18], a man yelled that he was ready to behead Jokowi. His action was recorded in a video, and his full statement was as follows:

> "From Poso, [I am] ready to behead Jokowi.... Jokowi, prepare to be slaughtered.... God willing," he said. The crowd around him responded with chants of "*Allahu Akbar*" (God is great)."

His statement never became a reality, as he made it spontaneously while engulfed in the euphoria of the protest[19]. According to Article 87 of the Indonesian Criminal Code, treason (*makar*) is considered a criminal act once there is an initial act that fulfils the intention or plan[20].

The Indonesian civil liberty index is also in an alarming state, as indicated by several laws passed by the government that curb freedom of speech rather than protect it. In August, the Ministry of Communication and Information (*Kementerian Komunikasi dan Informatika-KOMINFO*[21]) shut down the internet in Papua and West Papua Provinces due to protests and violence[22]. Without clear and legitimate reasons, this policy infringes on citizens' rights and blocks access to any information that the public seeks, whether true or false, useless or useful. This action does little to resolve the conflict in Papua itself[23].

In another instance, Prita Mulyasari's case was one of the earliest examples of online defamation under the ITE Law. Prita, a patient who wrote a consumer complaint, was charged with criminal defamation. Initially, the attorney charged her under Articles 310 and 311 of the Criminal Code (slander and libel). Later, charges under Article 27 Section 3 of the ITE Law, which regulates online defamation, were added. The harsh reality was how Prita faced multiple defamation charges under both the Criminal Code and ITE Law[24].

Prita's case, along with hundreds of other online defamation cases, shows the dangerous effect of the ITE Law on online expressions in Indonesia. Since the ITE Law was passed, there have been significant criticisms and questions about its criminalization of online expressions. The unclear scope of what is considered unprotected expressions and how the criminal punishment as a punitive damage mechanism is problematic. Moreover, it is also unclear why prison sentences for online defamation have a longer duration compared to those for online threats, which is another cybercriminal act regulated in the ITE Law (Article 27 Section 4)[25].

When the ITE Law was passed, types of online expressions, such as defamation, hate speech, pornography, and threats, began to be regulated under the statute. The distinctions between offline expressions and online expressions, along with their corresponding criminal provisions, were further emphasized after several judicial review processes for the ITE Law were not granted by the Indonesian Constitutional Court (*Mahkamah Konstitusi*-MK).

One of the Constitutional Court's judicial decisions was a verdict in 2008, just a few months after the ITE Law was officially passed, in which the Court stated that the ITE Law did not violate the Indonesian Constitution of 1945. The distinction between online and offline defamation is necessary as the court notes differences in how defamatory content is published both offline and online[26].

One reason the distinction between offline and online defamation laws is necessary, according to the Indonesian Constitutional Court, is the various acts that are defined differently in the Criminal Code and the ITE Law. The three terms in Article 27 Section 3 of the ITE Law, "to distribute," "to transmit," and "causes to be accessible" were not initially defined when the law was first enacted in 2008, which contributed to the high number of unnecessary criminalization of expressions.

The controversies surrounding the implementation of the ITE Law in relation to unnecessary criminal cases of online expressions led to further efforts to amend the ITE Law. In early February 2021, Indonesian President Joko Widodo ordered the Indonesian National Police (POLRI) to undertake a selective process in investigating online defamation cases and called for amendments to the ITE Law[27]. The President's instruction for a selective process stemmed particularly from the fact that many criminal defamation investigations lacked clear evidence of reputational harm, and it was expected that the police would carefully investigate online defamation cases.

The President's statement gained attention, and it seemed that the amendment of the ITE Law would be in motion. However, the attempt to pass the ITE Law revision into the National Legislation Program of the *DPR* failed in March 2021[28]. Eventually, the Indonesian Ministry of Communication and Information set a plan to make a guideline for interpreting the ITE Law[29] instead of pursuing its amendment.

Additionally, the Indonesian National Police published a Circular Letter on Awareness of Culture and Ethics to create a clean, healthy, and productive Indonesian digital space[30]. One of the instructions given by the Indonesian Head of National Police in the letter is not to detain a suspect of online defamation if the suspect has publicly apologized. The National Police also enacted a plan to activate a cyber police force, which would serve as a unit to warn internet users when they post expressions that potentially violate the ITE Law[31].

Eventually, after months of work, the ITE Law Research Team established by the government to investigate problems within the law decided that the ITE Law would not be repealed[32], something civil society organizations have also fought for over the years. The guidelines jointly drafted by the Ministry of Communication and Information, the Attorney General, and the National Police Chief may provide valuable content, but they still need more clarity regarding the provisions for online expressions in the ITE Law, which could ultimately be resolved through a comprehensive revision of the ITE Law[33].

The pending amendment of the ITE Law has imparted a chilling effect on Indonesians. Data shows that the most frequent plaintiffs in online defamation cases are public officials[34]. Therefore, this data shows that the ITE Law creates a power imbalance between the plaintiff and the defendant. These chilling effects have also turned the defendants' lives in turmoil.

Free speech also experienced a chilling effect during the pandemic. One concerning example of a new law suppressing free speech in the pandemic era was the enactment of the Regulation in Lieu of Law (*Perppu*) No. 1/2020 on the COVID-19 Pandemic Response. This law protects officials who authorize spending for programs related to pandemic management from any legal charges. The risk is that the law provides cover for authoritarian actions and greater consolidation of government power[35].

In addition to the Regulation in Lieu of Law, the Indonesian Head of the Police Force issued five telegram letters in response to the COVID-19 pandemic. One of the letters, unfortunately, declares that the police will conduct special internet patrols to monitor COVID-19 hoaxes and defamation against the President and public officials[36].

This set of regulations should be a concern for those who value free speech as a key component of democracy. While people already feel threatened by the outbreak, these additional regulations have a restricting effect, making it more difficult to criticize the actions taken by the Indonesian government.

Criminalizing expression laws also potentially contributes to Indonesia's overcriminalization problem. Although the most significant contributor to the inmate population comes from drug cases, Indonesia's jails are overcrowded[37] due to various criminal cases, including criminal defamation. Most criminal cases result in quick decisions for imprisonment, with sentences of less than a year[38]. Furthermore, the Criminal Code includes a provision that regulates simple defamation or insults as a type of defamation that can lead to the offender's imprisonment for up to four months and two weeks[39]. Not only does simple defamation often fail to result in reputational harm[40], but regulating insults as one of the criminal acts emphasizes the overcriminalization problem within the current Indonesian criminal law.

Despite the title of this section suggesting a rise in democratic institutions, this was only reflected in the early years of the Reformation Order. In recent years, democracy has declined, exacerbated by the political divide among Indonesians and the interference with dissenting expressions through laws that do not serve legitimate aims and are unnecessary, as they harm democracy.

Furthermore, the long-awaited amendment to the Indonesian Criminal Code eventually occurred in January 2023. Even though the new Indonesian Criminal Code is set to be officially enforced in 2026, many fear that this amended Act will harm the free press and free speech due to several vague provisions, such as hoaxes, pornography, and false accusations[41].

A year after the amendment of the new Criminal Code was passed, in January 2024, the Indonesian government passed the second amendment of the ITE Law, which, similar to the Criminal Code amendment process, was criticized for its closed-door meetings during the legislative process[42].

Heavy criticism of the latest amendment to the ITE Law has been directed at its content, which is still feared to pose a threat to freedom of expression[43]. With the First Amendment in 2016, a few changes were made, including the definitions of "to distribute" and "to transmit," which are part of the provisions for the criminalization of expression. The definition of "causes to be accessible" – that is, in one sentence of that provision – was finally defined through the second amendment to the ITE Law in 2024.

Unfortunately, neither of the two amendments included total revisions to the criminalization of expression in the law. Both amendments still contain provisions that criminalize expressions such as defamation, hate speech, and blasphemy. Ironically, shortly after the second amendment to the ITE Law was passed through Law No. 1 of 2024, investigations into online expression cases began, which seemed to justify the fear of threats to freedom of expression.

The first case was reported just 13 days after the second amendment of the ITE Law was passed. On 15 January 2024, the Sukabumi Police sent a summons to Dudy Syahprialdi for an investigation. Dudy, a father whose son had been physically bullied in school, had reported the incident to the school after identifying the bully. Unfortunately, Dudy was later reported by the father of the alleged bully for online defamation under the ITE Law[44].

The second case was allegedly reported in January 2023. Septia, a former employee of Hive Five, a company owned by a social media figure John LBF, was accused of online defamation. Her post on X, in which she shared details about the abuse of her employment rights while she was working there, consisted of the violation of Septia's rights as a worker, led to a police report, even though the Jakarta Labour Authority had recommended that the dispute be settled through the Industrial Dispute Court[45]. In just a few days after the second amendment of the ITE Law was passed, Septia was officially named a suspect in an online defamation case. In August 2024, Septia was detained for the controversial prosecution. Septia has also gone through her trial before the Central Jakarta Court, which, according to Septia's attorney, was problematic due to time stalling of the trial schedule and the public prosecutor who did not attach a claim of the evidence for the trial[46].

The aforementioned cases highlight some of the issues related to both the content and the implementation of the ITE Law. In addition to the ITE Law, both the current and the new Criminal Code contain draconian provisions that threaten freedom of expression. A detailed analysis of these laws will be provided in Chapter 3.

Notes

1 Tristam Pascal Moeliono, *Terjemahan Beberapa Bagian Risalah Pembahasan Wetboek van Strafrecht dan Wetboek van Strafrecht voor Nederlandsch Indie* [*Translation of Several Parts of the Minutes of Discussion of The Criminal Code and The Criminal Code for Dutch East Indies*], 614 (2021).

2 Franklin B Wenstein, 1971, *The Indonesian's Elite View of the World and the Foreign Policy of Development*, Indonesia, Oct. 1971, No. 12, 107.

3 Hwian Christianto, 2013, *The Significant Impact of Law of Number 1/PNPS/1965/ Freedom of Religion*, Jurnal Yudisial Vol.6., No.1, 3.
4 Asfinawati, Muhammad Isnur, Febi Yonesta, *Penodaan Agama [Blasphemy]*, 1 (2018).
5 BPHN, *Laporan Akhir Tim Analisa dan Evaluasi Hukum tentang Delik-Delik Penghinaan terhadap Pejabat Negara dan Simbol-Simbol Negara (Pasal 310-321 KUHP) [Final Report of the Legal Analysis and Evaluation Team on Offenses Against State Officials and State Symbols (Articles 310-321 of the Criminal Code)]*, 4 (n.d).
6 John H. McGlynn, 2000, *Silenced Voices, Muted Expressions: Indonesian Literatures Today*, Manoa Vol. 12 No. 1, 39.
7 Verelladevanka Adryamarthanio, 2022, *Pembredelan Media Massa pada Orde Baru [Banning of Mass Media during the New Order]*, Kompas.com (Mar., 19, 2023) https://www.kompas.com/stori/read/2022/06/21/110000079/pemberedelan-media-massa-pada-masa-orde-baru?page=all.
8 Felix Nathaniel, 2020, *Pembredelan Tempo, Detik dan Editor (Benih Penggulingan Soeharto)* [The Banning of Tempo, Detik and Editor (The Seeds of the Overthrow of Suharto)], TIRTO.ID (June 20, 2021) https://tirto.id/pemberedelan-tempo-detik-dan-editor-benih-penggulingan-soeharto-fJ79.
9 Wikrama I Abidin, 2007, *Saatnya Menggunakan Hak Jawab [Time to Use the Right of Reply]*, dewanpers.or.id (July 15, 2023). https://dewanpers.or.id/publikasi/opini_detail/46/Saatnya_Menggunakan_Hak_Jawab.
10 Politics and the Media in Twenty-First Century Indonesia: Decade of Democracy 182 (Krishna Sen & David T. Hill eds., 2011).
11 Politics and the Media in Twenty-First Century Indonesia: Decade of Democracy 182.
12 Airlangga Pribadi and Milda Istiqomah, 2021, *Indonesia's New Despotism*, Melbourne Asia Review, Edition 5 January 2021.
13 Indonesian Act, 1998, art. 1 Section 3(Indonesia), Freedom to Expressing Opinion in Public Spaces Act (Indon.).
14 Indonesian Act, 1998, art. 3(Indonesia), Freedom to Expressing Opinion in Public Spaces Act (Indon.).
15 Freedom House, 2020, *Freedom in the World: Indonesia*, Freedom House (August 3, 2020) https://freedomhouse.org/report/freedom-world/2019/indonesia.
16 Kate Lamb, 2019, *Indonesia Riots: Six Dead After Protesters Clash with Troops over Election Result*, The Guardian (May 22, 2020), https://www.theguardian.com/world/2019/may/22/indonesia-riots-protesters-clash-with-security-forces-over-election-result.
17 Ross Tapsell, 2019, *Arrest for Political Hoax News in Indonesia*, East Asia Forum (March 7, 2021) https://www.eastasiaforum.org/2019/11/08/arrests-for-political-hoax-news-in-indonesia/.
18 Telly Nathalia, 2019, *Man Threatening to Behead Jokowi Charged with Treason, May Face Life Sentence*, the Jakarta Globe (October 2, 2020) https://jakartaglobe.id/news/man-threatening-to-behead-jokowi-charged-with-treason-may-face-life-sentence/.
19 Ronald, 2019, *Tersangka Pengancam Penggal Kepala Jokowi Kirim Surat Minta Maaf dan Menyesal [Suspect Who Threatened to Behead Jokowi Sends Letter of Apology and Regret]*, Merdeka.com (October 2, 2020) https://www.merdeka.com/peristiwa/tersangka-pengancam-penggal-kepala-jokowi-kirim-surat-minta-maaf-dan-menyesal.html.
20 Criminal Code [C. Crim] [Criminal Code] art. 87 (Indon.).
21 The nomenclature of this Ministry is during the Jokowi's presidency from 2014 to 2024, under the Prabowo's regime that started since October 2024, the Ministry's name changed to Kementrian Komunikasi dan Digital-Ministry of Communication and Digital.
22 BBC News, 2019, *Indonesia Cuts Off Internet to Papua Following Protests*, BBC Indonesia (Aug 22, 2019), https://www.bbc.com/news/av/world-asia-49442819/indonesia-cuts-off-internet-to-papua-following-protests.

23 Ika Karlina Idris, 2019, *The Internet Shutdown In Papua Threatens Indonesia's Democracy And Its' People Right To Free Speech*, The Conversation Indonesia (April 23, 2021,), https://theconversation.com/the-internet-shutdown-in-papua-threatens-indonesias-democracy-and-its-peoples-right-to-free-speech-122333.
24 Siswantoro Sunarso, *Hukum Informasi dan Transaksi Elektronik [Information and Electronic Transaction Law]*, 7 (2009).
25 Anggara, Supriyadi W.E., and Ririn Sjafriani, *Kontroversi UU ITE: Menggugat Pencemaran Nama Baik di Ranah Maya [ITE Law Controversy: Suing for Defamation in Cyberspace]*, 16 (2010).
26 Mahkamah Konstitusi [MK] [The Indonesian Constitutional Court] 2008, Decision No. 50/PUU-VI/2008 (Indon.).
27 Budi Sutrisno and Marchio Irfan Gorbiano, 2021, *Ball in Jokowi's Court on ITE Law Revisions*, The Jakarta Post (June 4, 2022) https://www.thejakartapost.com/news/2021/02/17/ball-in-jokowis-court-on-ite-law-revisions.html.
28 CNN Indonesia, 2021 *Revisi UU ITE tak Masuk Prolegnas Prioritas 2021 [Revision of ITE Law Not Included in 2021 Priority National Legislation Program]*, CNN Indonesia (March 30, 2021) https://www.cnnindonesia.com/nasional/20210309132911-32-615485/revisi-uu-ite-tak-masuk-prolegnas-prioritas-2021.
29 VOI Editorial, 2021, Preventing Disputes, *Kominfo Produces Guidelines for the Electronic Information and Transaction Law*, voi.id (September 27, 2021) https://voi.id/en/news/34687/preventing-disputes-kominfo-produces-guidelines-for-the-ite-law.
30 Tsarina Maharani, 2021, *Kapolri Terbitkan SE soal UU ITE, Tersangka Minta Maaf tak Perlu Ditahan [Police Chief Issues Circular Regarding ITE Law, Suspect Apologizes, No Need to Detain]*, kompas.com (September 27, 2021) https://nasional.kompas.com/read/2021/02/22/21494101/kapolri-terbitkan-se-soal-uu-ite-tersangka-minta-maaf-tak-perlu-ditahan?page=all#page2.
31 Tsarina Maharani, 2021, *Polisi Virtual Indonesia Bakal Segera Patroli di Medsos [Indonesian Virtual Police Will Soon Patrol Social Media]*, kompas.com (March 21, 2021) https://tekno.kompas.com/read/2021/02/18/09480057/polisi-virtual-indonesia-bakal-segera-patroli-di-medsos.
32 Intan Umbari Prihatin, 2021, *Menko Polhukam: Tidak ada Pencabutan UU ITE karena masih sangat Diperlukan [Coordinating Minister for Political, Legal and Security Affairs: There will be no revocation of the ITE Law because it is still very Necessary]*, merdeka.com (May 4, 2022) https://www.merdeka.com/peristiwa/menko-polhukam-tidak-ada-pencabutan-uu-ite-karena-masih-sangat-diperlukan.html.
33 Putra, *SKB UU ITE Bawa Kemajuan tapi Revisi tetap Mutlak Dilakukan karena masih Banyak Kelemahan [Joint Decree on ITE Law Brings Progress but Revision is Still Absolutely Necessary as There Are Still Many Weaknesses]*.
34 Scholastica Gerintya, 2021, *Jerat UU ITE Banyak Dipakai oleh Pejabat Negara [The Snares of the ITE Law are Widely Used by State Officials*, tirto.id (July 13, 2022) https://tirto.id/jerat-uu-ite-banyak-dipakai-oleh-pejabat-negara-c7sk.
35 Ghina Ghaliya, 2020, *Intimidation of Government Critics Raises Concerns About Freedom of Speech*, The Jakarta Post (June 22, 2020), https://www.thejakartapost.com/news/2020/06/02/intimidation-of-government-critics-raises-concerns-about-freedom-of-speech.html.
36 Ghina Ghaliya, 2020, *Criticism 'Not an Insult': Polices Plan to Nab Slanderers of Govt over COVID-19 Questioned*, The Jakarta Post (June 22, 2020) https://www.thejakartapost.com/news/2020/04/06/criticism-not-an-insult-polices-plan-to-nab-slanderers-of-govt-over-covid-19-questioned.html.
37 Bayu Marhaenjati, 2021, *Indonesian Prison System at More than Double Its Capacity*, Jakarta Globe, (September 29, 2021) https://jakartaglobe.id/news/indonesian-prison-system-at-more-than-double-its-capacity.
38 VOA Editorial, 2019 *Indonesia Government Looks Alternatives Overcrowded Prisons*, VOA News, (September 15, 2021) https://www.voanews.com/east-asia/indonesia-government-looks-alternatives-overcrowded-prisons.

39 18 weeks, the term four months and two weeks is the term that used in the Article 315 Criminal Code.

40 Criminal Code [C. Crim] [Criminal Code] art. 315 (Indon.).

41 Memorandum Dewan Pers, *RUU KUHP: Mengancam Kebebasan Pers dan Berekspresi*, No.05/M-DP/V/2005 [Press Council Memorandum, Criminal Code Bill: Threatening Freedom of the Press and Expression, No.05/M-DP/V/2005].

42 Nur Janti, 2023 *Critics Slam Closed-Door Meetings on ITE Law Revision*, The Jakarta Post, (July 29, 2023) https://www.thejakartapost.com/indonesia/2023/07/13/critics-slam-closed-door-meetings-on-ite-law-revision.html.

43 International Federation of Journalist, 2023, *Indonesia: ITE Law Revision Retains Threat to Freedom of Expression*, International Federation of Journalist, (December 19, 2023) https://www.ifj.org/media-centre/news/detail/category/press-releases/article/indonesia-ite-law-revision-retains-threat-to-freedom-of-expression.

44 Anggraini, MA. 2024 [Twitter] 16 January 2024, https://twitter.com/MellisA_An/status/1747101956978688205 (22 January 2024).

45 "Konferensi Pers: Nasib Buruh Curhat, Berujung Dipidana Pengusaha [Press Conference: Workers' Fate Speaks Out, Ends in Criminal Prosecution by Employers]." Youtube, uploaded by PBHI_Nasional, 7 January 2024, https://www.youtube.com/watch?v=oCVtMy9Bl-M.

46 Erick Tanjung, 2024, *Kisah Kelam Septia: Curhat Soal Upah Berujung Kriminalisasi UU ITE [Septia's Dark Story: Complaining About Wages Leads to Criminalization under ITE Law]*, suara.com (November 4, 2024) https://liks.suara.com/read/2024/09/23/165918/kisah-kelam-septia-curhat-soal-upah-berujung-kriminalisasi-uu-ite.

Bibliography

Books

Asfinawati, Muhammad Isnur, Febi Yonesta, *Penodaan Agama [Blasphemy]* (2018).

Anggara, Supriyadi W.E., and Ririn Sjafriani, *Kontroversi UU ITE: Menggugat Pencemaran Nama Baik di Ranah Maya [ITE Law Controversy: Suing for Defamation in Cyberspace]* (2010).

Tristam Pascal Moeliono, *Terjemahan Beberapa Bagian Risalah Pembahasan Wetboek van Strafrecht dan Wetboek van Strafrecht voor Nederlandsch Indie [Translation of Several Parts of the Minutes of Discussion of The Criminal Code and The Criminal Code for Dutch East Indies]* (2021).

Politics and the Media in Twenty-First Century Indonesia: *Decade of Democracy 182* (Krishna Sen & David T. Hill eds., 2011).

Siswantoro Sunarso, *Hukum Informasi dan Transaksi Elektronik [Information and Electronic Transaction Law]* (2009).

Journals

Airlangga Pribadi and Milda Istiqomah, 2021, Indonesia's New Despotism, Melbourne Asia Review, doi: https://doi.org/10.37839/MAR2652-550X5.13.

Franklin B Wenstein, 1971, The Indonesian's Elite View of the World and the Foreign Policy of Development, *Indonesia*, Oct. 1971, No. 12, 102. https://www-jstor-org.libproxy1.nus.edu.sg/stable/3350661?seq=7

Hwian Christianto, 2013, The Significant Impact of Law of Number 1/PNPS/1965/Freedom of Religion, *Jurnal Yudisial* Vol.6., No.1, 3.

John H. McGlynn, 2000, Silenced Voices, Muted Expressions: Indonesian Literatures Today, *Manoa* Vol. 12 No. 1, 39.

Indonesian Law

Criminal Code [Crim. Code.], 1946, [Criminal Code] (Indon.).
Indonesian Act, 1998, (Indonesia), *Freedom to Expressing Opinion in Public Spaces Act (Indon.)*.

Indonesian Cases

Mahkamah Konstitusi [MK] [The Indonesian Constitutional Court] 2008, Decision No. 50/PUU-VI/2008 (Indon.).

Government Documents

Memorandum Dewan Pers, *RUU KUHP: Mengancam Kebebasan Pers dan Berekspresi*, No.05/M-DP/V/2005 [Press Council Memorandum, Criminal Code Bill: Threatening Freedom of the Press and Expression, No.05/M-DP/V/2005].

Reports

BPHN, *Laporan Akhir Tim Analisa dan Evaluasi Hukum tentang Delik-Delik Penghinaan terhadap Pejabat Negara dan Simbol-Simbol Negara (Pasal 310-321 KUHP) [Final Report of the Legal Analysis and Evaluation Team on Offenses Against State Officials and State Symbols (Articles 310-321 of the Criminal Code)]* (n.d.).

Internet

Bayu Marhaenjati, 2021, Indonesian Prison System at More than Double Its Capacity, *Jakarta Globe*, (September 29, 2021) https://jakartaglobe.id/news/indonesian-prison-system-at-more-than-double-its-capacity.
BBC News, 2019, Indonesia Cuts Off Internet to Papua Following Protests, *BBC Indonesia* (Aug 22, 2019), https://www.bbc.com/news/av/world-asia-49442819/indonesia-cuts-off-internet-to-papua-following-protests.
Budi Sutrisno and Marchio Irfan Gorbiano, 2021, Ball in Jokowi's Court on ITE Law Revisions, *The Jakarta Post* (June 4, 2022) https://www.thejakartapost.com/news/2021/02/17/ball-in-jokowis-court-on-ite-law-revisions.html.
CNN Indonesia, 2021 Revisi UU ITE tak Masuk Prolegnas Prioritas 2021 [Revision of ITE Law Not Included in 2021 Priority National Legislation Program], *CNN Indonesia* (March 30, 2021) https://www.cnnindonesia.com/nasional/20210309132911-32-615485/revisi-uu-ite-tak-masuk-prolegnas-prioritas-2021.
Erick Tanjung, 2024, Kisah Kelam Septia: Curhat Soal Upah Berujung Kriminalisasi UU ITE [Septia's Dark Story: Complaining About Wages Leads to Criminalization under ITE Law], *suara.com* (November 4, 2024) https://liks.suara.com/read/2024/09/23/165918/kisah-kelam-septia-curhat-soal-upah-berujung-kriminalisasi-uu-ite.
Felix Nathaniel, 2020, Pembredelan Tempo, Detik dan Editor (Benih Penggulingan Soeharto) [The Banning of Tempo, Detik and Editor (The Seeds of the Overthrow of Suharto)], *TIRTO.ID* (June 20, 2021) https://tirto.id/pemberedelan-tempo-detik-dan-editor-benih-penggulingan-soeharto-fJ79.
Freedom House, 2020, Freedom in the World: Indonesia, *Freedom House* (August 3, 2020) https://freedomhouse.org/report/freedom-world/2019/indonesia.
Ghina Ghaliya, 2020, Criticism 'Not an Insult': Polices Plan to Nab Slanderers of Govt over COVID-19 Questioned, *The Jakarta Post* (June 22, 2020a) https://www.

thejakartapost.com/news/2020/04/06/criticism-not-an-insult-polices-plan-to-nab-slanderers-of-govt-over-covid-19-questioned.html.

Ghina Ghaliya, 2020b, Intimidation of Government Critics Raises Concerns About Freedom of Speech, *The Jakarta Post* (June 22, 2020), https://www.thejakartapost.com/news/2020/06/02/intimidation-of-government-critics-raises-concerns-about-freedom-of-speech.html.

Ian Vazques and Tanja Porcnik, 2019, The Human Freedom Index, *Cato Institute* (February 11, 2020) https://www.cato.org/sites/cato.org/files/human-freedom-index-files/2019-human-freedom-index-update-2.pdf.

Ika Karlina Idris, 2019, The Internet Shutdown In Papua Threatens Indonesia's Democracy And Its' People Right To Free Speech, *The Conversation Indonesia* (April 23, 2021,), https://theconversation.com/the-internet-shutdown-in-papua-threatens-indonesias-democracy-and-its-peoples-right-to-free-speech-122333.

Intan Umbari Prihatin, 2021, Menko Polhukam: Tidak ada Pencabutan UU ITE karena masih sangat Diperlukan [Coordinating Minister for Political, Legal and Security Affairs: There will be no revocation of the ITE Law because it is still very Necessary], *merdeka.com* (May 4, 2022) https://www.merdeka.com/peristiwa/menko-polhukam-tidak-ada-pencabutan-uu-ite-karena-masih-sangat-diperlukan.html.

International Federation of Journalist, 2023, Indonesia: ITE Law Revision Retains Threat to Freedom of Expression, *International Federation of Journalist*, (December 19, 2023) https://www.ifj.org/media-centre/news/detail/category/press-releases/article/indonesia-ite-law-revision-retains-threat-to-freedom-of-expression.

Kate Lamb, 2019, Indonesia Riots: Six Dead After Protesters Clash with Troops over Election Result, *The Guardian* (May 22, 2020), https://www.theguardian.com/world/2019/may/22/indonesia-riots-protesters-clash-with-security-forces-over-election-result.

Nur Janti, 2023 Critics Slam Closed-Door Meetings on ITE Law Revision, *The Jakarta Post*, (July 29, 2023) https://www.thejakartapost.com/indonesia/2023/07/13/critics-slam-closed-door-meetings-on-ite-law-revision.html.

Ronald, 2019, Tersangka Pengancam Penggal Kepala Jokowi Kirim Surat Minta Maaf dan Menyesal [Suspect Who Threatened to Behead Jokowi Sends Letter of Apology and Regret], *Merdeka.com* (October 2, 2020) https://www.merdeka.com/peristiwa/tersangka-pengancam-penggal-kepala-jokowi-kirim-surat-minta-maaf-dan-menyesal.html.

Ross Tapsell, 2019, Arrest for Political Hoax News in Indonesia, *East Asia Forum* (March 7, 2021) https://www.eastasiaforum.org/2019/11/08/arrests-for-political-hoax-news-in-indonesia/.

Scholastica Gerintya, 2021, Jerat UU ITE Banyak Dipakai oleh Pejabat Negara [The Snares of the ITE Law are Widely Used by State Officials], *tirto.id* (July 13, 2022) https://tirto.id/jerat-uu-ite-banyak-dipakai-oleh-pejabat-negara-c7sk.

Telly Nathalia, 2019, Man Threatening to Behead Jokowi Charged with Treason, May Face Life Sentence, *the Jakarta Globe* (October 2, 2020) https://jakartaglobe.id/news/man-threatening-to-behead-jokowi-charged-with-treason-may-face-life-sentence/.

The Economist Intelligence Unit, 2019, Democracy Index 2019, *The Economis Intelligence Unit* (February 11, 2020) http://www.eiu.com/Handlers/WhitepaperHandler.ashx?fi=Democracy-Index-2019.pdf&mode=wp&campaignid=democracyindex2019.

Tsarina Maharani, 2021a, Kapolri Terbitkan SE soal UU ITE, Tersangka Minta Maaf tak Perlu Ditahan [Police Chief Issues Circular Regarding ITE Law, Suspect Apologizes, No Need to Detain], *kompas.com* (September 27, 2021) https://nasional.kompas.com/read/2021/02/22/21494101/kapolri-terbitkan-se-soal-uu-ite-tersangka-minta-maaf-tak-perlu-ditahan?page=all#page2.

Tsarina Maharani, 2021b, Polisi Virtual Indonesia Bakal Segera Patroli di Medsos [Indonesian Virtual Police Will Soon Patrol Social Media], *kompas.com* (March 21, 2021) https://tekno.kompas.com/read/2021/02/18/09480057/polisi-virtual-indonesia-bakal-segera-patroli-di-medsos.

Verelladevanka Adryamarthanio, 2022, Pembredelan Media Massa pada Orde Baru [Banning of Mass Media during the New Order], *Kompas.com* (Mar., 19, 2023) https://www.kompas.com/stori/read/2022/06/21/110000079/pemberedelan-media-massa-pada-masa-orde-baru?page=all.

VOA Editorial, 2019 Indonesia Government Looks Alternatives Overcrowded Prisons, *VOA News*, (September 15, 2021) https://www.voanews.com/east-asia/indonesia-government-looks-alternatives-overcrowded-prisons.

VOI Editorial, 2021, Preventing Disputes, Kominfo Produces Guidelines for the Electronic Information and Transaction Law, *voi.id* (September 27, 2021) https://voi.id/en/news/34687/preventing-disputes-kominfo-produces-guidelines-for-the-ite-law.

Wikrama I Abidin, 2007, Saatnya Menggunakan Hak Jawab [Time to Use the Right of Reply], *dewanpers.or.id* (July 15, 2023) https://dewanpers.or.id/publikasi/opini_detail/46/Saatnya_Menggunakan_Hak_Jawab.

Social Media Posts

Anggraini, MA. 2024 [Twitter] 16 January 2024, https://twitter.com/MellisA_An/status/1747101956978688205 (22 January 2024).

"Konferensi Pers: Nasib Buruh Curhat, Berujung Dipidana Pengusaha [Press Conference: Workers' Fate Speaks Out, Ends in Criminal Prosecution by Employers]." *Youtube, uploaded by PBHI_Nasional*, 7 January 2024, https://www.youtube.com/watch?v=oCVtMy9Bl-M

3 Legal Framework for Free Speech in Indonesia

3.1 International Human Rights Treaties

Despite the enactment of laws designed to protect free speech and uphold democracy, Indonesia continues to struggle in establishing a truly free and democratic society. Recent surveys and global studies on freedom and democracy have consistently ranked Indonesia in declining positions over the past few years.

In the 2019 Democracy Index issued by the *Economist*, Indonesia was ranked 64th with a civil liberty score of 5.59[1]. The 2019 Human Freedom Index, issued by the Cato Institute, ranked Indonesia even lower at 81st, with personal freedom and human freedom scores at 6.38 and 6.83, respectively[2]. Those low index scores for Indonesian freedom of speech indicate that, despite the Constitution being ratified in 1945 to regulate democracy and its practice, particularly free speech, Indonesia still faces many obstacles in this area.

Freedom House has indeed determined that Indonesia has made significant progress toward democracy since the fall of authoritarian in 1998, marking a total political reform[3]. However, more than 20 years after the reform, the rating of Indonesian freedom remains low. The country scored 62 out of 100, with a freedom rating of 3/7, political rights of 2/7, and civil liberties of 4/7[4].

Freedom House conducts research on each country's index of freedom based on two main elements: Civil liberties (60%) and political rights (40%). Civil liberties are measured by the protection of freedom of expression and belief, associational and organizational rights, the rule of law, personal autonomy, and individual rights. Political rights are determined by the electoral process, political pluralism, and participation, and the functioning of government.

According to the organization, Indonesia's index of freedom is categorized as "partly free," mainly due to the low civil liberties index. The overall index of freedom of Indonesia has been gradually declining. In 2019, the index was rated at 62 (partly free), with a civil liberties score of 32 out of 60. The decline continued in 2020 with an index of freedom of 61, and further decreased to 59 in both 2021 and 2022, and 58 in 2023. The civil liberties score also significantly decreased, which affected the index of freedom, with scores of 31 out of 60 in 2021, 29 out of 60 in 2022, and 28 out of 60 in 2023.

DOI: 10.4324/9781032661544-3

The concerning index of freedom suggests that, although Indonesia is a signatory to international human rights statutes, its implementation may still fall short of proper practices and should be analyzed in the context of national laws. Therefore, the second section of this chapter analyzes Indonesian laws regarding free speech. It begins with the Indonesian Constitution of 1945, which officially became the Indonesian Constitution on 18 August 1945 and was amended in 2002. This section will explore how the Constitution provides protection for free speech but does not clearly define what constitutes protected and unprotected speech. The Criminal Code analysis will be divided into two parts: The Current Criminal Code (1946 law) and the newly amended Criminal Code, which has been enacted but will only become official law in 2026, replacing the Current Criminal Code. The analysis will focus on several provisions that curb free speech in both versions of the Criminal Code. The section on the ITE Law will be divided into three different discussions. Considering that the ITE Law was partially amended in 2016 and 2024, these amendments did not replace the original 2008 ITE Law. The analysis will address issues with the language of the ITE Law provisions, which remain open to multiple interpretations and lead to inadequate implementation.

Freedom of speech is considered a fundamental human right, which means that it is recognized and protected by the highest authorities, regardless of the identity factors of a person, such as race, religion, sex, and nationality. Several international treaties regulate human rights and define the boundaries between protected and unprotected speech. These include the Universal Declaration of Human Rights (UDHR)[5], and the International Covenant on Civil and Political Rights (ICCPR)[6]. In addition, this section will analyze the 1998 Association of Southeast Asian Nations (ASEAN) Declaration of Human Rights to determine Indonesia's position on free speech protection in both international and ASEAN contexts.

3.1.1 Universal Declaration of Human Rights and International Covenant on Civil and Political Rights

In the UDHR, freedom of expression is regulated under Article 19, which states:

> Everyone has the right to freedom of opinion and expression; this right includes freedom to hold opinions without interference and to seek, receive and impart information and ideas through any media and regardless of frontiers.

Although the provision does not provide a specific explanation, free speech, and free expression are legal terms. Michel Verpeaux states that free speech is closely related to free expression, which is fundamental to the freedom to reside in a country and the elimination of privilege[7]. The placement of opinions and expression under one article means that they are protected in the same ways. The phrase "regardless of frontiers" is included to emphasize that freedom of opinion and expressions are rights that are protected globally. However, these freedoms still have limitations, which are enforced when the expression violates others' rights or poses harm to the public. These limitations are regulated under the ICCPR.

The ICCPR, which was passed in 1966 by the United Nations, also protects free expression. Article 19 of the ICCPR states:

1 Everyone shall have the right to hold opinions without interference.
2 Everyone shall have the right to freedom of expression; this right shall include freedom to seek, receive, and impart information and ideas of all kinds, regardless of frontiers, either orally, in writing or print, in the form of art, or through any other media of his choice.
3 The exercise of the rights provided for in paragraph 2 of this article carries special duties and responsibilities. It may, therefore, be subject to certain restrictions, but these shall only be such as are provided by law and are necessary: (a) For respect of the rights or reputations of others; (b) For the protection of national security or of public order (ordre public), or of public health or morals."

The ICCPR distinguishes between opinions and expression, even though both terms serve the same purpose as in the previous international agreements. This distinction is meant to differentiate the dissemination of opinions from expression. Opinions are usually not in a concrete form or abstract, representing views or thoughts on an issue while expression can take various concrete forms such as written communication, art, media, broadcasting, or commercial advertising.

The ICCPR emphasizes two main aspects: The right to reputations and public order, and the different wording for the national security matter. It strengthens the importance of freedom of expression in international law, recognizing it as part of the personal and social dimensions[8].

In establishing the scope of free speech, the ICCPR outlines a "three restrictions test," also known as the three-step test, which explores the limitations on free speech required to satisfy the three elements of the test. The test consists of restrictions that satisfy the following criteria[9]:

- It must be provided by law, which is clear and accessible to everyone.
- It must pursue one of the specific purposes set out in Article 19(3) of the ICCPR; and
- It must be necessary and the least restrictive means required to achieve its purported aim.

The three elements of the test, also known as the three-step test, regulate that any restrictions on free speech should be based on legality, legitimacy, and necessity. **Legality** means that the restrictions should be prescribed by law. The United Nations Human Rights Committee, through its General Comment No.

34 on Article 19 of the ICCPR, emphasizes that the first test of legality does not include traditional, religious, or other customary laws[10]. Although this may seem to overlook legal pluralism, it is meant to ensure the universality of human rights. Implementing the universality of human rights principle in any State parties of the ICCPR can be challenging, but an exclusive legal tradition may lead to discrimination and harm the universality of human rights principle itself, as noted in the General Comment No. 34[11].

Legitimacy, as the second test, means that the restrictions that are provided by law should serve legitimate purposes, such as protecting the rights and reputation of others, maintaining public order, safeguarding public moral, ensuring public health, and protecting national security. Last, **Necessity** test, which also aligns with the principle of proportionality, means that any restriction must not violate human rights principles and should not harm the values upheld in a democratic society.

Despite the overt language of the restrictions, it remains challenging to compose and apply the restrictions at a national level of human rights and free speech legislation. Although free speech is generally recognized as a human right, the universal value of human rights is still not globally accepted[12].

The debate on the universalism of human rights stems from two perspectives: A concept or idea and a normative reality[13]. The concept of universalism has evolved into normative structures through the international treaties. States have access to international norms on universal human rights, which can be ratified and adopted into their national laws. The actions of states to adopt and comply with these international laws can be assessed in several ways. According to international law, this may encompass the interpretation of internal laws, the willingness of national organizations to comply with the international laws, or bridging gaps in national laws with international law contents[14].

In defining universal human rights, including free speech, the ICCPR exemplifies how states can practice free speech legislation and apply it at the national level. The 172 countries that have ratified the ICCPR have agreed to its content and the universal concept of human rights. For instance, Indonesia, which ratified the ICCPR in 2005 and enacted Law Number 11 of 2005 on the ICCPR Ratification, has adopted several of its provisions, despite facing challenges in enforcing them[15].

Based on the definitions of free speech outlined in the international laws mentioned above, we can draw two conclusions. First, in the vertical relationship between the state and its citizens, public order or national security matters are the most restrictive limitations on free speech. In other words, speech that incites chaos or disrupts public order falls into law-violation conduct. Second, in the horizontal interactions between private individuals, speech is considered unlawful if it harms the rights and reputations of others.

Under the ICCPR, various civil and political rights are protected, including freedom of expression. ICCPR is considered as one of the most fundamental documents in international law. Along with the UDHR and the International Covenant on Economic and Social Rights (ICESCR), these three documents are collectively known as the International Bill of Rights.

Indonesia ratified the ICCPR in 2005 through Law Number 12 of 2005 on Ratification on the International Covenant on Civil and Political Rights, which declared the state's compliance with the ICCPR. Therefore, through the adoption of the ICCPR into Law Number 12 of 2005, Indonesia, as part of the international community, has pledged to respect, protect, and fulfil human rights principles.

Before the ratification of the ICCPR in 2005, Indonesia had already enacted its own human rights law. A year after the political reformation in 1998, which was marked by the fall of Suharto's 32-year authoritarian regime, the Indonesian government passed Law Number 39 of 1999 on Human Rights (The Human Rights Law). This law was passed not only in response to the long-standing democratic aspirations of Indonesians but also because of several issues, such as economic and monetary crises, human rights problems, and political conflict within society[16].

The human rights issues that united Indonesians in urging the new government to establish its own human rights legal regime were also supported by Presidential Decree Number 129 of 1998 on the National Action Plan for Indonesian Human Rights (1998–2003) and Presidential Instruction Number 26 of 1998 on the Elimination of Usage on "Native" and "Non-Native." The context of the latter law stems from Dutch colonization. During the colonial era, the policy of *Devide et Impera* was implemented, enforcing different laws for native Indonesians and non-native, such as those of Chinese descent. The polarization introduced by the colonizers continued to influence the Indonesian government even after the independence in 1945, reflected in the use of different legal and policy drafting terms. The 1998 Presidential Instruction eventually reinforced the commitment to a non-discrimination policy. In a bigger context, Indonesia passed Law Number 40 of 2008 on the Elimination of Racial and Ethnic Discrimination, which also influenced Presidential Decree No. 12 of 2004 on the Revocation of the 1967 Cabinet Decree, which replaced the term "Chinese" with "Tionghoa." This change was intended to erase the distinction between "native" and "non-native" and to strengthen efforts to combat ethnic racism.

In addition to the Presidential Decree and Instruction mentioned above, Indonesia also ratified the Convention Against Torture and Other Cruel, Inhuman, or Degrading Treatment and Punishment through Law Number 5 of 1998. These three legislations in 1998 demonstrate Indonesia's strong commitment to human rights obligations, particularly through the enactment of its own human rights law.

When Indonesia eventually complied with the international human rights regime in 2005 through the ratification of ICCPR, it, like other state parties, faced challenges in adopting human rights principles into the country's legal system. Hikmahanto Juwana, an international law expert from the University of Indonesia and President of Jendral Achmad Yani University, states that several challenges have emerged post-ratification of the ICCPR. These include uniformly adopting the provisions of the ICCPR into domestic law uniformly and raising awareness of Indonesian citizens and officials about human rights, especially civil and political rights[17].

After officially becoming one of the state parties of the ICCPR, Indonesia is required to report on its human rights situation. The United Nations Human Rights Committee (UNHCR) provides a mechanism called the Universal Periodic Review (UPR), which gives opportunities to all state parties to declare the actions they have taken to fulfill human rights obligations. The UPR is held once every cycle, which lasts four and a half years.

Since its first cycle of the UPR in 2008, Indonesia has actively participated in the process. Indonesia also highlighted the challenges of implementing the ICCPR in its National Report submitted for the first cycle of the UPR. The report states that, as one of the most recent countries to join the Third-Wave Democracy, which started in the mid-1970s, Indonesia has faced challenges in its political journey toward becoming a fully democratic country[18]. Indonesia successfully held its first election in 2004 peacefully[19] and regained economic and political stability, despite four changes in presidency between 1998 and 2002. However, the first cycle of the UPR recommended that Indonesia should provide education and training on human rights to promote civil and political human rights and raise awareness of human rights[20].

The first cycle of UPR in 2008 marked the ten-year anniversary of the Reformation Order and the passage of the ITE Law. By the second cycle of the UPR in 2012, the Indonesian government had made several legislative developments, particularly regarding civil and political rights, including the 2008 Law on Public Information Transparency and the implementation of the 1999 Press Law and the 2002 Broadcast Law[21].

Despite the Indonesian government's report that the Press Law and Broadcast Law promote press freedom, the implementation of these two laws has faced criticism. The Press Law is considered "inferior" because the ITE Law, especially its defamation provisions, often leads to criminal charges in defamation cases, including those involving news stories that should be protected by the Press Law[22]. Meanwhile, the Broadcast Law is criticized for failing to promote diversity of ownership in the radio and television industry, as mandated by the statute[23].

In the third cycle of the UPR in 2017, Indonesia passed Law Number 19 of 2016, as the Amendment of the ITE Law. However, the 2016 ITE Law only partially amended the provisions of the 2008 ITE Law. For example, it only reduced the prison term for online criminal defamation from 6 years under the 2008 ITE Law to 4 years in the 2016 ITE Law[24]. Meanwhile, civil society organizations have demanded the revocation of all criminal provisions in the ITE Law[25].

In its third cycle UPR report, Indonesia states that the country provides protection of freedom of expression under the 1945 Indonesian Constitution and the ITE Law. Furthermore, the freedom of assembly to express opinions is protected under Law Number 2 of 2002 on the Indonesian Police and the Regulation of the National Police Chief Number 7 of 2012 on Procedures for Implementation, Service, Security, and Case Management Delivery of Opinion in Public.

However, in practice, those aforementioned practices have not always been effectively implemented. For instance, the Indonesian government arrested 1,000 people from Papua and West Papua provinces who were demanding an independence referendum[26]. In addition, Basuki Tjahaja Purnama, also known as Ahok, an ethnic Chinese Christian and a candidate in the 2017 gubernatorial election, was criminally charged with blasphemy provisions under the Criminal Code for his allegedly blasphemous remarks[27]. The blasphemy provisions in the Criminal Code have been criticized for being inconsistent and for curbing freedom of expression and freedom of religion[28].

In the latest UPR report in 2022, Indonesia claimed that it is protecting human rights defenders as vital partners in promoting human rights in the country[29]. Human rights defenders, in turn, pointed out that the government has passed an Anti-Strategic Lawsuit Against Public Participation (Anti SLAPP) law through Chief Justice of the Supreme Court's Decree (Keputusan Mahkamah Agung) No. 36 of 2013 on the Implementation of Guidelines for Handling Environmental Cases.

Unfortunately, Indonesian human rights defenders continue to face threats of criminal charges. A recent case involves the defamation trial of two human rights activists, Haris Azhar and Fatia Maulidiyanti, following their discussion on YouTube about a potential conflict of interest involving Luhut Binsar Pandjaitan, an Indonesian four-star army General and Coordinating Minister for Maritime Affairs and Investment. Their comments were alleged to have defamed Luhut's reputation[30], which sparked concerns because the activists were simply quoting A research report. According to the Joint Decree on the ITE Law, such actions should not be investigated as criminal defamation. In addition, in September 2023, residents of Rempang island, part of the Riau Islands province, faced criminalization after they were fighting for protesting against forced evictions due to the government's plan to turn the 17,000-hectare area of the island into a new hub for glass and solar panel manufacturing plants[31]. The forced eviction in Rempang has added to the growing list of criminalization of Indonesian human rights and environmental activists[32].

Despite the Indonesian government's claim of strong human rights protection, the facts show the opposite, particularly regarding freedom of expression. The lack of serious commitment to human rights has raised concerns among various civil society organizations, both national and international, especially with Indonesia's re-election as a member of the United Nations Human Rights Council for 2024–2026[33]. One major concern is how Indonesia should implement the international human rights mechanisms, such as implementing UPR's recommendations on shrinking civic space and cooperating with the Special Procedures visits by the UN Special Rapporteurs on Freedom of Expression[34].

3.1.2 ASEAN Human Rights Declaration

In contrast to other regions, such as America with the Inter-American Convention on Human Rights and Europe with the European Convention on Human Rights, Asia does not have a single international human rights treaty. Asia adopted the Asian Human Rights Charter in 1998, but this charter was signed by a non-governmental organization, which may not have the same authority and strong legal binding compared to a treaty signed by the government. One of the reasons for the inexistence of regional human rights regimes in Asia is that, despite geographic proximity, trade and security issues still become problems for stronger regional cooperation. Hence, the cooperation is typically manifested in regional organizations, such as the ASEAN, instead of all Asian cooperation.

The ASEAN Human Rights Declaration (AHRD) was adopted in 2012 by the ASEAN Intergovernmental Commission on Human Rights (AICHR), which had been established three years earlier. The Declaration serves as the regional framework for cooperation on the promotion and protection of human rights in the ASEAN region. Notably, Article 23 of the ASEAN Declaration of Human Rights stipulates the rights of individuals to form, hold, and express their opinions without undue interference, particularly with regard to free speech.

In regional cooperation on human rights issues, particularly regarding free speech, Indonesia contributed by hosting the 2019 AICHR Consultation on Freedom of Expression and Opinion in ASEAN. Through its representative, Indonesia emphasized that freedom of expression is the precondition for a democratic society and highlighted how ASEAN countries should address disinformation and misinformation from a human rights perspective[35].

In the Declaration, freedom of expression is categorized as civil and political rights. Article 22 stipulates the rights to freedom of thought, conscience, and religion while also emphasizing the need for action against intolerance, discrimination, and hatred based on religion and beliefs. The provision in Article 22 implies that the limitation of freedom of expression is established if such expressions take the form of hate speech.

Meanwhile, Article 23 of the Declaration uses language similar to that of the ICCPR. It states that "every person has the right to freedom of opinion and expression, including freedom to hold opinions without interference and to seek, receive and impart information, whether orally, in writing or through any other medium of that person's choice."

Considering the absence of the ASEAN regional human rights treaty, the AHRD could serve as a new form of universalism for human rights, especially respecting Asian values[36], and, more specifically, Southeast Asian values. The idea emerges from the challenge of manifesting the universal values of human rights, since the current human rights regime is often seen as too Eurocentric, unequal, and power-fueled[37].

The actions carried out by the AICHR to promote Asian values of human rights are regularly recorded in its annual reports, with a focus on promoting and mainstreaming human rights in ASEAN countries[38]. Notably, in 2022, the AICHR marked the 10th year anniversary of the AHRD. The AICHR emphasized the importance of raising awareness about AHRD and urged its adoption and implementation within the legal system of each member state, which is in line with the Phnom Penh Statement on the Adoption of the ASEAN Human Rights Declaration[39].

3.2 The 1945 Indonesian Constitution (UUD 1945)

In 1998, Indonesian society finally gained the right to create and express their ideas freely. Political speech became easier to express in public and across various platforms, at least as promised by the government at the time. However, Indonesians still face the obstacles due to free speech restrictions.

After 32 years under Suharto's authoritarian regime, one of the obstacles faced by the Indonesian society is the ongoing wait for the government to fulfill its promise of democracy and free speech. Despite the 1998 political reform, some criminal provisions continue to limit freedom of speech, contradicting the 1945 Indonesian Constitution, which aims to protect free speech through its provisions.

Freedom of speech is protected in the 1945 Indonesian Constitution (Undang-Undang Dasar 1945-UUD 1945), which is the foundational Indonesian constitution. The importance of a state constitution in addressing the issue of freedom of expression is to set the limitations between protected and unprotected expressions. According to the aforementioned Articles 28 and 28F of the Constitution, the scope of freedom of expression in Indonesia includes the right to associate, the right to gather, the right to written and spoken ideas, and the right to access, communicate, and disseminate ideas.

Article 28F, part of the amendment of the Constitution, marked a significant change in Indonesian constitutional law. In 1998, following three decades of Suharto's authoritarian regime, Indonesia started a political reformation that brought changes in many aspects of the country. In law, it was the amendment of the 1945 Constitution that became the mandate of the 1998 reformation[40]. The idea of amending the Constitution was already manifested in Article 37 of the Constitution, but it was not until the 1998 reformation that both the public and the government urged amending the multi-interpreted provisions in the Constitution[41]. There are a total of four amendments to the Constitution of Indonesia. All of these occurred as a result of the General Assembly of the Indonesian Consultative Assembly (*Majelis Permusyawaratan Rakyat*-MPR) in 1999 (The First Amendment), 2000 (The Second Amendment), 2001 (The Third Amendment), and 2002 (The Fourth Amendment).

Article 28F was one of the new provisions in the Second Amendment to the Indonesian Constitution. By enacting this provision, Indonesia has expanded the scope of freedom of expression, which formerly focused on the rights to associate, gather, and express written and spoken ideas, to include the rights to access and disseminate ideas.

Constitutionally, not only did the Indonesian government expand the scope of freedom of expression, but it also marked the country's embrace of an era of public open access to information. Despite having several laws related to human rights and freedom of speech, no clear and specific scope has been defined for limiting free speech in Indonesia. In contrast, other countries outline several unlawful expressions in their constitutions, and the laws of these countries will be explored in this chapter. Additionally, Indonesian laws are often considered draconian regarding freedom of expression. Indonesian laws seem to impose limitations on free speech by recognizing defamation. However, only defamation that causes harm to a person's reputation and dignity is actionable, without a clear definition or specific standards. Obscenity[42] is also regulated as an unlawful expression, although the definitions in some laws are vague. Blasphemy, meanwhile, has sparked controversies and debates since the law was first established, as it has also evidently harmed certain religious minority groups[43].

While defamation serves as a limitation on forms of speech that are not constitutionally protected, Indonesia, with its civil law system, has not changed its defamation-related articles in the Indonesian Criminal Code. The whole Criminal Code has remained unchanged since it was first passed in 1946 by the Indonesian government as a legacy of Dutch colonial rule. Currently, in Indonesia, defamation laws still impose criminal prosecution as a sanction, although each defamation-related article also provides for civil sanctions.

The unchanged Criminal Code now presents challenges in Indonesian legal practice. For instance, as briefly discussed in the previous chapter, Prita Mulyasari faced multiple defamation charges under both the Criminal Code and the ITE Law.

The criminal charges for online defamation are not limited to Prita's case. Although limitations on free expression outlined in the Law Act were originally intended to serve a beneficial purpose, the definitions remain unclear, as the article does not provide specific elements that constitute online defamation. This lack of clarity has also led to consumer complaints, such as Prita's case, being prosecuted as online defamation. The case of Prita Mulyasari will be discussed in more detail in Chapter 4.

To provide a more in-depth analysis and keep this research aligned with the previously stated context and goals, the following sections will discuss offline defamation and offline hate speech in both the current and new Criminal, as well as Article 27 Section 3 of the ITE Law concerning online defamation and its provisions for online hate speech.

3.3 The Criminal Code (KUHP)

The earliest regulation on defamation in Indonesia can be found in the Indonesian Criminal Code. This statute, which was officially enacted during the Dutch colonial era in Indonesia on 1 January 1918, was originally named *Wetboek van Strafrecht voor Nederlands-Indië* (WvS). Even after gaining independence, Indonesia continued to use this colonial version of the Criminal Code, which was passed in 1946.

The government has made numerous attempts to reform the criminal justice system by amending the Criminal Code, beginning with discussion among Indonesian legal scholars in the 1st Law National Seminar in Semarang, Indonesia. This discussion led to the government's initiative to draft a new Criminal Code[44]. However, many of these efforts failed to result in a new official statute. The latest draft, presented by the Indonesian Council of Representatives (DPR) last year, was also rejected. Criticism toward the 2019 draft of the statute was mainly on the potential human rights violations in some of its provisions[45]. The controversial draft also sparked rally protests led by Indonesian students, which unfortunately resulted in chaos[46].

While the Indonesian Criminal Code covers various expressions such as treason, threats, and blasphemy, this book will focus specifically on defamation and hate speech. These two types of criminalized expressions are the primary issues discussed in this chapter, as they represent the highest number of criminal cases reported and investigated, especially with the advent of the internet and the enactment of the ITE Law. While it is challenging to obtain exact data on these cases, some available figures may help support the argument.

First is the massive dissemination of harmful online content, especially content based on race and ethnicity. The Indonesian Ministry of Communication and Information recorded that over a three-year period, from 2018 to 2021, 3,640 pieces of online content were taken down. These takedowns were based on three regulations: The ITE Law, the Governmental Decree No. 71 of 2019 on the Establishment of Electronic Systems and Transaction, and the Ministerial Decree No. 5 of 2020 on Private Electronic System Providers[47].

Second is data from the Southeast Asia Freedom Network (SAFENet), an organization advocating for digital rights in the Southeast Asia region. According to its report, by the third quarter of 2023 (July to September 2023), SAFENet recorded an 18.5% increase in reported cases compared to the previous quarter, which included incidents of online defamation and online hate speech[48].

Last, a search was conducted for reported cases on defamation and hate speech in the Indonesian Supreme Court's repository. The keywords used were "pencemaran nama baik" and "penghinaan" for defamation and "ujaran kebencian" for hate speech. The keywords for defamation resulted in 51,783 cases (51,140 for "pencemaran nama baik" and 733 for "penghinaan") decided in the First Degree Court in Indonesia, with the earliest case recorded in 1970. For hate speech, the keyword "ujaran kebencian" recorded 505 cases decided in the First Degree Court, starting in 2013.

Based on these figures, the discussion and analysis of defamation and hate speech will examine each provision within both the Criminal Code and the ITE Law.

3.3.1 Offline Hate Speech in the Current Criminal Code

Under the Chapter "Crimes Against Public Order," the Current Criminal Code regulates hate speech as a crime. There are currently five provisions for hate speech, even though there were originally eight. However, Articles 153 *bis* and Article 153 *ter* were revoked by Law No.1 of 1946 on Criminal Law Regulation.

The 1946 Law was passed a year after the country's independence to address several provisions that became irrelevant as they were passed during Dutch colonization. Some of these provisions also needed partial changes, such as using the terms "Indonesie" or "Indonesisch(e) for Indonesia instead of "Nederlandsch-Indie" or "Nederlandschindisch(e)" for the Netherlands[49].

Ironically, despite the fact that the 1946 Law was passed to revoke and change provisions that reflected colonization against Indonesians, several provisions with a colonial spirit that criminalize expressions still exist, namely those concerning hate speech and defamation.

3.3.1.1 Article 154 of the Current Criminal Code

While there is no exact definition of hate speech under international human rights law, the United Nations has defined it as any kind of communication that attacks or uses pejorative or discriminatory language against a person or a group based on identity-related factors[50].

The keywords in defining hate speech here are "pejorative" and "discriminatory," which, unfortunately, are not reflected in the hate speech provisions under Indonesian criminal laws. Article 154 reads:

> *Any person who publicly gives expression to feelings of hostility, hatred or contempt against the Government of Indonesia shall be punished by a maximum imprisonment of seven years or a maximum fine of three hundred Rupiahs.*

As can be seen in the language of the Article, this provision focuses on hostility, hatred, or contempt rather than on pejorative and discriminatory. It also suggests that the prosecuted offense involves declaring hostile, hatred, and contemptuous expressions, which is barely a crime unless it is manifested through a specific physical action, such as assault, in cases involving the Government of Indonesia.

The targeted subject in this provision is also problematic. It offers an obscure scope, suggesting that simple criticism toward the government can be considered a crime. There is no clear definition or distinction between criticism toward the government and hostile, hateful, or contemptuous expressions.

In addition, Article 154a focuses on defaming the Indonesian national flag and state symbols.

3.3.1.2 Article 155 of the Current Criminal Code

This Article consists of two Sections. Article 155 Section 1 reads:

> *Any person who disseminates, broadcasts or puts up a writing or an image where feelings of hostility, hatred or contempt against the Government of Indonesia are expressed with intent to give publicity to the contents or to enhance the publicity thereof, shall be punished by a maximum imprisonment of four years and six months or a maximum fine of three hundred Rupiahs.*

This provision has a similar meaning to Article 154. While the previous provision criminalizes spoken expression, this provision addresses offenses committed through writing and images. Section 2 of Article 155 emphasizes that if the offense is committed during the individual occupation or within five years after a previous verdict, the person's right would be revoked.

Despite this fact, the formulations of both Articles 154 and 155 have been used to criminalize expressions critical of the government. Both provisions are also known as *hazard artikelen* or criminal offenses for inciting hatred toward the government[51].

During the New Order under Suharto's authoritarian regime, there were numerous student protests that emerged, criticizing his administration. One example is a 1989 student protest at Institut Teknologi Bandung (ITB), where students boycotted the arrival of Rudini, the Minister of Internal Affairs, due to his policy of forced evictions related to land disputes in several areas of Indonesia. Another example is the 1992 White Group (*Golongan Putih*) movement, which called for abstaining from the election. All of these protests were ultimately investigated and prosecuted under Article 154, among other provisions.

Both Articles 154 and 155 were revoked in 2007 after being declared unconstitutional by the Indonesian Constitutional Court. The petition was originally filed to request the court to review several articles of the Criminal Code. However, through Decision No. 6/PUU-V/2007, the Court only granted the petition to revoke Articles 154 and 155, which means those provisions are no longer constitutional since they conflicted with the Indonesian Constitution. One of the court's main arguments was that the existence of Articles 154 and 155 was irrational because it is implausible for an Indonesian citizen to wage war against an official state and its government, except in cases of treason, which is already regulated under Article 107 of the Criminal Code[52].

3.3.1.3 Article 156 of the Current Criminal Code

This Article criminalizes hostile, hateful, and contemptuous expressions, similar to the two previous provisions, but the targeted victims of this crime are groups within the population of Indonesia. Article 156 reads:

> *Any person who publicly gives expression to feelings of hostility, hatred, or contempt against one or more groups of the population of Indonesia shall be punished by a maximum imprisonment of four years or a maximum fine of three hundred Rupiahs.*

One of the main elements in this criminal provision is the definition of "group of populations." The Indonesian Supreme Court states that it refers to groups of population based on tribe, region, religion, descent, origin, nationality, and status according to Indonesian constitutional law[53].

Additionally, the crime can be considered to have occurred if such expressions happen "in front of the public," which not only means that the offender may express hostile, hateful, and contemptuous expressions in public places, but also refers to expressions delivered by the offender in a way that the public can hear them. However, this latter element lacks clarity as the explanation provided does not precisely define it.

Another problem with this Article is that the provision does not specifically regulate blasphemy, but religion is included as one of the population groups under this provision. Given that Indonesia does not distinctively separate state and religious affairs, the State may refer to religious leaders to interpret "correctness" within respective religions[54], which can lead to unclear definitions and incorrect implementation.

The lack of a distinctive definition between hate speech and blasphemy led to the passage of Law No. 1 of 1965 on the Prevention of Misuse and/or Defamation of Religion (*Undang-Undang Pencegahan Penyalahgunaan dan/atau Penodaan Agama*-Law PNPS), adding Article 156a to the Criminal Code. Unfortunately, the incorrect implementation of this provision, along with Article 156a, causes a logical fallacy since it fosters enmity toward deviant religious teachings and practices in Indonesia. This situation acknowledges the religious beliefs of minority groups as victims and also positions them as sources of conflict[55].

3.3.1.4 Article 156a of the Current Criminal Code

This provision was added after Law PNPS was passed. It is not necessarily considered part of the hate speech provisions, even though hate speech and blasphemy may seem similar due to the slight differences between the two offenses. Hate speech targets various identity factors such as race, ethnicity, gender, disability status, and religion. However, while hate speech involves pejorative and discriminatory expressions regarding religion, blasphemy concerns the abuse of religion and/or its practices, which are classified as religious deviant.

That definition of blasphemy is at least applicable in the Indonesian context, especially after the passage of Law PNPS, which broadened the implementation of "blasphemy" from its original meaning, "speaking evil" about God, to include tainting, insulting, and defaming the teachings and/or practices of religions and beliefs[56].

3.3.1.5 Article 157 of the Current Criminal Code

Article 157 has similar elements regarding the punishable offense, specifically on the types of expressions and targeted victims. Section 1 of this Article reads:

> *Any person who disseminated, openly demonstrates or puts up a writing or portrait where feelings of hostility, hatred or contempt against or among groups of the population of Indonesia are expressed, with intent to give publicity to the contents or to enhance the publicity thereof, shall be punished by a maximum imprisonment of two years and six months or a maximum fine of three hundred Rupiahs.*

While Article 157 Section 2 states:

> *If the guilty person commits the crime in his position and at the time of committing the crime, it has not been more than five years since the decision of his previous sentence because a similar crime has also been decreed, then he can be dismissed from his position.*

The main difference with Article 156 is that it addresses punishable expressions through written words or images, specifically regulating both spoken and written hate speech. However, with the passing of the ITE Law in 2008, an overlap in hate speech criminal laws emerged. Criminal punishment for hate speech involving written material or images should fall under the Criminal Code, especially when the 2023 Criminal Code was officially implemented in 2026. However, the ITE Law, through Article 28 Section 2, also regulates hate speech through written material and images, which includes electronic information and/or documents, text messages, electronic messaging, and emails.

In 2018, this provision – along with Article 156 – was petitioned for revocation at the Indonesian Constitutional Court. One of the main arguments proposed by the petitioner was that the teachings and values of each religion are different, making it impossible to defame another religion[57]. The Court rejected the petition, arguing that the provision is necessary for implementing limitations on religious freedom, not to limit individual religious freedom in the private realm, but to prevent any potential conflicts[58].

3.3.2 Offline Defamation in the Current Criminal Code

The criminal provision of defamation lies in Book Two, "Crimes"[59]. Eleven articles regulate defamation as a criminal offense, covering various defamatory acts (from Article 310 to Article 321). These eleven Articles in the Criminal Code are categorized as general defamation, as the elements of these criminal offenses are the same[60]. For instance, the object of general defamation is someone's reputation and honor[61]. However, we can classify these general defamations into four significant types of offenses: slander (*smaad*), libel (*smaadschrift*), slander/fitnah (*calumny*), and insult/ordinary defamation (*eenvoudige belediging*).[62] While the first two are commonly known as spoken and written defamation, the latter two have more complicated definitions and implementations.

Under Indonesian law, *eenvoudige belediging*[63], refers to defamatory expressions that do not involve accusations of intentionally committing an act meant to harm someone's reputation. Thus, mocking, humiliation, and bullying based on someone's physical attributes or attitude are also considered criminal offenses under *eenvoudige belediging*. However, only a few existing cases fall under this category.

On the other hand, *calumny*[64] is a specific defamation or false accusation. The specific categorization of calumny arises from its elements as a crime (the accusation of deeds committed by someone), which should be tested by the judge to verify whether the accusations are true or false. In contrast, for other defamation offenses, the burden of proof falls on the defendant[65].

Calumny, as a certain defamation offense, is closely connected to libel and slander in Article 310. While a perpetrator of libel and slander is guilty whenever they spread defamatory content, calumny is considered to have fully occurred as a crime when the plaintiff cannot prove the defamatory content to be true before the court. However, this does not mean that the burden of proof lies fully on the defendant; according to the Criminal Procedure Code, the burden of proof rests with the prosecutor.

However, this ideal circumstance exists only in the provisions' text and is implemented differently in reality. Many criminal defamation cases are brought to the trial even though there is no sufficient evidence to support a defamatory statement. In some cases, Articles 310 and 311 are included together in one indictment, despite being interconnected. However, since there is no process for proving the truth of defamatory content, the trial process is unfair because it often places the burden on the defendant to prove that his or her expression was not intended to be defamatory.

Besides the classification of general defamation in Book Two of the Criminal Code, special defamation is also regulated as a criminal act. Additionally, the objects of these defamations are different from those of general defamation. Special defamation involves acts attacking the Indonesian president and/or vice president (Article 134, Article 136 *bis*, and Article 137) and Indonesian public officials (Article 154 and Article 155). The latter two provisions are also considered hate speech provisions. However, these two criminal defamation acts are no longer constitutional and have no binding legal force[66]. The Indonesian Constitutional Court has judicially reviewed these five provisions and upheld that they violate the freedom of speech principle under the Indonesian Constitution of 1945[67].

The revocation of criminal defamation provisions concerning the Indonesian government means that there is no longer special treatment for defamation against government officials, indicating that attacking the government's official reputation cannot be considered defamation under Article 310 of the Criminal Code. This revoked Article also means that there is no longer a provision for seditious libel. However, Indonesian criminal law still regulates treason, or "makar," as defined in the Criminal Code, which remains in effect and is considered a criminal act. The treason provisions are regulated under Section I, "Crimes Against State Security" of the Criminal Code.

Unfortunately, in recent times, defamation against government officials has indeed been legally processed, especially under Article 27 Section 3 of the ITE Law. The unclear definitions within these provisions contribute to unnecessary legal processes related to defamation. Until 2018, 35.92% of defamation plaintiffs were Indonesian government officials[68]. Article 27 Section 3 of the ITE Law will be discussed in the next section of this chapter. Another ironic fact regarding the Indonesian government's criminal defamation law is that Eggi Sudjana, one of the petitioners in the judicial review of Article 134, Article 136 *bis*, and Article 137 of the Criminal Code, has been in custody since 2019 due to allegedly treasonous conduct[69]. Although organizing a rally to protest the unfair results of the National Election should be protected under Article 28F of the Indonesian Constitution of 1945, the provision that protected Eggi's constitutional rights was removed in 2006.

3.3.2.1 Article 310 of the Current Criminal Code

Given the ongoing uncertainty surrounding the Criminal Code amendment, the current version of the Criminal Code is filled with obsolete provisions, particularly those related to offline defamation. The Current Criminal Code is considered obsolete because it was originally drafted in 1917 during the colonial regime, and no amendments have been made since it was passed in 1946.

Article 310 Section 1 states the following:

> *Whoever deliberately attacks the honor and reputation of someone while accusing them of an offense, with the intention so that the offense is publicly known, the verdict by defamation with a prison term up to nine months or fine sanction up to four thousand and five hundred rupiahs.*

Unfortunately, since there is no single official translation of the Current Criminal Code from the Dutch WvS, this provision exists in two different languages. While the first version is written above, the second one states, "someone accusing something toward someone, with the intention so that the accusation is publicly known."

In analyzing the language of the first version of the Article, the accusation against someone pertains to a specific offense. It cannot involve character attacks, mocking, ridiculing, or other accusations that are not related to any offense[70]. The offense that the accuser alleges must be specific, and the person accused must also be a specific person instead of a group of people[71].

There are a couple of problems with this article because it has not yet been amended. One example is the obsolete element in this provision, which can be seen in the amount of the fine sanction. The amount of 4,500 rupiahs is not even close to $1. In comparison, the fine sanction for online defamation under the ITE Law 2008 can reach up to 1 billion rupiahs (around $73,000). As one of the five criminal penalties regulated in the Criminal Code, the fine sanction is one of the oldest forms of punishment, alongside prison terms and the death penalty[72]. The fine is primarily intended to restore balance in legal inequality resulting from law violations[73]. However, in the Indonesian context, a fine sanction is typically mandated by the court for minor crimes (misdemeanors). Therefore, fine sanctions are applied as alternatives, with prison terms being the primary punishment.

The reasoning behind the fine sanction in the Indonesian legal system is clear. It classifies defamation as a criminal offense, especially regulating it with a prison term as the primary punishment for defamation categorized as a felony. A felony typically involves an element of violence and causes serious harm – greater than misdemeanors – such as physical injury.

In terms of the compensation rationale, physical injury is equated with prison terms, while psychological injury is extremely restricted to fines or tort claims[74]. Attacks on reputation and honor can also be considered forms of psychological injury. Based on this initial analysis, it can be concluded that categorizing defamation attacking honor and reputation as a criminal offense, with prison terms as the primary punishment, represents an inappropriate approach to defamation legislation.

Another problem in Article 310 Section 1 is the use of the phrase "accusing of an offense so that accusation is publicly known." Although the language of the whole Criminal Code is certainly obsolete, the terms "accusing" and "accusation" in this context suggest that the honor and reputation of the defamed person are already compromised. These words are also not entirely accurate in light of the modern definition of defamation. The term "accusing" has evolved in meaning, as it now tends to imply only negative deeds. Additionally, the overall language of the text suggests that the accusation negatively affects honor and reputation. In Indonesian cases, spreading rumors, stating false facts, and giving criticism are also considered forms of defamation.

In Article 310 Section 2, libel is regulated in terms of the specific flow of defamatory content through writing and images, as outlined in the following provision:

> *If those (defamations) are carried out through writing or images that are broadcast, shown, placed in public, a verdict by defamation (libel) with a prison term up to one year and four months or fine sanction up to four thousand and five hundred rupiahs.*

The dissemination of defamatory expressions mentioned in this Section influenced the Indonesian Constitutional Court's decision in 2008 regarding the judicial review of the revocation of Article 27 Section 3. Considering that defamatory expressions spread through conventional means, such as writing and images, and through digital platforms each have distinct characteristics, the court upheld that the defamation provision in the Criminal Code applies to offline defamation, while the ITE Law governs online defamation. However, years later, the application of these provisions remains confusing and burdensome for the Indonesian population, as many cases have shown that both provisions are often applied separately.

The latest constitutional change to this Article occurred in March 2024. Haris Azhar and Fatia Maulidiyanti, two Indonesian human rights defenders, filed a petition to revoke Articles 14 and 15 Law Number 1 of 1946 on Criminal Law Regulation, Article 310 Section 1 of the Current Criminal Code, and Articles 27 Section 3 and 45 Section 3 of the ITE Law.

Haris and Fatia were on trial for online defamation after their podcast video allegedly defamed Luhut Binsar Panjaitan, the Indonesian Coordinating

Minister for Maritime Affairs and Investment, due to a potential conflict of interest in a mining business in Papua, one of the provinces in Indonesia (More details on this case will be discussed in Chapter 4). Consequently, the petition to the Constitutional Court also requested that the Constitutional Court instruct the East Jakarta District Court to halt the trial process in their case.

The decision on their petition to the Constitutional Court was eventually made in March 2024, two months after they were found not guilty of online defamation by the East Jakarta District Court, which was described as an oasis for freedom of expression amid the criminal laws curbing it[75]. More importantly, however, is how the decision of the Constitutional Court brought a significant change to laws on freedom of expression in Indonesia.

In Decision No. 78/PUU-XXI/2023, the court partially granted Haris and Fatia's petitions. First, Articles 14 and 15 of Law Number 1 of 1946 on Criminal Law Regulation, which concerned the dissemination of hoaxes, were declared unconstitutional due to the unclear definition of "chaos" in the provision. Additionally, a mere public discourse on a sensitive issue should not be considered as inciting chaos or a riot[76].

Article 310 Section 1 on criminal defamation was not fully revoked but was deemed conditionally unconstitutional. The decision regarding Article 310 Section 1 stems from the differing norms between Article 310 Section 1 of the Current Criminal Code and Article 433 of the 2023 Criminal Code, particularly in the use of the phrase "verbally," which is absent from Article 310 Section 1 of the Current Criminal Code. Therefore, the court ruled that Article 310 Section 1 is not a valid law unless it is interpreted in line with the norm applied in Article 433 of the 2023 Criminal Code, which is now supposed to read as follows:

> *Anyone who intentionally attacks someone's honor or good name by accusing someone of something* ***verbally****, with the intention of making it clear to the public, is threatened with defamation by a maximum imprisonment of nine months or a maximum fine of four thousand five hundred Rupiah.*

Meanwhile, the petition to revoke Articles 27, Section 3, and 45, Section 3 of the ITE Law was rejected by the court due to an unclear object. The court's decision may have only partially granted the petition, but it is a good sign for a more robust protection for freedom of expression. Nevertheless, challenges remain because the ITE Law provisions and the 2023 Criminal Code are still valid laws.

Furthermore, a good law will not be effective if it is inadequately implemented, which is, unfortunately reflected in the statement by the Indonesian Police Force (*Kepolisian Republik Indonesia*-POLRI) regarding the Constitutional Court's decision on Article 310 Section 1, made just a few days after the verdict. The Indonesian Police Force stated that they would adjust to the changes in the law, but for ongoing investigation under ITE Law cases, they said that the changes would not be applied retroactively until a new law is passed[77]. The Indonesian Police Force's statement goes against the criminal law principle called *Lex Favor Reo*, which states that when there are changes in the law, the most favorable provision should be applied to the defendant[78]. This criminal law principle is also regulated in the Current Criminal Code Article 1 Section 2, which reads:

> *If there is a change in the law after the act is committed, the provisions that are most favorable to the defendant are applied to the defendant.*

Article 3 Section 1 also regulates the *Lex Favor Reo* principle, with an additional adjustment, which reads:

> *In the event that there are changes to statutory regulations after the act has occurred, new laws and regulations are applied, unless the provisions of the old laws and regulations are beneficial to the perpetrators and accomplices of the crime.*

An analysis of the Indonesian Police Force indicates that it remains unacknowledged of this principle, highlighting the need for more robust changes to ensure the adequate implementation of defamation laws.

3.3.2.2 Article 311 of the Current Criminal Code

This Article addresses *calumny*, and the text of Section 1 in this Article is as follows:

> Whoever commits crimes of *calumny* or *calumny* through writing is allowed to prove the accusation of *calumny*, but if he or she cannot prove it and if that accusation is not true, he or she shall be punished for a *calumny* crime with a prison term up to four years.

As mentioned in the previous section, this Article is a follow-up to Article 310 of the Current Criminal Code. It contains details of the procedure on how Article 310's legal process transitions into Article 311[79]:

1. *A defendant under trial for Article 310 Section 1 the Criminal Code or Article 310 Section 2*;
2. *The defendant files a motion for the dismissal of the criminal offense based on public interest or self-defense (Article 310 Section 3)*;
3. *Judges review the accusation of the defendant to validate the testimony that: (a) the offense was committed in the public interest or self-defense (Article 312 Section 1), or (b) the defendant is a public official who is accused of misconduct related to their task (Article 312 Section 2)*;
4. *Judges allow the defendant to prove that the accusations of slander or libel are factual (Article 311)*;
5. *If the defendant cannot prove the accusation and the accusation is opposed with what the defendant knows, then the defendant is punished for calumny with a prison term up to four years.*

3.3.2.3 Article 312 of the Current Criminal Code

This article serves as another follow-up to Article 310 and Article 311. It provides the conditions for proving the truth of allegations where the suspect of defamation is allowed to prove the opposite fact of the allegation (Article 311). The full text of the Article is:

> "Proving for the truth of allegations only allowed for the following:

1 *If judges see that it is necessary to check the truth to weigh the defendant's statement, that the alleged act was done to protect the public interest, or forced to defend themselves;*
2 *If a public official is accused of something in carrying out their duties."*

The definition of public interest might seem broad. However, R. Soesilo, a prominent Indonesian criminal law scholar who also translated the Indonesian Criminal Code from Dutch, outlines that protecting public interest in this Article is defined as "an effort that is intended to show misconducts and neglects that potentially harm or endanger society"[80]. Based on R. Soesilo's argument, press publication is part of Article 312, as press work is an effort to deliver facts, including misconducts and neglects. Press duties are also protected under the Indonesian Press Law Number 40 of 1999, which provides the Right to Answer[81] and a dispute mechanism that is handled by the Press Council[82] for any party who experiences a loss because of the news.

Although current laws do not regulate the criminalization of the press, ironically, many cases show the opposite. One such case happened in 2004[83] when Risang Bima Wijaya, the editor-in-chief of *Radar Jogja* newspaper, was jailed after publishing a story in the newspaper covering a sexual abuse incident involving Soemadi Martono Wonohito, a businessman who owned a local newspaper, and one of his employees. This case, which is going to be discussed deeper in Chapter 5 is an example of the violation of free press.

The reason for defending oneself against exclusion is regulated in Article 312. Exclusion applies when a person uses allegedly defamatory expressions to show misconduct by another person. However, even with these exceptions, the implementation of defamation laws is rare. One reason is the unclear definition of "public interest protection" and "defending themselves" written in the Criminal Code.

3.3.2.4 Article 313 of the Current Criminal Code

Building on the previous Article, Article 313 rules that the verification process outlined in Article 312 does not apply when the accusation can only be prosecuted based on a complaint. However, a complaint is not required to investigate the accusation. This ruling is based on Indonesian criminal law doctrine, which recognizes two types of criminal acts: ordinary crimes and complaint crimes. **Ordinary crimes** can be processed without any complaint submitted, allowing the police to start the investigation. Victims can also submit the complaint, but the police will continue the investigation even if the complaint is later withdrawn. Meanwhile, **complaint crimes** can only be investigated initially based on a victim's complaint, and the prosecution requires the consent of the crime's victim. R. Soesilo further categorizes complaint crimes into two distinct forms[84]:

a Absolute complaint crimes
These are crimes whose prosecution requires a complaint from the victim. The complaint should also specifically address the alleged criminal act, which means that any suspects (the offender, the helper, or anyone involved) should be prosecuted. Examples of such crimes are rape, sexual abuse, defamation, and abduction of women.
b Relative complaint crimes
These crimes are not classified as absolute complaint crimes. However, due to the provisions in Article 367 of the Criminal Code involving family members, they can be processed as complaint crimes. Examples include blackmail, threatening, and smuggling.

As mentioned above, defamation is classified as a criminal complaint provision, which means the investigation process can only start once a report or complaint is filed by the victim. Given that defamation can occur through speech or writing, the victim bears the burden of proving the defamatory content, so no investigation will proceed unless a complaint is formally submitted. This complaint must specify the defamatory expression in question. The alleged defamatory expression that the victim complains about often varies and may relate to other types of crimes such as robbery, rape, sexual abuse, smuggling, or corruption. The Criminal Code contains various offenses that can occur in defamation, ranging from Article 27 to Article 488.

3.3.2.5 Article 314 of the Current Criminal Code

This Article provides another exception for defamation. Section (1) of this Article addresses the person accused of defamation, stating that if the person is found guilty of the alleged deed through a judicial decision, it is not considered defamation. This means the accusation is based on fact and supported by the court.

However, in Section (2), if the person is not found guilty of the accusation through a judicial decision, the expression is considered defamation and falls under the category of Article 311. The verdict serves as evidence against the defamation complaint, and the accused may even file a complaint against the individual who spread the defamatory expression. Last, Section (3) rules that the prosecution for defamation can be held until the prosecution of the original accusation comes to a verdict.

3.3.2.6 Article 315 of the Current Criminal Code

This Article addresses "simple" defamation. Unlike other types of defamation in the Criminal Code, simple defamation does not fall under slander or libel categories. In this type of defamation, there is no direct accusation against the victim. Instead, it involves mocking, insulting, or bullying statements that, due to their vague nature, may still be considered criminal acts.

Mocking and insults are cruel and disrespectful expressions that can hurt someone. Bullying, on the other hand, can involve not only verbal expression but also physical acts intended to harm, intimidate, or coerce the victim.

It is difficult to identify criminal elements in mocking or insults that would qualify them as actual criminal acts. For instance, if someone calls another person names, it is generally considered an opinion. Even though the opinion may be hurtful, as long as it does not result in physical harm or involve violence, it should be treated as merely an opinion. Generally, mocking or insulting someone is not considered a crime.

However, in several countries, mocking and insulting are considered crimes, especially when directed at a police officer. For example, in St. Lucia, a Caribbean Island, a defendant was initially not imposing any physical force. However, after resisting arrest and making an insulting gesture toward a police officer, he was found guilty under local law[85]. Another example can be seen in countries that are part of the Organization for Security and Cooperation in Europe (OSCE), such as the Czech Republic, where insults can be punishable acts. Insults specifically become a crime when directed at public officials, government institutions, national institutions, and/or the state[86]. Such actions are considered punishable crimes as they attack the honor and dignity of these entities. The situation becomes more complex in that, unlike defamation laws, an expression may still be considered a crime even if it is factual[87]. Although the classification of mocking and insults as crimes is still debatable, most countries around the world do not regulate these acts in their national laws.

Bullying, however, should be treated very differently. As mentioned earlier, bullying is not only an opinion that disheartens someone; most of the time, it involves a physical act directed at the victim. In these circumstances, it is not appropriate to rule bullying as defamation because it should be regulated as a separate criminal act. Physical damage in bullying indicates that harm has occurred, which is sufficient to consider it one of the crime elements that make bullying a criminal offense.

In Indonesia, however, bullying is not fully regulated as a crime. Although minor defamation under Article 315 of the Current Criminal Code could be enforced for bullying cases, this provision is rarely utilized. Instead, petty and debatable cases, such as name-calling or referring to someone by animal names, are often processed as minor defamation under Article 315 of the Current Criminal Code or Article 27 Section 3 of the ITE Act, which will be discussed in the next chapter.

Calling someone a racial slur is a crime, and unfortunately, this type of offense has been prevalent in Indonesia for a long time[88]. In many cases, however, the victims of this racial act have been the ones investigated and even convicted of treasonous crimes[89]. If an insult is not racially based, such as name-calling, it should be treated as a mere opinion. Yet, in Indonesia, the insults are frequently reported as defamation and investigated by the police, even when they could simply be viewed as harsh criticism[90] or making fun of someone.

3.3.2.7 Article 316 of the Current Criminal Code

This Article provides a ruling on a one-third enhancement of the punishment in the preceding Articles if the expression directed toward an official occurs during or pertains to their office's legal duties. This provision emphasizes what is discussed in the previous subsection (Article 315)-the fact that Indonesia is one of the countries that regulate citizens defaming public officials. This includes mocking or insulting (Article 315) a police officer, although it might be debatable whether such actions should be considered a crime. For example, stating that a police officer is "stupid" is an opinion rather than a fact, and it does not depict the police as an institution. In Indonesia, the defamation laws do not include a provision for "defamation to a legal subject."

3.3.2.8 Article 317 of the Current Criminal Code

This provision regulates charges of calumnious submission to the authorities. An act falls into the category of calumnious acts if it fulfills these requirements[91]:

a *The person who submits or causes the submission of the charge must know that the charge is false.*

In filing a crime report to the police, one does not hold the responsibility to gather any evidence, but he or she must ensure that the reported offense truly happened. If the crime report is false and was deliberately submitted, it is considered calumnious. This provision and the provision in Article 311 of the Current Criminal Code are similar in regulating false accusations, but the degree of offense in Article 317 is higher, as the offense is reported to the police.

b *The charge must contain an offense against the honor or reputation of a person, not an institution.*

Honor and reputation are attributes possessed only by a person (natural subject). Unfortunately, there are fallacies in many cases investigated in Indonesia. Defamations directed at government institutions, companies, or even cities in Indonesia have been processed by authorities, even though these cases do not satisfy the elements of the defamation law. Generally, the reputation of a legal entity can be damaged by defamation, but the plaintiff must prove it. For instance, a da maged reputation can occur if a company's services are affected by a defamatory expression[92]. One example of a controversial case that failed to fulfill the requirement for demonstrating damage to the reputation of a legal entity occurred in 2014 when Yogyakarta, a city in Indonesia, was labeled "idiotic" in a social media post by Florence, a law graduate student[93].

Section 2 of this Article regulates the revocation of rights from individuals charged with calumnious conduct. The rights revoked include those specified in Article 35 Section 1, such as the right to hold any occupation or position, the right to be enrolled in the Indonesian military, and the right to vote and be elected in an election.

3.3.2.9 Article 318 of the Current Criminal Code

Like the previous Article, this Article addresses calumnious insinuations made against another person. The false accusation involves someone being accused of engaging in a criminal offense. There is no requirement for the act to have damaged honor and reputation, but if the accusation is false, it falls into the category of this Article.

The language of this Article does not specifically describe the form of the act that constitutes a false accusation. For instance, an act of simply placing a gun in a house and then claiming that the gun was used to kill someone would count. The act of planting evidence alone is enough to satisfy the offense regulated in this Article. The main element in this Article is the suspicion that someone could rationally do the criminal act[94].

3.3.2.10 Article 319 of the Current Criminal Code

Article 319 does not specify a particular form of defamation. Instead, it emphasizes that all forms of defamation under the Criminal Code are generally criminal complaint-based, except for those covered under Article 316. This means that an investigation can only proceed if the plaintiff files a complaint based on the defamation act.

3.3.2.11 Article 320 of the Criminal Code

Under Article 320, defaming a deceased person is considered a criminal offense and is classified as slander or libel toward a person who has passed away. Specifically, if the person being defamed were still alive, the expression would be categorized slander or libel. This is referred to as special defamation, as it includes additional and specific elements that are absent from general defamation under Article 310. The accusation pertains to an offense allegedly committed when the person was still alive, making it publicly known[95]. Under Article 320, defaming a deceased person is considered a criminal offense and is classified as a slander or libel toward a person who has passed away. Specifically, if the person being defamed were still alive, the expression would be categorized slander or libel.

Although defamation is typically based on the victim's feelings (subjective), and the deceased does not have feelings, the complaint-based stipulation might not seem applicable. However, under Indonesian law, the right of the plaintiff to file a defamation complaint transfers to the closest family members of the deceased. This is possible because Indonesian law is influenced by Islamic law, which allows certain rights and obligations to be passed on to the family members of the deceased. Regarding the filing of a defamation complaint, as regulated in Article 320 Section 2, these rights can be exercised by:

a *Blood relatives: Children, parents, grandchildren, grandparents*
b *Siblings in the nuclear family*
c *Second-degree relatives: Parents-in-laws and siblings-in-law*
d *Spouse of the deceased (widow or widower)*

3.3.2.12 Article 321 of the Current Criminal Code

Articles 320 and 321 are similar in that both regulate defamation against the deceased. However, while the elements of broadcasting, publicly displaying, or posting information containing defamatory content are required, there is no stipulation that the content must intentionally attack the reputation or honor of the deceased. The defamation offense is considered fulfilled once the defamatory content is disseminated, even if it does not directly accuse the deceased of committing an act. Article 321 is fulfilled if the defamatory content against the deceased has become publicly known. This form of defamation is similar to that defined in Article 315[96], which involves name-calling or insulting the character of the deceased.

Similar to the previous Article, the basis for filing a defamation complaint consults the provision in Article 319, while the family members who can exercise their right to be plaintiffs are regulated in Article 320, Sections 2 and Section 3.

3.4 The 2023 Criminal Code (KUHP 2023)

After decades of attempts to amend the outdated Criminal Code, in December 2022, the Indonesian Government finally passed a new Criminal Code. The statute is officially named Law No. 1 of 2023 on the Criminal Code.

Although the new Criminal Code has been passed, it has not yet been implemented. Considering the transition and synchronization process among legal enforcers, the new Criminal Code (hereinafter referred to as the 2023 Criminal Code) will officially come into effect on 2 January 2026.

The 2023 Criminal Code has expanded its content and now contains 624 Articles compared to the old version, which has 569 Articles. While the old Criminal Code was divided into three chapters -General Norms, Crimes, and Offenses, the 2023 Criminal Code only has two chapters, namely General Norms and Criminal Offenses. Therefore, unlike the old Criminal Code, the new one will no longer recognize the differences between crimes and offenses.

Particularly regarding criminal provisions regarding freedom of expression, some provisions still pose potential threats to this freedom. The following sections will discuss and analyze each of the provisions for offline defamation and offline hate speech.

3.4.1 Offline Defamation in the 2023 Criminal Code

3.4.1.1 Article 218 of the 2023 Criminal Code

This Article has two Sections. Section 1 reads:

> *Any person who in public attacks the honor or dignity of the President or Vice President, shall be punished by a maximum imprisonment of 3 (three) years or a fine at most category IV.*

Meanwhile, Section 2 reads:

> *It does not constitute an attack on honor or dignity as intended in paragraph (1), if the act is carried out in the public interest or self-defense.*

This Article is one of the controversial provisions that has sparked controversies and debates among the public and scholars regarding the necessity of its reinstatement. The controversy arises from the fact that the criminal offense of defaming the President or Vice President was declared unconstitutional by the Indonesian Constitutional Court in 2006. In Decision No. 013-022/PUU-IV/2006, the Court ruled that several provisions on defamation of the President (Articles 134, 136bis, and 137) are no longer valid and are in violation of the Indonesian Constitution[97].

In its argument, the Court emphasized that the criminal provisions on defamations of the President and Vice President are irrelevant and could obstruct the process of addressing potential legal violations by the President and/or Vice President as regulated under Article 7A of the Indonesian Constitution.

Article 7A of the Constitution states:

> *The President and/or Vice President can be impeached during their term of office by the People's Consultative Assembly on the recommendation of the House of Representatives, either if they are proven to have committed a violation of the law in the form of treason against the state, corruption, bribery, other serious criminal acts, or disgraceful acts or if they are no longer proven fulfill the requirements as President and/or Vice President.*

From the text of the provisions, it is clear that this article can only be implemented on serious crimes. Furthermore, Article 7B states that the proposal for impeachment can be brought by the House of Representatives to the Constitutional Court to analyze the claim, ensuring that the President and/or President can indeed be impeached.

Reinstating the defamation provisions for the President and/or Vice President in the new Criminal Code is ironic. Another argument the Constitutional Court delivered in its 2006 decision was the protection of freedom of expression, and the proposed amendments to the Criminal Code is to decolonize it[98].

The provisions on defamation against the President and/or Vice President, or generally against authorities, are indeed a colonial legacy. As discussed in Chapter 2, the current Indonesian Criminal Code was formerly known as *Wetboek von Strafrecht* (WvS), which was drafted by the Dutch during their colonialization of Indonesia. Despite a few minor adjustments, the Current Criminal Code still largely reflects the provisions that were enforced during the Dutch colonial period.

Articles 134, 136bis, and 137, which were declared invalid by the Constitutional Court originated from Article 111 of the WvS, which addressed defamation against the King and Queen of the Netherlands. Unfortunately, the provision from WvS was adopted blatantly, which merely replaced "the King and Queen" with "the President and Vice President.[99]"

3.4.2 Article 219 of the 2023 Criminal Code

Although the substance of this provision is similar to Article 218, the provision of Article 219 regulates the use of images and/or written materials that are used to defame the President and Vice President. The language of Article 219 states: Although the substance of this provision is similar to Article 218, the provision of Article 219 regulates the use of images and/or written materials that are used to defame the President and Vice President. The language of Article 219 states:

> *Any person who broadcasts, displays or attaches writing or images so that they are visible to the public, listens to recordings so that they can be heard by the public, or disseminates using information technology means an attack on the honor or honor and dignity of the President and/or Vice President with the intention of making its contents known or more publicly known, shall be punished with a maximum imprisonment of 4 (four) years or a maximum fine of category IV.*

As discussed in the previous section, Articles 218 and 219 reinstate defamation against the President and/or Vice President, which was revoked by the Indonesian Constitutional Court in 2006. These provisions seem to ignore the long struggle to decolonize the criminal legal system in Indonesia.

The attempt to amend the Criminal Code started in 1958 with the establishment of the National Legal Development Institute (*Lembaga Pembinaan Hukum Nasional*-LPHN). The drafting process started during the first National Seminar in 1963, and after 50 years, the draft underwent several revisions. However, the latest draft issued in 2019 sparked major debates and controversies, with Articles 218 and 219 being among the most controversial provisions.

On the one hand, public concern about the reinstatement of these provisions is that they could be "weaponized" to silence critics of the President, Vice President, and the government. On the other hand, the government argues that in some countries, criminal provisions exist to protect the dignity of their leaders. Edward Omar Sharif Hiariej, the Deputy Minister of Law and Human Rights, stated that it does not make sense for the dignity of Indonesia's leaders to remain unprotected in the Criminal Code.

The statement about protecting the dignity of the country's leaders through criminal provisions is hardly justified. First, according to the Constitution, being elected as the President or Vice President in Indonesia means that these individuals hold the top positions as head of state and head of government. Additionally, under Law No. 29 of 1954 on State Defense, the President acts as the Supreme Commander of the Armed Forces of the Republic of Indonesia. Given these roles, it is difficult to see how an expression, especially one that criticizes policies, will affect the high positions held by the President or Vice President. Additionally, defamation as an offense should be proven based on whether any actual damage or actual malice occurred after the alleged defamatory expression. For instance, could criticizing the President demote him/her from the position? Even if so, as discussed in the previous section, there is a high threshold for such a process according to the Constitution, which cannot merely stem from an alleged defamatory expression.

The second reason provided by the government for the criminal defamation provision in the new Criminal Code is that, unlike the old provisions that regulated defamation as an ordinary offense, the new provision classifies it as a complaint-based offense[100]. While ordinary offenses, such as robbery or fraud, can be investigated without any consent or report from the victim, a complaint-based offense requires the victim to report the offense for an investigation to proceed.

However, formulating defamation as a complaint-based offense directed at the President and Vice President is also problematic. Criticisms of the President and Vice President pertain to their roles as head of state and head of government, not their personal character. Therefore, without a clear definition of protected and unprotected expressions within the Indonesian legal system, the criminalization of expressions, as reflected in this provision, remains likely.

3.4.3 Article 240 of the 2023 Criminal Code

There are four sections in the Article. While the other three sections explain the criminal aggravation for this offense, Section 1 regulates the main element of this offense, which reads as follows:

> *Any person who defames public authority or state institutions in public, verbally, or in writing shall be punished with a maximum imprisonment of 1 year and six months or a maximum fine of category II.*

The Article contains a regulation on offenses similar to Article 154 of the Current Criminal Code, which addresses hate expressions toward the government. The difference between this provision and Article 154 of the Current Criminal Code is that this provision includes both verbal and written expressions that contain insults, while Article 154 regulates offenses involving only verbal expressions.

However, the most concerning aspect of this provision is the use of "defame" as an element of the criminal act. In Article 154, hate speech is the alleged unprotected expression. Despite the unclear scope of hateful expression, hate speech theoretically has its own limits as a criminal offense, meaning that such speech could encourage or incite crimes motivated by it. Moreover, in the context of the Indonesian criminal legal system, some scholars agree that hate speech is a *formil* offense (*delik formil*), which means that as long as the elements of the act have occurred, it is punishable under the provision.

Unfortunately, defamation does not share the same element as hate speech. Defamation requires a threshold in which reputational harm is what makes it punishable. However, the term used in Article 240, "*menghina*," is closer in meaning to insult." Insult does not attack the reputation or honor of a person.

The Elucidation Section of Article 240 provides further explanation, which states that "*menghina*" is any act that degrades or damages the honor or image of the government and state institutions, including insult and slander.

First of all, honor and reputation can only be held by a person as a natural legal subject, not by a legal entity, which is usually referred to as an artificial legal subject due to its lack of feelings and emotional attachment, qualities that only a person can possess. Secondly, including insult in the definition of defamation is contradictory since insult is a simple act, like name-calling that does not damage honor and reputation. Even though it may be ethically wrong, it does not violate the law.

3.4.4 Article 241 of the 2023 Criminal Code

Same as Article 240, Sections 2, 3, and 4 of this provision are about the criminal aggravation of the offense. The main element of the crime is regulated under Section 1 as follows:

> *Any person who distributes, displays, or pastes writing or images so that they are visible to the public and can be heard recording so that it can be heard by the public or disseminate widely information technology means that contain defamation to the government or state institutions become known, with the intention of making the contents of defamation public, shall be punished with a maximum imprisonment of 3 (three) years or a criminal offense the maximum fine is category IV.*

Similar to the element of crime regulated in Article 240, Article 241 addresses visual expressions (such as images or pictures) and written expressions that contain defamatory expression. In this provision, written expression is also regulated, but the punishable expressions regulated here are the ones that are disseminated through information technology in the form of electronic information and/or documents.

The provision text raises questions due to its potential overlap with Article 27 Section 3 of the ITE Law (further analysis is provided in the next section) because both use similar language to regulate online defamatory expression. However, Article 622 Section r states that several provisions in the ITE Law, including Article 27 Section 3, will be revoked and will no longer be valid. Therefore, the law on criminal online expression will primarily fall under the Criminal Code.

Interestingly, Articles 218 and 219, along with 240 and 241, have been petitioned for revocation through a judicial review in the Constitutional Court. Early in January 2023, the petition was filed and proceeded to trial as the Court assessed the constitutionality of these provisions. One of the petitioners' main arguments for revocation is that, while offensive expressions may be common, this does not necessarily justify the need for a specific provision under the Criminal Code[101].

However, the Court rejected the petition on the grounds that the Criminal Code is a legal norm that has not yet been implemented because it will officially take effect in 2026. Additionally, the Court argued that the petitioners lack legal standing because there is no urgency due to a legal vacuum, given that the Current Criminal Code is still in effect. The Court cited its verdict on the Criminal Justice System Law of 2012 in Decision No. 110/PUU-X/2012, which noted an urgent situation due to the potential criminalization of law enforcers[102].

3.4.5 Article 433 of the 2023 Criminal Code

Article 433 is the first provision under the Chapter XVII titled "Defamation." The Article has four Sections, but the main elements of the crime are regulated under Section 1, which reads as follows:

> *Any person who verbally attacks the honor or good name of another person by accusing him of something, with the intention of making the matter known to the public, shall be punished for defamation, with a maximum imprisonment of nine months or a maximum fine of category II.*

Compared to the defamation law in the Current Criminal Code (Article 310), there is only a slight difference between Article 310 of the Current Criminal Code and Article 433 of the 2023 Criminal Code, specifically regarding the phrase "verbally," which distinguishes Articles 433 Section 1 (spoken defamation) from Section 2 (written defamation). This distinction was already present in the Current Criminal Code, but adding the phrase "verbally" will likely strengthen the distinction in defamation law.

In addition, there is a difference in penalties, which now include a Category II fine. In the 2023 Criminal Code, there are eight categories of fines, with Category II of Rp. 10.000.000 (ten million Rupiahs)[103]. Another difference is that the provision, through the Elucidation Section, asserts that there must be actual harm, and the law applies only to individuals, not to legal entities such as companies or corporations.

In this context, this is a positive direction because criminal defamation laws have often been implemented incorrectly in cases of alleged defamatory expression toward corporations. In criminal law, however, such entities are artificial subjects and cannot possess feelings like human beings. Ironically, alleged defamation cases involving corporations have still been investigated and brought to trial. Further analysis of the law's implementation will be discussed in Chapter 4.

Section 3 of this Article also emphasizes, similar to the Current Criminal Code, that an act is not punishable if it is in the public interest or in self-defense. Unfortunately, the Elucidation Section does not clearly explain what qualifies as "public interest." By regulating "public interest" as a defense in these criminal defamation laws, the 2023 Criminal Code could suggest a recognition of the international human rights framework, as outlined in the General Comment 34 of Article 19 of the ICCPR. However, the General Comment also states that state parties, including Indonesia, should avoid excessive punitive measures and penalties and consider the decriminalization of defamation, which is not the case in the Indonesian context.

3.4.6 Article 434 of the 2023 Criminal Code

This Article addresses "fitnah", also known as false accusation, Section 1 explains the main elements as follows:

> *If every person, as intended in Article 433, is given the opportunity to prove the truth of the matter alleged but cannot prove it, and the accusation is contrary to what he knows, he will be punished for false accusation, with a maximum imprisonment of 3 (three) years or a maximum fine of category IV.*

Compared to the same offense that is regulated under Article 311 of the Current Criminal Code, there is not much difference. Both Article 311 of the Current Criminal Code and Article 434 of the 2023 Criminal Code consist of the main elements of the offense, namely libel and slander, harming the reputation and good name of a person when such expressions are made publicly.

Therefore, a statement expressed in private communication does not fall into the category of this provision. Furthermore, if the statement is made publicly and is based on fact, it is also not actionable.

In Section 2 of the provision, the law states that proving the truth of the expression can be done under two conditions. The court needs to assess whether the statement is made in the public interest or to defend oneself or in a condition where an officer is conducting the investigation due to his or her occupation. The Elucidation Section also emphasizes that the process of proving the truth of the statement can be applied to public officials.

While there are no clearer explanations on this, in the context of a public official accused of an offense, the type of offense is based on Chapter XXX of the 2023 Criminal Code, titled "Crime by Officials." This chapter consists of Articles 527 to 541, which regulate various criminal acts, such as neglecting instructions from a superior or abusing the power held due to one's position.

The importance of regulating false accusations against state officials stems from the need for these state officials to perform their duties for the government in governing the country. Hence, the limitation on the aforementioned criminal offenses aims to ensure that the officials do not act beyond the mandate of their positions.

3.4.7 Article 435 of the 2023 Criminal Code

This provision is a continuation of Article 434 concerning false accusations. Therefore, there is not much difference between this Article and Article 312 of the Current Criminal Code. Article 435 emphasizes the regulation of false accusations that conflict with established facts. In Section 1, if the accusation has been ruled upon in a court verdict, it is not actionable as a false accusation offense. Meanwhile, Section 2 emphasizes that the accusation is considered false if there is a court verdict that states that the accused is not guilty. In Section 3, the provision states that if the trial regarding the accusation is still ongoing, the legal proceedings for the false accusation offense should be postponed.

3.4.8 Article 436 of the 2023 Criminal Code

Article 436 addresses minor defamation, which may also be considered as an insult. The full text of the provision is as follows:

> *Insults that are not in the nature of slander or libel committed against another person, whether in public orally or in writing, or directly to the person insulted verbally or by deeds or in writing sent or received to him or her, are accepted as light insults with criminal penalties. imprisonment for a maximum of 6 (six) months or a maximum fine of category II.*

This provision is not significantly different from Article 315 of the Current Criminal Code, which also regulates insult. However, it highlights the ongoing problem of regulating minor defamation or insults as criminal offenses. The language of the provision suggests that minor defamation does not harm reputation or good name as defamation does, nor does it specify any specific harm necessary to be considered a criminal offense.

The core idea of an offense regulated under criminal law is that it causes physical, mental, or financial harm. Furthermore, the offense should also cause disorder within society because criminal law is drafted by the state to maintain public order. Therefore, individual, societal, and state interests should be protected.

Minor defamation does not require an accusation. It includes name-calling based on physical appearance or social status and may be considered a form of sociological defamation[104]. A key consideration is whether minor defamation causes any harm to a person's reputation and good name.

In ordinary defamatory, reputation and good name can be tainted because such expressions may affect someone's position, particularly in relation to his occupation or job. For example, if someone loses his job due to a defamatory expression labeling him as a thief, this could the trust of his or her boss. On the other hand, minor defamation does not cause such impacts, which means that it lacks the degree of harm necessary to be considered a crime.

However, in bullying, where name-calling is also quite common, different treatment may occur. As a crime, bullying targets vulnerable groups, especially children, and imposes an intimidating effect on the victims. This intimidation can happen due to the power imbalance between the bully and the bullied.

In summary, regarding the difference between minor defamation and bullying, Indonesian criminal law currently does not have any specific formula or test to determine whether the element of minor defamation truly has a harmful effect, similar to that of bullying.

3.4.9 Article 437 of the 2023 Criminal Code

Article 437 pertains to fraud reporting. Section 1 of the provision reads as follows:

> *Any person who submits a false complaint or notification in writing or asks another person to write a false complaint or notification to an authorized official about another person so that the person's reputation or good name is harmed shall be punished for making a slanderous complaint with a maximum imprisonment of 3 (three) 6 (six) months or a maximum fine of category IV.*

While the language of the provision aligns with the elements of false accusation, the Article specifically addresses individuals complicit in fraud reporting, which involves making false accusations. In this provision, the crime occurs in two different types, which are the false accusation itself and the act of reporting that is actually untrue, as it involves an incorrect accusation.

In addition, Section 2 of this article includes an accumulation penalty in the form of rights revocation. Rights revocation is regulated under Article 86 of the 2023 Criminal Code, which specifies seven different rights that may be revoked. However, two of these revocations can be applied to violations of

Article 437 Section 2, namely the right to hold a public official position and/or the right to become a member of the Indonesian Police or Indonesian Army[105].

3.4.10 Article 438 of the 2023 Criminal Code

Article 438 pertains to false suspicion. The provision reads as follows:

> *Any person who by an act creates a false suspicion against another person that the person has committed a criminal act shall be punished for creating a false suspicion, with a maximum imprisonment of three (3) years and six (6) months or a maximum fine of category IV.*

According to this provision, the punishable action is not the statement itself, either spoken or written, but any action that causes suspicion against another person, leading to the allegation that he or she has committed a criminal act.

The Elucidation Section of the provision provides an example in which A put C's watch inside B's drawer, causing B to be accused of stealing C's watch. Interestingly, based on the language of the provision and the example provided, Article 438 is the only defamation law that does not regulate statements as actionable defamation.

3.4.11 Article 439 of the 2023 Criminal Code

Defaming the dead is regulated by this Article. It contains four sections, with Section 1 reading as follows:

> *Any person who commits written defamation or defamation against a dead person shall be punished with a maximum imprisonment of 6 (six) months or a maximum fine of category II.*

Despite the fact that the person who was defamed has already passed away, Indonesian criminal law holds that the reputation and good name of the deceased are still important matters to protect. As reflected in this Article, a criminal complaint can be filed by the spouse or other family members of the deceased[106].

The reputation of the deceased is related to the late person's status within the family and how he or she will be remembered by society; hence, this regulation addresses the offense. Similar to minor defamation regulated under Article 436 of the 2023 Criminal Code, this provision can also be considered sociological defamation because it does not occur directly in front of the person since the person has already passed away.

However, the reputation of the deceased can be viewed from two perspectives: Subjective and objective. The subjective perspective refers to how a person feels his or her reputation has been harmed due to the alleged defamatory expression, which does not apply in cases of defamation against the deceased. The objective perspective relates to reputational harm measured by common sense and logical reasoning, as assessed by family members and society at large[107]. The latter is reflected in how the family reacts to the alleged defamatory expression.

Article 439 has three other sections. Section 2 addresses the accumulation of penalties, Section 3 regulates that this offense is a criminal complaint-based, and Section 4 specifies that a complaint can be filed by whoever holds the father's authority in a matriarchal society. For example, in Minangkabau, the largest ethnic group on Sumatra Island, domestic matters and inheritance are traced through the female line[108]. Given this societal background, Article 439 Section 4 can be implemented in Minangkabau society.

3.4.12 Article 440 of the 2023 Criminal Code

The last three articles on defamation in the 2023 Criminal Code are regulations concerning criminal complaints, criminal aggravation, and cumulative punishment. Article 440 reads as follows:

> *Criminal acts as regulated in Article 433, Article 434, and Articles 436 to 438 are not prosecuted if there is no complaint from the victim of the crime.*

As reflected in the language of the provisions, the criminal offenses of slander and libel (Article 433), calumny (434), minor defamation (436), fraudulent reporting (437), and false suspicion (438) are based on criminal complaints. Article 440 is a new provision not present in the previous Criminal Code, emphasizing that defamation investigations must be filed by the victim – the person who feels defamed – and cannot be represented by others, such as friends or family members. The only exception is Article 439 concerning defamation of the deceased, as discussed in the previous section.

3.4.13 Article 441 of the 2023 Criminal Code

Two provisions in this Article regulate punishment aggravation. However, specific conditions apply to the implementation of the punishments. For criminal offenses under Articles 433 to 439, both the duration of the imprisonment and the fine amount will be increased by 1/3 if the offenses are committed using information technology.

Article 441 Section 1 emphasizes that online defamation will be regulated under one law, the Criminal Code, thereby revoking all criminal provisions for online defamation in the ITE Law. These changes and revocations will take effect once the 2023 Criminal Code is officially imposed in 2026, as mandated in Article II of the 2023 Criminal Code.

Meanwhile, Section 2 increases the punishment by 1/3 for Articles 433 (slander and libel), 434 (calumny), and 436 (minor defamation) if the offenses are directed against public officials who are running their duties. As discussed in the section on hate speech, regulating banned expressions toward government officials requires a specific standard to delineate the scope of what unprotected expressions are actionable as criminal offenses. Furthermore, a higher standard applies to public officials, since they hold more power. If they wish to report defamation, they must provide evidence that meets a high legal threshold to demonstrate that defamation has occurred and that their reputation has been harmed. Unfortunately, no specific scope is provided, nor does the Elucidation Section provide any explanation.

3.4.14 Article 442 of the 2023 Criminal Code

An additional punishment is regulated in the last provision of defamation in the 2023 Criminal Code. This Article states that the individuals convicted of offenses under Articles 434, 436, and 439 will have certain rights revoked. According to Article 86, these revoked rights include the right to hold a position as a public official, the right to join the Indonesian National Army and Indonesian National Police, the right to be elected and vote in elections, and the right to serve as a guardian or guardian supervisor for a child.

3.5 Offline Hate Speech in the 2023 Criminal Code

There are only two provisions for offline hate speech in the 2023 Criminal Code, which are Articles 242 and 243. In the new Criminal Code, hate speech provisions are included under "Defamation Against Groups of People," which likely overlaps with defamation.

However, the elements of the criminal act consist of identity factors that are associated with the victim, making it more identifiable as hate speech provisions. Furthermore, specifying the scope of identity factors within the provisions should establish a precise, actionable definition of hate speech. In addition to Articles 242 and 243, there are a few more criminal provisions related to hate speech, specifically Articles 244 and 245, which regulate racial and ethnic discrimination. However, this section does not discuss these provisions, given that they punish actions rather than hateful expressions.

3.5.1 Article 242 of the 2023 Criminal Code

The provision in Article 242 reads as follows:

> *Any person who publicly expresses feelings of hostility, hatred, or contempt towards one or several groups or groups of the Indonesian population based on race, nationality, ethnicity, skin color, gender, mental disability, or physical disability shall be punished by a maximum imprisonment of three years or a maximum fine of category.*

This provision of the 2023 Criminal Code introduces a section entitled "Group Defamation," which consists of defamatory offenses. followed by a section called "Crime Based on Racial and Ethnic Discrimination." Both sections are part of the "Crimes Against Public Order" chapter. Regulating specific criminal acts based on racial and ethnic discrimination is understandable, especially since Indonesia has ratified the International Convention on the Elimination of All Forms of Racial Discrimination 1965 through Law No. 29 of 1999. Indonesia has also passed Law No. 40 of 2008 on Racial and Ethnic Discrimination as *lex specialis* for such offenses.

Interestingly, while this Article uses the term "*penghinaan*," which translates to "defamation," the elements it regulates are directed toward hate speech, even though the term "group defamation" is used. The Elucidation Section does not provide further explanation of the criminal act's elements, but based on the language of the provision and also its placement under the chapter on "Crime Against Public Order," it remains unclear whether this Article regulates the offense as a *formil* offense (*delik formil*) or as a *materiil* offense (*delik materiil*).

The language of Article 242 does not require an effect on public order for an offense to occur, and the Elucidation Section does not provide an explanation on this point. This suggests that the Article may classify as a formal offense, where an effect is not required for the offense to be considered complete. However, Article 242 is located within the chapter "Crime Against Public Order," which implies that the harm of offenses under this chapter pertains to public order. Harm to public order is the effect resulting from the crime, which would define it as *materiil* offense. In summary, there remains inconsistency from the lawmakers of the new Criminal Code in regulating this offense, despite the need to protect social harmony.

3.5.2 Article 243 of the 2023 Criminal Code

The provision has two Sections. Article 243 Section 1 reads:

> *Any person who broadcasts, displays, or posts writing or images so that they are visible to the public or plays recordings so that they are audible to the public or disseminates them using information technology, which contains statements of feelings of hostility with the intention that the contents are known or more widely known by the public, towards one or several groups or groups of Indonesian residents based on race, nationality, ethnicity, skin colour, religion, belief, gender, mental disability, or physical disability that results in violence against people or property, shall be punished with a maximum imprisonment of 4 years or a maximum fine of category IV, for 200 million Rupiahs.*

This provision has a similar formulation to the Current Criminal Code regarding the elements of hateful expression, which must consist hostile expression. However, the provision provides a broader scope regarding the medium used by potential perpetrators, allowing for broadcast (such as radio, television, podcast), display (poster), or posting of writings or images (such as social media posts or websites), including information technology media. The identity factors are also broadened to include gender, belief, skin color, and disability status.

While the provision is a more well-drafted law on hate speech, one element remains unclear, particularly regarding the distinction between the creator and the disseminator. For example, should there be a distinct punishment for those who create hateful content in a video versus those who disseminate it? This distinction is not about the platform where the content is usually spread; rather, there is a high possibility that content is shared by others who think it is worth sharing or who support the hateful ideas in the content without understanding the legal consequences related to hate speech.

However, there is also a possibility that the Indonesian government may take broader action in combating hate speech by "ignoring" the distinction between creators and disseminators, as long as hateful expression exists within society. If this is the case, any expression that incites hostility, either created or spread, would need to align with the standards imposed by the United Nations[109], which in application should also respect the three-step test to determine that the restriction is legal, legitimate, and necessary[110].

Meanwhile, Article 243 Section 2 regulates the possibility of additional punishment for hate speech perpetrators if they commit hate speech as part of their occupation or as a repeated criminal offense. The provisions reads:

> *If any person as referred to in paragraph (1) commits the crime in carrying out his profession and at that time it has not yet passed 2 (two) years since the criminal decision which has obtained permanent legal force for committing the same crime, the perpetrator may be subject to additional punishment in the form of revocation of rights as referred to in Article 86 Letter f.*

With these two provisions on hate speech, the government has made a few changes in addressing hate speech as a criminal offense. A further comparison is provided in the following section to determine the differences between the provisions in the current and new Criminal Codes.

3.6 Comparison of the Criminal Codes

To summarize and provide context for comparison, the following table outlines the criminal provisions for offline defamation in the Current Criminal Code and the 2023 Criminal Code:

Table 3.1 Comparison of Offline Defamation and Offline Hate Provisions on the Current Criminal Code and the 2023 Criminal Code

Provisions	*The Current Criminal Code*	*The 2023 Criminal Code*
Offline Defamation	- Punishable for defamation with a prison term up to nine months and a fine of four thousand and five hundred rupiahs (Article 310). - Punishable for libel with a prison term up to four years (Article 311).	- Punishable for defamation with a prison term up to nine months and a fine of Category II (Article 433 Section 1). - Punishable for libel with a prison term up to three years and a fine of Category IV (Article 434 Section 1).
Offline Hate Speech	- Focus on expressions of hostility, hatred, or contempt instead of pejorative and discriminatory remarks toward one or more groups within the Indonesian population. - There is no specific definition for one or more groups that are victims of hate speech. - Act against the Government of Indonesia (Articles 154 and 155) or against one or more groups within the population of Indonesia (Articles 156 and 157). - Punishable by a prison term of up to four years and a fine of 4.5 million rupiahs (Article 156).	- Focus on expressions of hostility, hatred, or contempt toward one or more groups within the Indonesian population. - Groups are defined by several identity factors, including race, nationality, ethnicity, skin color, gender, and disability status. - Punishable by a prison term of up to three years and a fine of Category IV of 200 million rupiahs Article 242).

3.7 The Information and Electronic Transactions Law (the ITE Law)

In 2008, the ITE Law was passed as national legislation, marking the first law regarding the internet in Indonesia. The idea to draft a law on Information and Electronic Transactions started in 2013 when the Indonesian Representative Council (*Dewan Perwakilan Rakyat*-DPR) discussed the draft law on Information Electronic and Electronic Transactions. The law was drafted in response to the need for specific legislation to address technological advancements and the rise of the internet. In general, the ITE Law was passed to facilitate the development of the digital economy and to provide safety, justice, and legal certainty for internet users and providers in Indonesia[111]. In addition, the ITE Law was intended to replace Law Number 36 of 1999 on Telecommunications, which had become outdated, as the ITE Law also regulates communication over the internet[112].

In the early stages of drafting the ITE Law, the Ministry of Communication and Information drafted the ITE Law based on an academic manuscript, a manuscript written as a result of discourse and research on a particular issue, which can be justified scientifically as a basis for legislation. This manuscript, drafted in 2005, already incorporated the Information and Electronic Transaction Law. It included a discussion of criminal offenses occurring digitally. However, all the offenses focused on crimes harming either data or systems, such as phishing, hacking, carding, and fraud, instead of criminalizing content. The only content subject to criminalization includes pornography, copyright infringement, and online organized crime for terrorism[113].

Unfortunately, the ITE Law has become more widely recognized for its criminal provisions and for prosecuting online expressions, such as online defamation[114], even though the government has acknowledged that the current defamation laws in the Criminal Code are obsolete[115].

Before conducting a deeper analysis of the provisions in the law, this chapter will provide context by noting that the ITE Law has been amended twice. After being passed in 2008, the law was amended in 2016, and the latest amendment was in 2024.

The Amendment of Information and Electronic Transaction Number 19 of 2016 (the ITE Law 2016) partially revised the Information and Electronic Transaction Number 11 of 2008 (the ITE Law 2008), but the ITE Law 2016 did not revoke the 2008 Law. Both statutes remain valid, and Indonesian legal enforcers should consult these laws when investigating any offenses that are regulated under the ITE Laws (2008 and 2016).

Between the 2008 and 2016 ITE Laws, there were no significant differences regarding criminal offenses, but changes were made to the penalties[116]. For example, under the 2008 ITE Law, online criminal defamation (Article 27 Section 3) was punishable by 6 years of imprisonment and a fine of 1 billion rupiahs. This penalty was reduced in the 2016 ITE Law to 4 years of imprisonment and a fine of 750 million rupiahs. Meanwhile, the penalties for online hate speech (Article 28 Section 2) in the 2016 ITE Law remained unchanged at 6 years imprisonment and a fine of one billion rupiahs.

In the first amendment of the ITE Law, the 2016 ITE Law did not revoke any provisions related to criminal offenses, despite the increasing number of criminal cases related to alleged offensive expressions and the potential for "rubber provision" – a term coined by the public to scrutinize the criminal provisions in the ITE Law that can be elastically abused for elite interests[117]. Many cases were also controversial, such as unnecessary prosecutions and trials for consumer complaints, which will be discussed in detail in Chapter 4. Despite only slight changes to the legal norms, the 2016 ITE Law emphasizes that online defamation is now a criminal-based complaint.

Five years after its first amendment, President Joko Widodo presented an idea in his speech to the Indonesian Police, stating that the ITE Law, especially the "rubber provision" needs to be amended. He also stated that he would ask the Indonesian Representative Council to initiate the process of the second amendment if the implementation of the ITE Law is deemed unfair[118].

Upon the President's instruction, the government responded by forming two teams related to the ITE Law: The Guideline Implementation of the ITE

Law team and the ITE Law Amendment team. These teams operate under the supervision of the Minister of Coordination of Political, Legal, and Human Rights, Mahfud MD[119].

However, even though some members of the Indonesian Representative Council agreed on the idea of amending the ITE Law[120], the Law was ultimately not submitted in the 2021 Priority National Legislation. Instead, there was a Joint Decree between the Minister of Communication and Information, the Indonesian Attorney General, and the Indonesian Chief of National Police (*Surat Keputusan Bersama-SKB*).

The 2021 Joint Decree on the ITE Law Guidelines, issued by the Indonesian Ministry of Communication and Information, the Attorney General, and the National Police Chief (herein referred to as the 2021 Joint Decree), resulted from the Guideline Implementation of the ITE Law team. However, the 2021 Joint Decree is not legally binding, as it is not a formal legal product and merely serves as a guideline for legal enforcers in implementing the legal norms of the ITE Law[121]. This means the Joint Decree does not enable any changes to the ITE Law. There is also no requirement for judges to use the ITE Law Guidelines as a legal source[122].

Following the 2021 Joint Decree, the ITE Law was amended in January 2024, introducing more changes than the 2016 version, especially in the section on criminalizing expressions.

Due to the partial amendment, most provisions of the 2008 ITE Law remain valid constitutionally. While the subsequent amendments made some changes and revoked certain articles in the 2008 ITE Law, they also established a conjunction between the 2008 ITE Law and its amendment in 2016 and 2024.

The following sections will discuss each provision from the 2008 ITE Law, 2016 ITE Law, and 2024 ITE Law, particularly focusing on the criminal provisions for online defamation and online hate speech, as mentioned in Chapter 2, given the high number of such cases. However, some provisions may be excluded if there are no substantial changes among the three versions of the laws.

3.7.1 Online Defamation in the 2008 ITE Law

The criminal provision for online defamation is part of Chapter VII, titled "Prohibited Acts" of the Law. Article 27 consists of four sections, each addressing a differing offense: Online pornography (Article 27 Section 1), online gambling (Article 27 Section 3), online defamation (Article 27 Section 3), and online blackmail and threats (Article 27 Section 4). The four offenses formulated in one provision of Article 27 share the same criminal elements: "to distribute," "to transmit," and "causes to be accessible."

The full language of the provision in Article 27 Section 3 is as follows:

> *Any person who deliberately and without authority distributes and/or transmits and/or causes to be accessible Electronic Information and/or Electronic Records with contents of insult and/or defamation.*

The three phrases "to distribute," "to transmit," and "causes to be accessible" were not initially defined in the 2008 ITE Law, despite being essential to the dissemination of online defamation. In addition, the norms of this provision are linked to Article 310 of the Current Criminal Code because Article 310 is *lex superior* – a law with a greater legitimacy due to its higher position in the hierarchy – while Article 27 Section 3 of the 2008 ITE Law is *lex inferior* because it has a lower position in the hierarchy in relation to the Criminal Code.

Because of the *lex superior* and *lex inferior* doctrines, the definition of defamation should be based on Articles 310 and 311 of the Current Criminal Code. The Constitutional Court also encourages the formulation of a primary norm for defamation in the Criminal Code in its Decision Number 50/PUU-VI/2008. This judicial decision stipulates that defamation should be distinctively regulated for offline defamation (Articles 310 and 311 of the Criminal Code) and online defamation (Article 27 Section 3). In addition, the Court emphasizes that *genus delict* – as a general principle in criminal law – in Articles 310 and 311 requires that both offline and online defamation be treated as criminal-based complaints.

The distinction in the regulation of defamation may appear appropriate, but the norms attached to Articles 310 and 311 present problems. The offense in the provision is labeled as "insult and/or defamation." However, following the logic that the definitions in these Articles should align with those in the Criminal Code, it is important to note that defamation falls under Chapter XVI (Articles 310 to 321) of the Criminal Code. Article 310 addresses slander and libel, while Article 311 pertains to calumny. At this point, the definition of online defamation in the 2008 ITE Law appears incompatible, as the ITE Law regulates insult and defamation as equal offenses, while insult is defined in the Criminal Code as one of the defamation offenses (Article 315). Moreover, the concept of insult in Article 315 does not serve as the basis for Article 27 Section 3 of the ITE Law, particularly when considering the element of unharmed reputation in the so-called crime, as discussed in Section 3.2.6.

Due to unclear norms in the provision, online defamation is subject to harsh punishment. Article 45, in conjunction with Article 27, part of the "Criminal Regulation" Chapter, states that all offenses under Article 27 are punishable by up to 6 years of imprisonment and/or a fine of up to 1 billion rupiahs.

Article 45 provides the criminal sanction for Article 27 Section 3, stating that the perpetrator will be punished with a prison term of up to six years and a fine sanction of up to 1 billion rupiahs[123]. Meanwhile, in the Criminal Code, the prison term in Article 310 is up to 9 months with a fine sanction of 4,500 rupiahs.

To ensure the fine amount is relevant and has a deterrent effect, the Indonesian Supreme Court passed a law in 2012 stating that every maximum amount in the Criminal Code should be multiplied by 1000[124]. This means that if a defendant is found guilty in a criminal defamation case based on Article 310 and the court instructs him or her to pay a fine, the fine amount would be 4,500,000 rupiahs, which is equal to $316.98.

Harsh penalties for criminalizing expression are one of the reasons the law comes under scrutiny, leading the public to criticize the ITE Law. One of the criticisms of Article 27 Section 3 comes from the ICJR (Institute for Criminal Justice Reform), an Indonesian research institute that focuses its work on criminal law and justice reform in Indonesia. ICJR's criticisms aim to address three issues[125]:

1 The Article has multiple interpretations and duplications of criminal offenses with the Criminal Code. These multiple interpretations arise from the phrase "causes to be accessible," which remains unclear. Even though the amendment of the ITE Law in 2016 attempts to clarify this, the explanation of "any act that causes to be accessible" does not provide a specific meaning. Meanwhile, the concepts of attacking honor and reputation are also interpreted differently because their definitions under the law are unclear.
2 Some criminal offenses are duplicated between this Article and Articles 310 and 311 of the Criminal Code. If defamation is already regulated in the Criminal Code, there is no need to regulate it in another regulation.
3 The multiple interpretations bring uncertainty into the entire legal process. Particularly during the court proceedings, the Indonesian criminal justice system relies on the judges' ability to interpret the legislation, so clear provisions are required.

In 2008, a couple of months after the ITE Law was enacted, Article 27 Section 3 was judicially reviewed by the Indonesian Constitutional Court. This was the very first time the controversial provision was filed to the Constitutional Court for repeal. The plaintiff in the lawsuit was Iwan Piliang, an Indonesian journalist. His legal standing as a journalist is valid because the law was officially passed, and people fear that such a law threatens press freedom[126]. The multiple interpretations of Article 27 Section 3 are raised in this lawsuit, which contributes to the term "rubber provision," – which became popular due to the high number of online defamation cases under the ITE Law. The plaintiff argued that the provision contradicts the Indonesian Constitution of 1945, particularly Articles 28D Section 1, 28E Sections 2 and 3, and 28F[127]. However, the Constitutional Court rejected the lawsuit, reasoning that the provision is still aligned with the Indonesian Constitution, even though the provision of criminal defamation is necessary to differentiate and regulate offline and online defamation.

Not only are the penalties harsh due to the combination of prison terms and fines, but it is also illogical to allocate state resources to address an offense that occurs between private individuals. Naturally, defamation can only occur between two individuals, as a legal subject is the one who can feel offended, and the determination of whether an expression is defamatory can only be made by the victim.

Criminal penalties consist of two types of punishment provided by the state: A prison term, which means that the convicted individual will be incarcerated in a state facility, and a fine, which is paid and becomes part of the state fund, as regulated under Article 42 of the Current Criminal Code. Additionally, Government Regulation Number 39 of 2016 on Types and Rates of Non-Tax State Revenue Applicable to the Indonesian Prosecutor's Office also regulates that one source of non-tax state revenue is fines derived from penalties for criminal offenses[128].

On the basis that both prison terms and fines are state resources, these penalties do not repair any reputational harm resulting from defamation, which is illogical. If a reputation is neither repaired nor restored, then using criminal penalties does not fulfill justice for the victim, suggesting that the legal system in defamation cases heavily relies on a retaliation process against the convicted instead of delivering true justice. This retaliation process stems from the retributive justice doctrine, which is applied in formulating criminal sanctions and compensation, with the severity of punishments based on the seriousness of the crime[129]. However, this doctrine has been criticized as obsolete, as restoring the condition prior to the crime may only occur if that prior condition was justified[130], raising issues of proportionality regarding the punishment itself[131].

In an online defamation case in Indonesia, the provisions indicate that reputational harm is measured by a prison term and a fine. However, these penalties do not effectively remediate the loss experienced by the victim. Hence, questionable punishments exist, which can serve as a tool for retaliation by the rich and powerful.

3.7.2 Online Hate Speech in the 2008 ITE Law

Online hate speech is regulated under Article 28, which covers two offenses, namely consumer fraud (Article 28 Section 1) and online hate speech (Article 28 Section 2). Both offenses do not include the elements "to distribute," "to transmit," and "causes to be accessible," but both use the term "to disseminate" regarding the alleged information that violates the provisions.

Article 28 Section 2 reads as follows:

> *Every person intentionally and without right to disseminate information intended to arouse feelings individual and/or group hatred or enmity certain communities based on ethnicity, religion, race, and intergroup (SARA)*[132].

While there is no explanation for "disseminate" in this provision or in the Elucidation Section, it appears that "disseminate" here refers specifically to online expressions of hate toward ethnicity, religion, race, and intergroup. However, the ITE Law is also unclear as to why online defamation uses distinctive terms like "to distribute," "to transmit," and "causes to be accessible," which are not applied to online hate speech. Defining – and, if possible, justifying – the different terms used for online defamation and online hate speech is essential because, even though the international human rights framework uses "disseminate" in supporting rights to expression, the scope of freedom of expression itself remains very broad[133]. Therefore, a clear limitation is needed when formulating proper laws to address potential violations of the right to expression.

Another unclear element in the provision is the definition of "intergroup." While ethnicity, religion, and race are clearly defined as identity factors that belong to an individual since he or she is born, "intergroup" has never been constitutionally defined. Hence, there is ambiguity when hate speech is classified as a crime and penalties are imposed. Several judicial decisions that used "intergroup" to determine online hate speech in the trials also did not define the term specifically; instead, the judicial decisions assessed "intergroup" as equivalent to "group," making "intergroup" the same as "interethnic," "interrace," and "interreligious"[134].

"Intergroup," as part of the term "SARA," is a legacy of the authoritarian regime during the New Order era, particularly during the events of 1965 related to the alleged coup by the Indonesian Communist Party (*Partai Komunis Indonesia*-PKI)[135]. That year, Sudomo, the Chief of the Operational Command for the Restoration of Security and Order (*Komando Operasi Pemulihan Pengamanan dan Ketertiban*-KOPKAMTIB), oversaw investigations, arrests, and even prosecutions of citizens suspected of being affiliated with communism and the Indonesian Communist Party without proper trials[136].

The term "SARA," which was used in an authoritarian manner and did not have a scientific basis, was one of the reasons the phrase "and intergroup" in the 2008 ITE Law and the 2016 ITE Law was requested to be revoked and deemed unconstitutional in 2017. The Constitutional Court acknowledged that "intergroup" is not firmly and clearly defined[137]. However, the Constitutional Court also argued that the ITE Law is a *lex specialis* because the context in which the term "intergroup" is used differs between the ITE Law and the Criminal Code. The distinction emphasizes the principle already applied in deciding online defamation cases: The ITE Law addresses online hate speech, while the Criminal Code is used for offline hate speech[138]. Based on this, the Court decided to reject the petition to revoke the term "and intergroup," and Article 28 Section 2 of the ITE Law remains valid.

While the Constitutional Court's decision provided a basis for distinguishing laws governing online and offline expressions, it does not clarify the clear meaning of "intergroup," which is understandable since it is not the Constitutional Court's duty as a judicial body to define such a term. However, the term "intergroup" has evidently caused confusion in implementation and represents yet another "rubber provision" due to its overly broad scope in several cases. The implementation of the provision of Article 28 Section 2 of the ITE Law will be discussed in detail in Chapter 4 of this book.

Because no changes were made to Article 28 Section 2 in the 2016 ITE Law, the discussion of this provision will be covered in the section on the 2024 ITE Law.

3.7.3 Online Defamation in the 2016 ITE Law

There are not many significant changes in the criminal provisions of the 2016 ITE Law. After the partial amendment, which allowed two laws to coexist in the area of Internet law in Indonesia (ITE Law 2008 and ITE Law 2016), the terms "to distribute," "to transmit," and "causes to be accessible" were provided with definitions in the Explanation Section of the Law.

The updated Elucidation Section for these three deeds is a positive step in narrowing the scope of actionable defamation. "To distribute" is defined as sending electronic information to a group of people, while "to transmit" means to send electronic information individually. However, "causes to be accessible" still has a broad definition, as it is merely defined as all other deeds not included in distributing and transmitting through an electronic system that causes electronic information and/or documents to be known by other parties or the public[139].

It is concerning that while "to distribute" and "to transmit" now have firm definitions, "causes to be accessible" is still broadly defined and may be inadequately implemented due to its ambiguous nature, which contradicts the principle of *lex certa*. *Lex certa*, or legal certainty, is a principle in criminal law that mandates lawmakers to carefully draft laws, ensuring that the law regarding violations is formulated clearly[140]. Clear formulations will limit the authority of the government and reduce the potential for abuse of the law.

Lex certa is a bigger part of the legality principle that is also mandated in Article 1 of the current and 2023 Criminal Code. There are three big concepts of the legality principle[141], which are: *nulla poena sina lege* (punishment should be based on criminal law), *nulla poena sine crimine* (punishment can only be imposed if the act is regulated as a criminal offense in a law), and *nullum crimen sine poena legali* (any criminal offense in law, if violated, is punishable as regulated by the law).

In the context of "causes to be accessible a narrow limitation should be provided, similar to that provided for "to distribute" and "to transmit." Defining it simply as "any other acts…" seems like oversimplification that could lead to potential abuse by law enforcers and may harm individual rights. From a deterrence perspective, compliance to *lex certa* would help both individual citizens and law enforcers to understand the limits and scope of the violated acts,[142] discouraging individuals from committing offenses because of clear limitations.

Another change was the reduction of criminal punishment for online defamation. Under the 2008 ITE Law, the penalties were 6 years of imprisonment and a fine of 1 billion Rupiahs. Despite the lack of significant changes in the provision and its potential for multiple interpretations, the penalties were reduced to 4 years of imprisonment, and a fine of 750 million Rupiahs.

To conclude, the 2016 ITE Law has not effectively changed the criminal provisions, despite concerns about curbing freedom of expression and scrutiny over unnecessary criminal provisions regarding online expressions.

3.7.4 Online Defamation in the 2024 ITE Law

After the 2016 ITE Law, it took another eight years for the government to amend it. In terms of structure, there are various changes to the provisions.

However, substantially, the draconian criminal provisions regarding expressions still exist in the law[143].

In the 2008 and 2016 ITE Laws, Article 27 Section 3 contains the criminal provision for online defamation. In the 2024 ITE Law, the provision has been removed and replaced with Articles 27A and 27B. Criminal online defamation has now been moved to Article 27A, which reads:

> *Every person intentionally attacks the honor or good name of another person by accusing him of something, with the intention of making the matter known to the public in the form of electronic information and/or electronic documents carried out through an electronic system.*

Meanwhile, Article 27B reads as follows:

Section 1:

> *Every person intentionally and without right distributes and/or transmits Electronic Information and/or Electronic Documents, with the intention of unlawfully benefiting himself or another person, forcing someone with threats of violence to*:
>
> *a giving an item, which partly or wholly belongs to that person or to another person; or*
> *b giving debt, making an acknowledgment of debt, or writing off a receivable.*

Section 2:

> *Every person intentionally and without right distributes and/or transmits Electronic Information and/or Electronic Documents with the intention of benefiting himself or another person unlawfully, with the threat of contamination or with the threat of disclosing secrets, forcing someone to*:
>
> *a giving an item which partly or wholly belongs to that person or to another person; or giving debt, making an acknowledgment of debt, or writing off a receivable.*
> *b to give credit, to acknowledge debt, or to write off receivables*

Substantially, the criminal online defamation provision in Article 27A added the phrase "by accusing him of something," which is essential for demonstrating that the dissemination of an alleged defamatory expression damages a reputation through a specific accusation. This added phrase introduces a specific element that must be proven when investigating online defamation. Therefore, the intention behind distributing, transmitting, or enabling access to defamatory content is emphasized by these changes.

Changes are also provided in the Elucidation Section, such as the definition of "known by the public," which is as follows:

> *What is meant by "publicly known" is to be or so that it can be accessed by a large group of people, most of whom do not know each other.*

While the above definition is clear and emphasizes the act of "to distribute," it does not provide a clearer meaning for "to transmit" and "causes to be accessible." The phrase "to transmit" is defined as the act of sending information from one individual to another. Therefore, this constitutes private communication that does not fall within the scope of "known by the public." Using the logic in the Elucidation Section for "to distribute" and "causes to be accessible," the definition of "known by the public" can also be applied to "to distribute" because it involves sending information to many individuals. For example, uploading a YouTube video allows electronic information to be accessed by a large group of people. However, the definition of "causes to be accessible" has not changed in the Elucidation Section, which, as discussed in section 3.5.3, is inconsistent with t the *lex certa* principle.

Another change in the Elucidation Section is the definition of "attacks the honor and good name" in Article 27A, which is defined as an act that demeans or damages another person's good name or self-esteem to the detriment of that person, including sacrilege and/or vilification[144]. Meanwhile, Article 27B essentially reformulates the norm in Article 27 Section 4 of the 2008 ITE Law, incorporating additional elements from Articles 368 and 369 of the Current Criminal Code regarding blackmail and threats. The added elements in Article 27B clarify the norms for online blackmail and threats as the language of the former provision lacks clarity on the scope of these offenses in the digital age.

3.7.5 Online Hate Speech in the 2024 ITE Law

Substantially, the 2024 ITE Law does not change the provisions for online hate speech as it does for online defamation. Article 28 Section 2 remains the governing law for online hate speech. However, compared to the previous version, it now reads as follows:

> *Any person intentionally and without right distributes and/or transmits Electronic Information and/or Electronic Documents that are inciting, inviting, or influencing other people so as to create feelings of hatred or enmity towards certain individuals and/or community groups based on race, nationality, ethnicity, skin color, religion, creed, gender, mental disability, or physical disability.*

The Law is no longer simply referred to as "disseminating," as regulated in the 2008 ITE Law. Instead, it now uses "to distribute" and "to transmit," which, as discussed earlier and defined in the Elucidation Section, refer to sending information to many individuals and to a single individual, respectively.

Another change in the 2024 ITE Law is the addition of more specific terms like "inviting" or "influencing to the provision that covers generating hostility and hatred. This change is important because the previous term "generate" was unclear regarding whether it implied punishable conduct as a deliberate action, which is a required element for hate speech to qualify as a criminal act. By using "inviting" and "influencing" in the provision, the law now emphasizes that the offender acts with clear intention and has full awareness of the effect.

Lastly, the term "intergroup" has been removed from the current provision and replaced with a list of specific identity factors that are more clearly defined. The formulation of online hate speech in the 2024 ITE Law is notably more substantial, especially considering that the previous provision was one of the most frequently used since the 2016 ITE Law was passed[145].

However, one major issue is how the provision should ideally incorporate international human rights principles into the text. This should be addressed in the Elucidation Section of the 2024 ITE Law, rather than simply stating that it is "adequately clear." One of the international human rights principles that could be adopted is the threshold on hate speech that was formulated in the 2012 Rabat Plan of Action. The Rabat Plan of Action document resulted from an expert workshop organized by the Office of the High Commissioner of Human Rights (OHCHR) in Rabat, Morocco. The document recommends that countries implement laws prohibiting advocacy of national, racial, or religious hatred that constitutes incitement to discrimination, hostility, or violence. The six-part threshold should be adopted and implemented by countries is as follows[146]:

- a **Context** of the statement
- b **Speaker**'s position or status
- c **Intent** to incite audience against a target group
- d **Content** and the form of the statement
- e **Extent** of its dissemination
- f **Likelihood** of harm, including imminence

At a glance, the current online hate speech provision under the 2024 ITE Law may align with this threshold, but it allows for multiple interpretations if a narrower scope is not provided. For example, the test on the speaker's position or status in the Rabat Plan of Action considers both the status or the position of the speaker and the nature of the audience. While the phrase "*influencing other people…*" in Article 28 Section 2 of the 2024 ITE Law may appear similar to the threshold, it remains open to broad interpretation because the provision can also be applied to ordinary individuals without specific status, potentially leading to charges of online hate speech.

3.8 Comparisons of the ITE Laws

To summarize and provide a clearer context on how the three versions of the ITE Law serve as draconian laws regarding free expression in the digital age, the following table presents a comparison of several main elements related to

Table 3.2 Comparison of Online Defamation and Online Hate Provisions in the 2008 ITE Law, 2016 ITE Law, and 2024 ITE Law

Provisions	*The 2008 ITE Law*	*The 2016 ITE Law*	*The 2024 ITE Law*
Online Defamation	- Article 27 Section 3 - Criminal punishment is 6 years of imprisonment and a fine up to 1 billion rupiahs (Articles 27 Section 3 in conjunction with Article 45 Section 1) - No explanation is provided for the phrases "to distribute," "to transmit," and "causes to be accessible."	- Article 27 Section 3 - The prison term is only reduced to 4 years, and the fine sanction is lowered to 750 million rupiahs (Article 45 Section 3) - The phrases "to distribute," "to transmit," and "causes to be accessible" are explained in the Elucidation Section - Online defamation is confirmed as a complaint-based crime.	- Article 27 Section is revoked and inserted with two different provisions: Articles 27A (online defamation) and 27B (online threat) - Article 27A is added as the provision for online defamation - The phrase "accusing something…" ia added for a clearer context regarding punishable online defamation - Criminal penalties are reduced to 2 years of imprisonment and a fine of 400 million rupiahs (Article 27A in conjunction with Article 45 Section 4) - Definitions for "known by the public" and "harming honor and good name" are added in the Elucidation Section, but there are no changes on "to distribute," "to transmit," and "causes to be accessible."
Online Hate Speech	- Article 28 Section 2 - The term "disseminate…" is used to refer to the punishable action - The term "intergroup" is used to refer to the victims of hate speech - Criminal penalties include 6 years of prison term and a fine up to 1 billion rupiahs	- There are no changes on Article 28 Section 2 - There are also no changes to the criminal penalties, but the provision is now under Article 45A Section 2	- punishable deeds have been changed to ""to distribute," "to transmit," and "causes to be accessible." - The terms "incite," "encourage," and "influence" have been added as intention elements to formulate the offense. - The term "intergroup" has been replaced with a list of identity factors. - There are no changes to the criminal penalties (Article 45A Section 2).

both online defamation and online hate speech. The table illustrates how the ITE Law was amended, despite ongoing concerns that these changes may still curb the freedom of expression in Indonesia. It focuses on the provisions related to online defamation and online hate speech, highlighting the penalties and differences in the language used in each provision.

Based on this table, it is evident that while changes were made through the two amendments of the ITE Law, criminal provisions restricting expression are still imposed. Some changes were also made to clarify the scope of unprotected expressions in defamation cases. However, the main issue lies in the unclear and "elastic" definition of "causes to be accessible," which poses a bigger problem in implementing the law, especially considering that criminalizing expression should not be enforced at all.

Similar to online defamation, online hate speech also faces challenges with defining the act of "causes to be accessible." The list of identity factors may help specify the scope of hate speech, but unfortunately, it does not clarify whether this criminal act is classified as a formal (*formil*) or material (*materiil*) offense.

This chapter has discussed the issues of free speech limitations at the legislative level, which provides clearer indications of how draconian these laws are when their implementation is considered. Chapter 4 will present case studies on both defamation and hate speech that occurred in offline and online contexts. The analysis shows that the problematic implementation of these laws, which overlooks the interests of the vulnerable groups, allows them to protect the interest of the rich and powerful while eventually ignoring the public interest.

Notes

1 The Economist Intelligence Unit, 2019,, *Democracy Index 2019*.
2 Ian Vazques and Tanja Porcnik, 2019, *The Human Freedom Index*, Cato Institute, https://www.cato.org/sites/cato.org/files/human-freedom-index-files/2019-human-freedom-index-update-2.pdf.
3 Freedom House, 2019, *Freedom in the World: Indonesia*, Freedom House (April 3, 2020) https://freedomhouse.org/report/freedom-world/2019/indonesia.
4 Freedom House, 2019, *Freedom in the World: Indonesia*, Freedom House (April 3, 2020) https://freedomhouse.org/report/freedom-world/2019/indonesia.
5 G.A. Res. 217A (III) art.19, U.N. Doc. A/810 (Dec. 10, 1948).
6 International Covenant on Civil and Political Rights, Art. 19, Dec. 16, 1966, 999 U.N.T.S. 171 (Mar. 23, 1976).
7 Michel Verpeaux, *Freedom of Expression in Constitutional and International Case Law*, 11 (2010).
8 See Emily Howie, 12, doi https://doi.org/10.1080/17549507.2018.1392612.
9 The International Center for Not-For-Profit Law, 2015, *The Right to Freedom of Expression: Restriction on a Foundational Right*, 3 global-ngo-law_trends6-1.pdf.
10 Human Rights Committee, General Comment No. 34, Article 19, Freedoms of Opinion and Expression, U.N. Doc. CCPR/C/GC/34 (2011).
11 Human Rights Committee, General Comment No. 34, Article 19, Freedoms of Opinion and Expression, U.N. Doc. CCPR/C/GC/34 (2011).

12 Matthew Lower, 2013, *Can and Should Human Rights be Universal?*, International Relations Info (Jan 4, 2022) https://www.e-ir.info/pdf/44590.
13 Rainer Arnold, *The Universalism of Human Rights*, 3 (2013).
14 *Id.*
15 Asian Human Rights Commission, 2006, *INDONESIA: Ratification of Key Human Rights Instruments must be Followed by Legal Reform*, human rights asia (August 26, 2022) http://www.humanrights.asia/news/ahrc-news/AS-044-2006/.
16 Nurjalal, 2018, *Analisis UU No. 39 Tahun 1999 tentang HAM [Analysis of Law No. 39 of 1999 on Human Rights]*, Jurnal Pahlawan, Vol. 1, No. 1, 32:30-35.
17 Hikmahanto Juwana, 2008, *Tantangan Indonesia Pasca Ratifikasi ICCPR [Indonesia's Challenges After ICCPR Ratification]*, Kompas (April 18, 2008) http://www.kompas.com/kompas.cetak/0506/08/opini/1799437.htm.
18 United Nations, 2008, Indonesia's National Report Submitted in Accordance with Paragraph 15(a) of the Annex to Human Rights Council Resolution 5/1, 17.
19 United Nations, Indonesia's National Report Submitted in Accordance with Paragraph 15(a) of the Annex to Human Rights Council Resolution 5/1, 19.
20 United Nations, 2008, Indonesia's Universal Periodic Review: Report of the Working Group on the Universal Periodic Review, 16.
21 United Nations, 2012, Indonesia's National Report Submitted in Accordance with Paragraph 15(a) of the Annex to Human Rights Council Resolution 16/21, 9.
22 Herlambang P. Wiratraman, 2022, *Indonesian Law Systematically Stifles Journalists*, the Jakarta Post (May 4, 2022) https://www.thejakartapost.com/opinion/2022/05/04/indonesian-law-systematically-stifles-journalists.html.
23 Kartika Singarimbun, et.al., 2019, *Broadcasting Law 32/2002: A Case of the Indonesian Government's Indecisiveness towards the Implementation of Radio Network*, Library and Philosophy Practice (E-Journal), 2966, https://digitalcommons.unl.edu/libphilprac/2966.
24 Indonesian Act, 2008, Art. 27 Section 3 (Indonesia), Information and Electronic Transaction Act (Indon.).
25 ICJR, 2016, *Respon atas Rencana Penetapan Revisi UU ITE: Lima Masalah Krusial dalam Revisi UU ITE yang Mengancam Kebebasan Ekspresi di Indonesia [Response to the Plan to Revise the ITE Law: Five Crucial Issues in the Revised ITE Law that Threaten Freedom of Expression in Indonesia]*, ICJR (October 27, 2016), https://icjr.or.id/respon-atas-rencana-penetapan-revisi-uu-ite-lima-masalah-krusial-dalam-revisi-uu-ite-yang-mengancam-kebebasan-ekpresi-di-indonesia/.
26 Oliver Holmes, 2016, *Indonesia Accused of Arresting more than 1000 in West Papua*, the Guardian (June 17, 2016) https://www.theguardian.com/world/2016/jun/17/indonesia-accused-of-arresting-more-than-1000-in-west-papua.
27 Kate Lamb, 2017, *Jakarta Governor Ahok Sentenced to Two Years in Prison for Blasphemy*, the Guardian (May 9, 2017) https://www.theguardian.com/world/2017/may/09/jakarta-governor-ahok-found-guilty-of-blasphemy-jailed-for-two-years.
28 Eka Nugraha Putra, 2023, *Blasphemy Cases Highlight Legal Inconsistencies*, Indonesia at Melbourne (June 27, 2023) https://indonesiaatmelbourne.unimelb.edu.au/blasphemy-cases-highlight-legal-inconsistencies/.
29 United Nations, 2022, Indonesia's National Report Submitted in Accordance with Paragraph 15(a) of the Annex to Human Rights Council Resolution 5/1 and 16/21, 19.
30 Manushya Foundation, 2023, *The Defamation Trial Against Fatia Maulidiyanti and Haris Azhar is Ongoing!*, Manushya Foundation (June 19, 2023) https://www.manushyafoundation.org/post/the-defamation-trial-against-fatia-maulidiyanti-and-haris-azhar-is-ongoing.
31 Dio Suhenda, 2023, *Rempang Sheds Light on Jokowi's "Land Hungry" National Projects*, The Jakarta Post (September 28, 2023) https://asianews.network/rempang-sheds-light-on-jokowis-land-hungry-national-projects/.

32 Kontras, 2022, *Putus Daftar Panjang Upaya Kriminalisasi terhadap Pejuang Lingkungan Hidup! [End the Long List of Criminalization Attempts against Environmental Activists!]*, Kontras (February 2, 2022) https://kontras.org/2022/02/02/putus-daftar-panjang-upaya-kriminalisasi-terhadap-pejuang-lingkungan-hidup/.

33 Asian Forum for Human Rights and Development, 2023, [*Joint Open Letter] Indonesia: Indonesia's Candidacy for Election to the UN Human Rights Council*, Forum Asia (September 14, 2023) https://forum-asia.org/?p=38629.

34 Asian Forum for Human Rights and Development, 2023, [*Joint Open Letter] Indonesia: Indonesia's Candidacy for Election to the UN Human Rights Council*, Forum Asia (September 14, 2023) https://forum-asia.org/?p=38629.

35 AICHR, 2019, The 2019 AICHR Consultation on Freedom of Opinion and Expression in ASEAN, asean.org (December 101 2019) https://asean.org/the-2019-aichr-consultation-on-freedom-of-opinion-and-expression-in-asean/.

36 Rachminawati, 2014, *ASEAN Human Rights Declaration: A New Form of Universalism*, Indonesian Journal of International Law, Vol. 11 No.3, 397.

37 Janne Mende, 2019, *Are Human Rights Western-And Why Does it Matter? A Perspective from International Political Theory*, Journal of International Political Theory, doi: https://journals.sagepub.com/doi/10.1177/1755088219832992.

38 ASEAN Intergovernmental Commission on Human Rights, 2022, *The ASEAN Intergovernmental Commission on Human Rights Annual Report 2022*, aichr, https://aichr.org/wp-content/uploads/2023/04/ADOPTED-AICHR-Annual-Report-2022-AICHR-Special-Meeting-1-2022-2.pdf.

39 Phnom Penh Statement on the Adoption of the ASEAN Human Rights Declaration. ASEAN. Nov. 18, 2012.

40 Majda el Muhtaj, Hak Asasi Manusia dalam Konstitusi Indonesia [Human Rights in The Indonesian Constitution], 84 (2017).

41 Majda El Muhtaj, Hak Asasi Manusia dalam Konstitusi Indonesia [Human Rights in The Indonesian Constitution], 84.

42 Under Indonesian law, acts considered as obscenity or attack morality is all about sexuality and pornography. In Indonesia, the proper term would be "pornography" even there is a bill entitled 'Pornography Act' enacted in 2008. However, there is an inconsistency as in the Criminal Code (the Criminal Code), the criminal offenses regulated under the Chapter of "Immoral Offenses.".

43 Ian Kumekawa, 2010, *Blasphemous Pluralism: Examining Indonesia's Blasphemy Law*, Harvard International Review, Vol. 32: 2, 8.

44 Admin, 2017 *Sekilas Sejarah dan Problematik Pembahasan RKUHP [A Glimpse of the History and Problems of Discussing the RKUHPA Glimpse of the History and Problems of Discussing the RKUHP]*, Reformasi the Criminal Code (Dec. 21, 2022) http://reformasikuhp.org/sekilas-sejarah-dan-problematika-pembahasan-rkuhp/.

45 HRW, 2019, *Indonesia: Draft Criminal Code Disastrous for Rights*, Human Rights Watch (Sep. 19, 2022) https://www.hrw.org/news/2019/09/18/indonesia-draft-criminal-code-disastrous-rights.

46 Kate Lamb, 2019, *Thousands Protest Against New Criminal Code in Indonesia.*

47 Kominfo, 2021, *Sejak 2018 Kominfo Tangani 3640 Ujaran Kebencian Berbasis SARA di Ruang Digital [Since 2018, Kominfo Has Handled 3640 SARA-Based Hate Speeches in Digital Space]*, kominfo.go.id (April 28, 2022) https://www.kominfo.go.id/content/detail/34136/siaran-pers-no-143hmkominfo042021-tentang-sejak-2018-kominfo-tangani-3640-ujaran-kebencian-berbasis-sara-di-ruang-digital/0/siaran_pers.

48 Anton Muhajir, *Laporan Triwulan Pemantauan Hak-Hak Digital di Indonesia Periode Juli-September 2023 [Quarterly Report of Digital Rights Monitoring in Indonesia Period July-September 2023]*, safenet.or.id, https://mega.nz/file/1g8TUaCK#uQ_azzncmUDMy4cwvdCyleJ-nnkl22vh_UULd-ym3y0.

49 Indonesian Act, 1946, Art. 1 (Indonesia), Criminal Law Regulation (Indon.).

50 United Nations, (n.d) *Understanding Hate Speech*, un.org (Jan. 30, 2024) https://www.un.org/en/hate-speech/understanding-hate-speech/what-is-hate-speech#:~:text=To%20provide%20a%20unified%20framework,person%20or%20a%20group%20on.

51 Supriyadi Widodo Eddyono, Fajrimei A. Gofar, and Adiani A. Viviana, 2020, *Tindak Pidana terhadap Pemerintah yang Sah dalam RKUHP [Criminal Acts against Legitimate Government in the Draft Criminal Code]*, icjr.or.id (Oct. 15, 2022) https://icjr.or.id/wp-content/uploads/2016/12/TINDAK-PIDANA-PENGHINAAN-Pemerintah.pdf.

52 Mahkamah Konstitusi [MK] [The Indonesian Constitutional Court] 2007, Decision No. 6/PUU-V/2007 (Indon.).

53 Puslitbang Mahkamah Agung Indonesia, *Kompilasi dan Republikasi Putusan-Putusan Perkara Pidana Penista Agama [Compilation and Republication of Criminal Case Decisions on Blasphemy]*, vii (2017).

54 Melissa Crouch, 2012, *Law and Religion in Indonesia: The Constitutional Court and the Blasphemy Law*, Asian Journal Comparative Law, Vol. 7, Issue 1, 45.

55 Zainal Abidin Bagir, 2013, *Defamation of Religion Law in Post-Reformasi Indonesia: Is Revision Possible?* Australian Journal of Asian Law, Vol. 13, No. 2, 153-168, 158.

56 Zainal Abidin Bagir, *Defamation of Religion Law in Post-Reformasi Indonesia: Is Revision Possible?*, 156.

57 Mahkamah Konstitusi [MK] [The Indonesian Constitutional Court] 2018, Decision No. 76/PUU-XVI/2018 (Indon.).

58 Mahkamah Konstitusi [MK] [The Indonesian Constitutional Court] 2018, Decision No. 76/PUU-XVI/2018 (Indon.).

59 The Indonesian Criminal Code consists of three books (chapters): Book One "General Provisions" (From Article 1 to Article 103), Book Two "Crimes" (From Article 104 to Article 488) and Book Three "Violation" From (Article 489 to Article 569).

60 Adami Chazawi, *Hukum Pidana Positif Penghinaan [Positive Criminal Law on Insult]*, 155 (2013).

61 Under Indonesian law, defamation is an act that attacking either *kehormatan* (honour) or nama baik (reputation) or both.

62 Dali Mutiara, *Tafsir Kitab Undang-Undang Hukum Pidana [Interpretation of the Criminal Code]*, 218 (1962).

63 *Eenvoudige belediging* is a Dutch. In Indonesian, the term means *penghinaan biasa/ringan*, which is translated as "minor defamation" in English. "Minor defamation formed as "insult" or "humiliation." While those two are not associated with a criminal act in English and have different meanings and contexts in Dutch and Indonesian, this book will proceed with using "minor defamation.".

64 Upon a similar reason with the usage of "*eenvoudig belediging,*" the term *"calumny"* will be used in this book. "Calumny" is a dutch word and used to differentiate it with libel and slander in Article 310 Sections 1 and 2 the Criminal Code.

65 Adami Chazawi, *Hukum Pidana Positif Penghinaan [Positive Criminal Law on Insult]*, 102–103 (2013).

66 The verdict of Article 134, Article 136 bis and Article 137, was in Indonesian Constitutional Court Judicial Decision Number 013-022/PUU-IV/2006. The verdict of Article 154 and Article 155 was in Indonesian Constitutional Court Judicial Decision Number 6/PUU-V/2007.

67 Undang-Undang Dasar [UUD] [Constitution] Aug. 18, 1945 art. 28 F (Indon.).

68 Scholastika Gerintya, *Jerat UU ITE Banyak Dipakai Oleh Pejabat Negara [The Snares of the ITE Law are Widely used by State Officials]*.

69 Bayu Marhaenjati and Christian Lee, 2019, *Police Arrest Eggi Sudjana for Treason*, Jakarta Globe (June 14, 2022), https://jakartaglobe.id/context/police-arrest-eggi-sudjana-for-treason.

70 Adami Chazawi, *Hukum Pidana Positif Penghinaan [Positive Criminal Law on Insult]*, 84 (2013).
71 Adami Chazawi, *Hukum Pidana Positif Penghinaan [Positive Criminal Law on Insult]*, 84 (2013).
72 Aisah, *Eksistensi Pidana Denda Menurut Sistem KUHP [The Existence of Criminal Fines According to the Criminal Code System]*, Lex Crimen Vol. IV No. 1, 215 (2015).
73 Aisah, *Eksistensi Pidana Denda Menurut Sistem KUHP [The Existence of Criminal Fines According to the Criminal Code System]*, 216.
74 John L. Diamond, Lawrence C. Levine, Anita Bernstein, *Understanding Torts*, 13 (2013).
75 Dian Dewi Purnamasari, 2024, *An Oasis of Freedom of Opinion from the Free Sentences of Haris and Fatia*, Kompas.Id (January 29, 2024) https://www.kompas.id/baca/english/2024/01/08/en-oase-kebebasan-berpendapat-dari-vonis-bebas-haris-dan-fatia.
76 Mahkamah Konstitusi [MK] [The Indonesian Constitutional Court] 2023, Decision No. 78/PUU-XXI/2023 (Indon.).
77 Ayu Mumpuni, 2024, *Polri: Kasus UU ITE Tak Berlaku Surut Meski Pasal Dihapus [Police: ITE Law Cases Not Retroactive Even Though Articles Are Removed]*, Tirto.Id (April 22, 2024). https://tirto.id/polri-kasus-uu-ite-tak-berlaku-surut-meski-pasal-dihapus-gXac.
78 Henny Saida Flora, Fradhana Putra Disantara, Mac Thi Hoai Thuong, 2023, *The Lex Favor Reo Principle After New Criminal Code: A Corrective Justice's Perspective*, Pena Justisia: Vol. 22, No. 02, 2.
79 Jeverly Jhosua Rumengan, *Delik Fitnah dalam Pasal 311 Ayat (1) KUHP sebagai Delik Kelanjutan dari Delik Pencemaran (Putusan Mahkamaha Konstitusi Nomor 14/PUU-VI/2008 [The crime of slander in Article 311 Paragraph (1) of the Criminal Code as a crime that is a continuation of the crime of defamation (Constitutional Court Decision Number 14/PUU-VI/2008]*, Lex Privatum Vol. V, Nomor 3, Mei 2017, 145-146 (2017).
80 R. Soesilo, *Kitab Undang-Undang Hukum Pidana serta Komentar-Komentarnya Lengkap Pasal Demi Pasal [Criminal Code and its Complete Commentaries Article by Article]*, 227 (1990).
81 Indonesian Act, 1999, art. 5 (Indonesia), Press act (Indon.).
82 Indonesian Act, 1999, art. 15 (Indonesia), Press act (Indon.).
83 Tempo.co, 2014, *Wartawan Jawa Post Group Divonis Sembilan Bulan Penjara [Jawa Post Group Journalist Sentenced to Nine Months in Prison]*, Tempo.co (Dec. 22, 2022), https://nasional.tempo.co/read/53509/wartawan-jawa-post-grup-divonis-sembilan-bulan-penjara.
84 R. Soesilo, *Kitab Undang-Undang Hukum Pidana serta Komentar-Komentarnya Lengkap Pasal Demi Pasal [Criminal Code and its Complete Commentaries Article by Article]*, 88.
85 SNO Staff, 2018, *Surprise? It's A Crime To Insult, Mock Or Call A Person Names Anywhere In Saint Lucia Criminal Code*, St. Lucia News Online, (Oct 8, 2021) https://www.stlucianewsonline.com/surprise-its-a-crime-to-insult-mock-or-call-a-person-names-anywhere-in-saint-lucia-criminal-code/.
86 CSCE, 2002, *Criminal Defamation and Insult Laws: Summary of Free Speech Developments in the Czech Republic*, csce.gov (Jan. 9, 2022,), https://www.csce.gov/international-impact/criminal-defamation-and-insult-laws-summary-free-speech-developments-czech.
87 CSCE, 2002, *Criminal Defamation and Insult Laws: Summary of Free Speech Developments in the Czech Republic*, csce.gov (Jan. 9, 2022,), https://www.csce.gov/international-impact/criminal-defamation-and-insult-laws-summary-free-speech-developments-czech.
88 Rebecca Henschke and Ayomi Amindo, 2019, *Papua Protest: Racist Taunts Open Deep Wounds*, BBC.com (Aug. 23, 2021), https://www.bbc.com/news/world-asia-49434277.

89 Tri Indah Oktavianti, 2020, *Prosecutors Seek up to 17 Years for Papuan Protesters Accused of Treason*, The Jakarta Post (Jun. 7, 2020) https://www.thejakartapost.com/news/2020/06/07/prosecutors-seek-up-to-17-years-for-papuan-protesters-accused-of-treason.html.
90 Coconuts Jakarta, 2020, *If I'm a Frog then My Mother is a Frog: Surabaya Mayor Tri Rismaharini Reports Woman to the Polic for Online Slander*, Coconuts.co (Feb.16,2021)https://coconuts.co/jakarta/news/if-im-a-frog-then-my-mother-is-a-frog-surabaya-mayor-tri-rismaharini-reports-woman-to-the-police-for-online-slander/.
91 Criminal Code [Crim. Code.], 1946,[Criminal Code] art. 317 (Indon.).
92 Gary KY Chan, 2013, *Corporate Defamation: Reputation, Rights and Remedies*, Legal Studies Vol. 33 No.2, June 2013, 264-288, https://onlinelibrary.wiley.com/doi/pdf/10.1111/j.1748-121X.2012.00258.x264.
93 BBC Trending, 2020, *Arrested for Calling Indonesian City "Idiotic,"* BBC.com (May 15, 2021) https://www.bbc.com/news/blogs-trending-29035858.
94 Adami Chazawi, 133.
95 Adami Chazawi, 141.
96 Adami Chazawi, 146.
97 Mahkamah Konstitusi [MK] [The Indonesian Constitutional Court] 2006, Decision No. 013/PUU-IV/2006 (Indon.).
98 *Id.*
99 Pusat Studi Hukum dan Kebijakan, 2021, *5 Alasan Menolak Pasal Penghinaan Presiden dimasukkan Kembali ke dalam RKUHP [5 Reasons to Reject the Article on Insulting the President from Being Reinserted into the RKUHP]*, pshk.or.id, https://pshk.or.id/publikasi/siaran-pers/5-alasan-menolak-pasal-penghinaan-presiden-dimasukkan-kembali-ke-dalam-rkuhp/ (July 17, 2021).
100 Rofiq Hidayat, 2022, *Alasan Pemerintah Pertahankan Pasal Penghinaan Kepala Negara dalam RKUHP [The Government's Reason for Maintaining the Article on Insulting the Head of State in the RKUHP]*, hukumonline.com, https://www.hukumonline.com/berita/a/alasan-pemerintah-pertahankan-pasal-penghinaan-kepala-negara-dalam-rkuhp-lt62a17f49e4d5a/ (June 29, 2022).
101 Mahkamah Konstitusi [MK] [The Indonesian Constitutional Court] 2023, Decision No. 7/PUU-XXI/2023 (Indon.).
102 Mahkamah Konstitusi [MK] [The Indonesian Constitutional Court] 2023, Decision No. 7/PUU-XXI/2023 (Indon.).
103 Criminal Code [Crim. Code.], 2023, [Criminal Code] art. 79 (Indon.).
104 Mahrus Ali, 2010, *Pencemaran Nama Baik Melalui Sarana Informasi dan Transaksi Elektronik [Defamation Through Electronic Information and Transaction Facilities]*, Jurnal Konstitusi Volume 7, Nomor 6, 131.
105 Criminal Code [Crim. Code.], 2023, art. 86 Sections a and b [Criminal Code] (Indon.).
106 Criminal Code [Crim. Code.], 2023, The Elucidation section art. 439 [Criminal Code] (Indon.).
107 J. Satrio, Gugat Perdata atas Dasar Penghinaan sebagai Tindakan Melawan Hukum [Civil Lawsuit on the Basis of Defamation as an Unlawful Act], 53 (2005).
108 Virginia Gorlinski, 2023, *Minangkabau*, britannica.com (March 12, 2024) https://www.britannica.com/topic/Minangkabau.
109 See United Nations, 2023, Countering and Addressing Online Hate Speech: A Guide for Policy Makers and Practicioners.
110 The three-step test is provided by Article 19 Section 3 of the ICCPR to assess whether any restrictions on expressions are not against human rights protection.
111 Soemarno Partodihardjo, *Tanya Jawab Sekitar Undang-Undang No. 11 Tahun 2008 tentang Informasi dan Transaksi Elektronik [Questions and Answers about Law No. 11 of 2008 on Electronic Information and Transactions]*, 14 (2009).

112 Moh. Afaf El Kurniawan, 2023, *Sejarah UU ITE di Indonesia: Perkembangan Regulasi dan Kontroversi di Dunia Digital [History of ITE Law in Indonesia: Regulatory Developments and Controversies in the Digital World]*, Narasi.tv (September 14, 2023) https://narasi.tv/read/narasi-daily/sejarah-uu-ite.

113 The Indonesian Ministry of Communication and Information, *Naskah Akademik Rancangan Undang-Undang tentang Informasi dan Transaksi Elektronik [Academic Manuscript of the Draft Law on Electronic Information and Transactions]*, 56-62 (2005).

114 Anggara Suwahju, 2021,*Bagaimana Mereformasi UU ITE dan Hukum Pidana Penghinaan yang lain di Indonesia [How to Reform the ITE Law and Other Criminal Defamation Laws in Indonesia]*, The Conversation Indonesia (April 1, 2022) https://theconversation.com/bagaimana-mereformasi-uu-ite-dan-hukum-pidana-penghinaan-yang-lain-di-indonesia-125204.

115 Anggara Suwahju, 2021,*Bagaimana Mereformasi UU ITE dan Hukum Pidana Penghinaan yang lain di Indonesia [How to Reform the ITE Law and Other Criminal Defamation Laws in Indonesia]*, The Conversation Indonesia (April 1, 2022) https://theconversation.com/bagaimana-mereformasi-uu-ite-dan-hukum-pidana-penghinaan-yang-lain-di-indonesia-125204.

116 Kemenkominfo, 2023, *Matriks Perbandingan Perubahan Undang-Undang Republik Indonesia Nomor 11 Tahun 2008 Tentang Informasi Dan Transaksi Elektronik Dengan Undang-Undang Republik Indonesia Nomor 19 Tahun 2016 Tentang Perubahan Atas Undangundang Nomor 11 Tahun 2008 Tentang Informasi Dan Transaksi Elektronik [Comparison Matrix of Amendments to Law of the Republic of Indonesia Number 11 of 2008 Concerning Electronic Information and Transactions with Law of the Republic of Indonesia Number 19 of 2016 Concerning Amendments to Law Number 11 of 2008 Concerning Electronic Information and Transactions]*, jdih.kominfo.go.id (April 24, 2024) https://jdih.kominfo.go.id/storage/files/mp-1491878641-matriks_perbandingan_perubahan_undang_undang_tentang_ite.pdf.

117 Arditho Ramadhan and Bayu Galih, 2023, *Melihat Lagi Revisi UU ITE pada 2016 yang tak Cabut Pasal-Pasal Karet [Reviewing the 2016 Revision of the ITE Law That Does Not Revoke the Rubber Articles]*, Kompas.com (December 11, 2023) https://nasional.kompas.com/read/2021/02/17/09330501/melihat-lagi-revisi-uu-ite-pada-2016-yang-tak-cabut-pasal-pasal-karet?page=all.

118 Fitria Chusna Farisa and Dani Prabowo, 2021, *Jokowi Bakal Minta DPR Revisi UU ITE Jika Implementasinya Tak Adil [Jokowi Will Ask DPR to Revise ITE Law If Its Implementation is Unfair]*, Kompas.com (August 8, 2023) https://nasional.kompas.com/read/2021/02/15/22160541/jokowi-bakal-minta-dpr-revisi-uu-ite-jika-implementasinya-tak-adil.

119 Rahmat Nur Hakim, 2021, *Revisi UU ITE: Berawal dari Keresahan Jokowi namun Batal Masuk Prolegnas Nasional 2021 [Revision of ITE Law: Starting from Jokowi's Concerns but Not Included in 2021 National Legislation Program]*, Kompas.com (September 9, 2023) https://nasional.kompas.com/read/2021/03/12/20521121/revisi-uu-ite-berawal-dari-keresahan-jokowi-namun-batal-masuk-prolegnas?page=all.

120 Rahmat Nur Hakim, 2021, *Revisi UU ITE: Berawal dari Keresahan Jokowi namun Batal Masuk Prolegnas Nasional 2021 [Revision of ITE Law: Starting from Jokowi's Concerns but Not Included in 2021 National Legislation Program]*, Kompas.com (September 9, 2023) https://nasional.kompas.com/read/2021/03/12/20521121/revisi-uu-ite-berawal-dari-keresahan-jokowi-namun-batal-masuk-prolegnas?page=all.

121 VOI, 2021, *SKB Guidelines for the ITE Law are not Legal Products, their Application isnot Retroactive*, Voi.id(April 14,2022), https://voi.id/en/news/61698/skb-guidelines-for-the-ite-law-are-not-legal-products-their-application-is-not-retroactive.

122 Normand Edwin Elnizar, 2021, *SKB UU ITE tak bisa Mengikat Penafsiran Hakim, Apakah Berfaedah*? [Joint Decree on ITE Law Cannot Bind Judges' Interpretation, Is It Useful?], hukumonline (April 14, 2022), https://www.hukumonline.com/stories/article/lt60eeb6125ce8c/skb-uu-ite-tak-bisa-mengikat-penafsiran-hakim--apakah-berfaedah.

123 Equal to USD 52,609.80.
124 Supreme Court Regulation on Limitation Adjusment of Misdemeanor and Fine Sanction in the the Criminal Code (Regulation No. 2/2012) art. 2 (Indon.).
125 ICJR, 2020, *Catatan atas RUU Perubahan Pasal 27 Ayat 3 UU ITE dan Sikap Fraksi-Fraksi di Komisi I DPR [Notes on the Draft Law on Amendments to Article 27 Paragraph 3 of the ITE Law and the Attitudes of the Factions in Commission I of the DPR]*, icjr.or.id (August 18, 2022) https://icjr.or.id/catatan-atas-ruu-perubahan-pasal-27-ayat-3-uu-ite-dan-sikap-fraksi-fraksi-di-komisi-i-dpr/.
126 Bambang Muryanto, 2020, *ITE Law Increasingly Threatens Press Freedom*, The Jakarta Post (November 17, 2022) https://www.thejakartapost.com/news/2014/11/17/ite-law-increasingly-threatens-press-freedom.html.
127 Mahkamah Konstitusi [MK] [The Indonesian Constitutional Court] 2008, Decision No. 7/PUU-XXI/2023 (Indon.).
128 Indonesian Act, 2016, (Indonesia), Government Regulation No. 39 of 2016 on Types and Rates of Non-Tax State Revenue that Apply to The Indonesian Prosecutor's office. Art. 1C (Indon.).
129 Jon'a F. Meyer, 2014, *Retributive Justice*, britannica.com (December 22, 2023) https://www.britannica.com/topic/retributive-justice.
130 David Lyons, 2005, *Punishment as Retribution*, Vice, Crime, and American Law (July 11, 2023) https://web.uncg.edu/dcl/courses/viceCrime/m7/part3.asp.
131 Alec Walen, 2020, *Challenges to the Notion of Retributive Proportionality*, Stanford Encyclopedia of Philosophy (November 3, 2023) https://plato.stanford.edu/entries/justice-retributive/challenges.html.
132 SARA is abbreviation for *Suku, Agama, Ras dan Antar Golongan* which the identity factors of hate speech as the criminal offenses in Indonesian criminal laws.
133 Article 19, *Penjelasan "Ujaran Kebencian": Panduan ["Hate Speech" Explanation: A Guide]*, article19.org (January 5, 2024) https://www.article19.org/wp-content/uploads/2019/12/Hate-Speech-Toolkit-Bahasa-Indonesia.pdf.
134 Ronny and Dian Adriawan Dg Tawang, 2023, *Kajian Konsep Antar Golongan dalam Pasal 28 Ayat 2 UU ITE [Study of Inter-Group Concepts in Article 28 Section 2 of the ITE Law]*, Amnesti Jurnal Hukum, Vol 5. No. 2, 249.
135 Mahkamah Konstitusi [MK] [The Indonesian Constitutional Court] 2017, Decision No. 76/PUU-XVI/2017 (Indon.).
136 Mahkamah Konstitusi [MK] [The Indonesian Constitutional Court] 2017, Decision No. 76/PUU-XVI/2017 (Indon.).
137 Mahkamah Konstitusi [MK] [The Indonesian Constitutional Court] 2017, Decision No. 76/PUU-XVI/2017 (Indon.).
138 Mahkamah Konstitusi [MK] [The Indonesian Constitutional Court] 2017, Decision No. 76/PUU-XVI/2017 (Indon.).
139 Indonesian Act, 2016, (Indonesia), Information and Electronic Transaction Act, The Elucidation Section of Article 27 Section 3 (Indon.).
140 Nella Sumika Putri, 2021, *Memikirkan Kembali Unsur "Hukum yang Hidup dalam Masyarakat" dalam Pasal 2 RKUHP Ditinjau Perpsektif Asas Legalitas [Rethinking the Element of "Living Law in Society" in Article 2 of the Draft Criminal Code Reviewed from the Perspective of the Principle of Legality]*, Indonesia Criminal Law Review, Vol. 1, No.1, 62.
141 Nella Sumika Putri, 2021, *Memikirkan Kembali Unsur "Hukum yang Hidup dalam Masyarakat" dalam Pasal 2 RKUHP Ditinjau Perpsektif Asas Legalitas [Rethinking the Element of "Living Law in Society" in Article 2 of the Draft Criminal Code Reviewed from the Perspective of the Principle of Legality]*, Indonesia Criminal Law Review, Vol. 1, No.1, 62.
142 Michael Faure, Morag Goodwin, and Franziska Weber, 2012, *The Lex Certa Principle in Criminal Law: Reconciling Economics and Human Rights?*, Alabama Law Journal of Science & Technology, Vol. 24.2, 361.

143 Mochamad Januar Rizki, 2024, *Pasal Karet dalam UU ITE Terbaru Masih Mengancam Masyarakat yang Kritis [Rubber Articles in the Latest ITE Law Still Threaten Critical Society]*, hukumonline.com (April 3, 2024) https://www.hukumonline.com/berita/a/pasal-karet-dalam-uu-ite-terbaru-masih-mengancam-masyarakat-yang-kritis-lt6597e40be9b8c.

144 Indonesian Act, 2024, (Indonesia), Information and Electronic Transaction Act, The Elucidation Section Number 9 (Indon.).

145 Adhigama A. Budiman, et.al, 2021, *Mengatur Ulang Kebijakan Pidana di Ruang Siber [Reregulate Criminal Policy in Cyberspace]*, icjr.or.id (February 1, 2024) https://icjr.or.id/wp-content/uploads/2021/03/ICJR_Mengatur-Ulang-Kebijakan-Pidana-di-Ruang-Siber.pdf.

146 Human Rights Council, Report of the United Nations High Commissioner for Human Rights on the Expert Workshop on the Prohibition of Incitement to National, Racial or Religious Hatred, U.N. Doc. A/HRC/22/17 (Jan. 11, 2013).

Bibliography

Books

Adami Chazawi, *Hukum Pidana Positif Penghinaan [Positive Criminal Law on Insult]* (2013).

Dali Mutiara, *Tafsir Kitab Undang-Undang Hukum Pidana [Interpretation of the Criminal Code]* (1962).

J. Satrio, *Gugat Perdata atas Dasar Penghinaan sebagai Tindakan Melawan Hukum [Civil Lawsuit on the Basis of Defamation as an Unlawful Act]* (2005).

John L. *Diamond, Lawrence C. Levine, Anita Bernstein, Understanding Torts* (2013).

Majda El Muhtaj, *Hak Asasi Manusia dalam Konstitusi Indonesia [Human Rights in The Indonesian Constitution]* (2017).

Michel Verpeaux, *Freedom of Expression in Constitutional and International Case Law* (2010).

Puslitbang Mahkamah Agung Indonesia, *Kompilasi dan Republikasi Putusan-Putusan Perkara Pidana Penista Agama [Compilation and Republication of Criminal Case Decisions on Blasphemy]* (2017).

R. Soesilo, *Kitab Undang-Undang Hukum Pidana serta Komentar-Komentarnya Lengkap Pasal Demi Pasal [Criminal Code and its Complete Commentaries Article by Article]* (1990).

Rainer Arnold, *The Universalism of Human Rights* (2013).

Soemarno Partodihardjo, *Tanya Jawab Sekitar Undang-Undang No. 11 Tahun 2008 tentang Informasi dan Transaksi Elektronik [Questions and Answers about Law No. 11 of 2008 on Electronic Information and Transactions]* (2009).

Journals

Aisah, Eksistensi Pidana Denda Menurut Sistem KUHP [The Existence of Criminal Fines According to the Criminal Code System], *Lex Crimen* Vol. IV No. 1, 215, (2015).

Henny Saida Flora, Fradhana Putra Disantara, Mac Thi Hoai Thuong, 2023, The Lex Favor Reo Principle After New Criminal Code: A Corrective Justice's Perspective, *Pena Justisia* Vol. 22, No. 02, 2.

Jeverly Jhosua Rumengan, Delik Fitnah dalam Pasal 311 Ayat (1) KUHP sebagai Delik Kelanjutan dari Delik Pencemaran (Putusan Mahkamaha Konstitusi Nomor 14/PUU-VI/2008 [The crime of slander in Article 311 Paragraph (1) of the Criminal Code as a crime that is a continuation of the crime of defamation (Constitutional Court Decision Number 14/PUU-VI/2008], *Lex Privatum* Vol. V, Nomor 3, 145–146, (2017).

Nurjalal, 2018, Analisis UU No. 39 Tahun 1999 tentang HAM [Analysis of Law No. 39 of 1999 on Human Rights], *Jurnal Pahlawan*, Vol. 1, No. 1, 30–35.

Rachminawati, 2014, ASEAN Human Rights Declaration: A New Form of Universalism, *Indonesian Journal of International Law*, Vol. 11 No.3.

Ian Kumekawa, 2010, Blasphemous Pluralism: Examining Indonesia's Blasphemy Law, *Harvard International Review*, Vol. 32: 2.

Mahrus Ali, 2010, Pencemaran Nama Baik Melalui Sarana Informasi dan Transaksi Elektronik [Defamation Through Electronic Information and Transaction Facilities], *Jurnal Konstitusi* Volume 7, Nomor 6, 131.

Ronny and Dian Adriawan Dg Tawang, 2023, Kajian Konsep Antar Golongan dalam Pasal 28 Ayat 2 UU ITE [Study of Inter-Group Concepts in Article 28 Section 2 of the ITE Law], *Amnesti Jurnal Hukum*, Vol 5. No. 2, 249.

Melissa Crouch, 2012, Law and Religion in Indonesia: The Constitutional Court and the Blasphemy Law, *Asian Journal Comparative Law*, Vol. 7, Issue 1, 45.

Michael Faure, Morag Goodwin, and Franziska Weber, 2012, The Lex Certa Principle in Criminal Law: Reconciling Economics and Human Rights?, *Alabama Law Journal of Science & Technology*, Vol. 24.2, 361.

Nella Sumika Putri, 2021, Memikirkan Kembali Unsur "Hukum yang Hidup dalam Masyarakat" dalam Pasal 2 RKUHP Ditinjau Perpsektif Asas Legalitas [Rethinking the Element of "Living Law in Society" in Article 2 of the Draft Criminal Code Reviewed from the Perspective of the Principle of Legality], *Indonesia Criminal Law Review*, Vol. 1, No.1, 62.

Zainal Abidin Bagir, 2013, Defamation of Religion Law in Post-Reformasi Indonesia: Is Revision Possible? *Australian Journal of Asian Law*, Vol. 13, No. 2, 158.

International Laws

G.A. Res. 217A (III) art.19, U.N. Doc. A/810 (Dec. 10, 1948).

Human Rights Committee, General Comment No. 34, Article 19, Freedoms of Opinion and Expression, U.N. Doc. CCPR/C/GC/34 (2011)

International Covenant on Civil and Political Rights, Art. 19 Dec. 16, 1966, 999 U.N.T.S. 171 (Mar. 23, 1976).

Indonesian Legislations

Undang-Undang Dasar [UUD] [Constitution] 1945 (Indon.).

Criminal Code [Crim. Code.], 1946,[Criminal Code] (Indon.).

Indonesian Act, 1946, (Indonesia), Criminal Law Regulation (Indon.).

Indonesian Act, 1999 (Indonesia), Press Act (Indon.).

Indonesian Act, 2008, (Indonesia), Information and Electronic Transaction Act (Indon.).

Criminal Code [Crim. Code.], 2023, [Criminal Code] (Indon.).

Indonesian Act, 2016a, (Indonesia), Information and Electronic Transaction Act (Indon.).

Indonesian Act, 2016b, (Indonesia), Government Regulation No. 39 of 2016 on Types and Rates of Non-Tax State Revenue that Apply to The Indonesian Prosecutor's Office (Indon.).

Supreme Court Regulation on Limitation Adjustment of Misdemeanor and Fine Sanction in the Criminal Code (Regulation No. 2/2012) (Indon.).

Indonesian Act, 2024, (Indonesia), Information and Electronic Transaction Act (Indon.).

Indonesian Cases

Mahkamah Konstitusi [MK] [The Indonesian Constitutional Court] 2006, Decision No. 013-022/PUU-IV/2006 (Indon.).

Mahkamah Konstitusi [MK] [The Indonesian Constitutional Court] 2007, Decision No. 6/PUU-V/2007.

Mahkamah Konstitusi [MK] [The Indonesian Constitutional Court] 2017, Decision No. 76/PUU-XVI/2017 (Indon.).
Mahkamah Konstitusi [MK] [The Indonesian Constitutional Court] 2018, Decision No. 76/PUU-XVI/2018 (Indon.).
Mahkamah Konstitusi [MK] [The Indonesian Constitutional Court] 2023a, Decision No. 7/PUU-XXI/2023 (Indon.).
Mahkamah Konstitusi [MK] [The Indonesian Constitutional Court] 2023b, Decision No. 78/PUU-XXI/2023 (Indon.).

Reports

Human Rights Council, Report of the United Nations High Commissioner for Human Rights on the Expert Workshop on the Prohibition of Incitement to National, Racial or Religious Hatred, U.N. Doc. A/HRC/22/17 (Jan. 11, 2013).
The Indonesian Ministry of Communication and Information, *Naskah Akademik Rancangan Undang-Undang tentang Informasi dan Transaksi Elektronik [Academic Manuscript of the Draft Law on Electronic Information and Transactions]* (2005).
The International Center for Not-For-Profit Law, 2015, *The Right to Freedom of Expression: Restriction on a Foundational Right* global-ngo-law_trends6-1.pdf.
Phnom Penh Statement on the Adoption of the ASEAN Human Rights Declaration. ASEAN. Nov. 18, 2012.
United Nations, 2008a, Indonesia's National Report Submitted in Accordance with Paragraph 15(a) of the Annex to Human Rights Council Resolution 5/1.
United Nations, 2008b, Indonesia's Universal Periodic Review: Report of the Working Group on the Universal Periodic Review.
United Nations, 2012, Indonesia's National Report Submitted in Accordance with Paragraph 15(a) of the Annex to Human Rights Council Resolution 16/21.
United Nations, 2022, Indonesia's National Report Submitted in Accordance with Paragraph 15(a) of the Annex to Human Rights Council Resolution 5/1 and 16/21.
United Nations, 2023, Countering and Addressing Online Hate Speech: A Guide for Policy Makers and Practitioners.

Internet

Adhigama A. Budiman, et.al, 2021, Mengatur Ulang Kebijakan Pidana di Ruang Siber [Reregulate Criminal Policy in Cyberspace], *icjr.or.id* (February 1, 2024) https://icjr.or.id/wp-content/uploads/2021/03/ICJR_Mengatur-Ulang-Kebijakan-Pidana-di-Ruang-Siber.pdf.
Admin, 2017 Sekilas Sejarah dan Problematik Pembahasan RKUHP [A Glimpse of the History and Problems of Discussing the RKUHPA Glimpse of the History and Problems of Discussing the RKUHP], *Reformasi the Criminal Code* (Dec. 21, 2022) http://reformasikuhp.org/sekilas-sejarah-dan-problematika-pembahasan-rkuhp/.
AICHR, 2019, The 2019 AICHR Consultation on Freedom of Opinion and Expression in ASEAN, *asean.org* (December 10, 2019) https://asean.org/the-2019-aichr-consultation-on-freedom-of-opinion-and-expression-in-asean/.
Alec Walen, 2020, Challenges to the Notion of Retributive Proportionality, *Stanford Encyclopedia of Philosophy* (November 3, 2023) https://plato.stanford.edu/entries/justice-retributive/challenges.html.
Anggara Suwahju, 2021,Bagaimana Mereformasi UU ITE dan Hukum Pidana Penghinaan yang lain di Indonesia [How to Reform the ITE Law and Other Criminal Defamation Laws in Indonesia], *The Conversation Indonesia* (April 1, 2022) https://theconversation.com/bagaimana-mereformasi-uu-ite-dan-hukum-pidana-penghinaan-yang-lain-di-indonesia-125204.

Anton Muhajir, Laporan Triwulan Pemantauan Hak-Hak Digital di Indonesia Periode Juli-September 2023 [Quarterly Report of Digital Rights Monitoring in Indonesia Period July-September 2023], *safenet.or.id*, https://mega.nz/file/1g8TUaCK#uQ_azzncmUDMy4cwvdCyleJ-nnkl22vh_UULd-ym3y0.

Arditho Ramadhan and Bayu Galih, 2023, Melihat Lagi Revisi UU ITE pada 2016 yang tak Cabut Pasal-Pasal Karet [Reviewing the 2016 Revision of the ITE Law That Does Not Revoke the Rubber Articles], *Kompas.com* (December 11, 2023) https://nasional.kompas.com/read/2021/02/17/09330501/melihat-lagi-revisi-uu-ite-pada-2016-yang-tak-cabut-pasal-pasal-karet?page=all.

Article 19, Penjelasan "Ujaran Kebencian": Panduan ["Hate Speech" Explanation: A Guide], *article19.org* (January 5, 2024) https://www.article19.org/wp-content/uploads/2019/12/Hate-Speech-Toolkit-Bahasa-Indonesia.pdf.

ASEAN Intergovernmental Commission on Human Rights, 2022, The ASEAN Intergovernmental Commission on Human Rights Annual Report 2022, *AICHR*, https://aichr.org/wp-content/uploads/2023/04/ADOPTED-AICHR-Annual-Report-2022-AICHR-Special-Meeting-1-2022-2.pdf.

Asian Forum for Human Rights and Development, 2023, [Joint Open Letter] Indonesia: Indonesia's Candidacy for Election to the UN Human Rights Council, *Forum Asia* (September 14, 2023) https://forum-asia.org/?p=38629.

Asian Human Rights Commission, 2006, INDONESIA: Ratification of Key Human Rights Instruments must be Followed by Legal Reform, *Human Rights Asia* (August 26, 2022) http://www.humanrights.asia/news/ahrc-news/AS-044-2006/.

Ayu Mumpuni, 2024, Polri: Kasus UU ITE Tak Berlaku Surut Meski Pasal Dihapus [Police: ITE Law Cases Not Retroactive Even Though Articles Are Removed], *Tirto.Id* (April 22, 2024). https://tirto.id/polri-kasus-uu-ite-tak-berlaku-surut-meski-pasal-dihapus-gXac.

Bambang Muryanto, 2020, ITE Law Increasingly Threatens Press Freedom, *The Jakarta Post* (November 17, 2022) https://www.thejakartapost.com/news/2014/11/17/ite-law-increasingly-threatens-press-freedom.html.

Bayu Marhaenjati and Christian Lee, 2019, Police Arrest Eggi Sudjana for Treason, *Jakarta Globe* (June 14, 2022), https://jakartaglobe.id/context/police-arrest-eggi-sudjana-for-treason.

BBC Trending, 2020, Arrested for Calling Indonesian City "Idiotic", *BBC.com* (May 15, 2021) https://www.bbc.com/news/blogs-trending-29035858.

Coconuts Jakarta, 2020, If I'm a Frog then My Mother is a Frog: Surabaya Mayor Tri Rismaharini Reports Woman to the Polic for Online Slander, *Coconuts.co* (Feb. 16, 2021)https://coconuts.co/jakarta/news/if-im-a-frog-then-my-mother-is-a-frog-surabaya-mayor-tri-rismaharini-reports-woman-to-the-police-for-online-slander/.

CSCE, 2002, Criminal Defamation and Insult Laws: Summary of Free Speech Developments in the Czech Republic, *csce.gov* (Jan. 9, 2022,), https://www.csce.gov/international-impact/criminal-defamation-and-insult-laws-summary-free-speech-developments-czech.

David Lyons, 2005, Punishment as Retribution, *Vice, Crime, and American Law* (July 11, 2023) https://web.uncg.edu/dcl/courses/viceCrime/m7/part3.asp.

Dian Dewi Purnamasari, 2024, An Oasis of Freedom of Opinion from the Free Sentences of Haris and Fatia, *Kompas.Id* (January 29, 2024) https://www.kompas.id/baca/english/2024/01/08/en-oase-kebebasan-berpendapat-dari-vonis-bebas-haris-dan-fatia.

Dio Suhenda, 2023, Rempang Sheds Light on Jokowi's "Land Hungry" National Projects, *The Jakarta Post* (September 28, 2023) https://asianews.network/rempang-sheds-light-on-jokowis-land-hungry-national-projects/.

Eka Nugraha Putra, 2023, Blasphemy Cases Highlight Legal Inconsistencies, *Indonesia at Melbourne* (June 27, 2023) https://indonesiaatmelbourne.unimelb.edu.au/blasphemy-cases-highlight-legal-inconsistencies/.

Fitria Chusna Farisa and Dani Prabowo, 2021, Jokowi Bakal Minta DPR Revisi UU ITE Jika Implementasinya Tak Adil [Jokowi Will Ask DPR to Revise ITE Law If Its Implementation is Unfair], *Kompas.com* (August 8, 2023) https://nasional.kompas.com/read/2021/02/15/22160541/jokowi-bakal-minta-dpr-revisi-uu-ite-jika-implementasinya-tak-adil.

Freedom House, 2019, Freedom in the World: Indonesia, *Freedom House* (April 3, 2020) https://freedomhouse.org/report/freedom-world/2019/indonesia.

Gary Ky Chan, 2013, Corporate Defamation: Reputation, Rights and Remedies, *Legal Studies* Vol. 33 No.2, June 2013, https://onlinelibrary.wiley.com/doi/pdf/10.1111/j.1748-121X.2012.00258.x264.

Herlambang P. Wiratraman, 2022, Indonesian Law Systematically Stifles Journalists, *the Jakarta Post* (May 4, 2022) https://www.thejakartapost.com/opinion/2022/05/04/indonesian-law-systematically-stifles-journalists.html.

Hikmahanto Juwana, 2008, Tantangan Indonesia Pasca Ratifikasi ICCPR [Indonesia's Challenges After ICCPR Ratification], *Kompas* (April 18, 2008) http://www.kompas.com/kompas-cetak/0506/08/opini/1799437.htm.

HRW, 2019, Indonesia: Draft Criminal Code Disastrous for Rights, Human Rights Watch (Sep. 19, 2022) https://www.hrw.org/news/2019/09/18/indonesia-draft-criminal-code-disastrous-rights.

Ian Vazques and Tanja Porcnik, 2019, The Human Freedom Index, Cato Institute, https://www.cato.org/sites/cato.org/files/human-freedom-index-files/2019-human-freedom-index-update-2.pdf.

ICJR, 2016, Respon atas Rencana Penetapan Revisi UU ITE: Lima Masalah Krusial dalam Revisi UU ITE yang Mengancam Kebebasan Ekspresi di Indonesia [Response to the Plan to Revise the ITE Law: Five Crucial Issues in the Revised ITE Law that Threaten Freedom of Expression in Indonesia], *ICJR* (October 27, 2016), https://icjr.or.id/respon-atas-rencana-penetapan-revisi-uu-ite-lima-masalah-krusial-dalam-revisi-uu-ite-yang-mengancam-kebebasan-ekpresi-di-indonesia/.

ICJR, 2020, Catatan atas RUU Perubahan Pasal 27 Ayat 3 UU ITE dan Sikap Fraksi-Fraksi di Komisi I DPR [Notes on the Draft Law on Amendments to Article 27 Paragraph 3 of the ITE Law and the Attitudes of the Factions in Commission I of the DPR], *icjr.or.id* (August 18, 2022) https://icjr.or.id/catatan-atas-ruu-perubahan-pasal-27-ayat-3-uu-ite-dan-sikap-fraksi-fraksi-di-komisi-i-dpr/.

Janne Mende, 2019, Are Human Rights Western-And Why Does it Matter? A Perspective from International Political Theory, *Journal of International Political Theory*, doi:https://journals.sagepub.com/doi/10.1177/1755088219832992.

Jon'a F. Meyer, 2014, Retributive Justice, *britannica.com* (December 22, 2023) https://www.britannica.com/topic/retributive-justice.

Kartika Singarimbun et.al., 2019, Broadcasting Law 32/2002: A Case of the Indonesian Government's Indecisiveness towards the Implementation of Radio Network, *Library and Philosophy Practice (E-Journal)*, https://digitalcommons.unl.edu/libphilprac/2966.

Kate Lamb, 2017, Jakarta Governor Ahok Sentenced to Two Years in Prison for Blasphemy, *the Guardian* (May 9, 2017) https://www.theguardian.com/world/2017/may/09/jakarta-governor-ahok-found-guilty-of-blasphemy-jailed-for-two-years.

Kemenkominfo, 2023, Matriks Perbandingan Perubahan Undang-Undang Republik Indonesia Nomor 11 Tahun 2008 Tentang Informasi Dan Transaksi Elektronik Dengan Undang-Undang Republik Indonesia Nomor 19 Tahun 2016 Tentang Perubahan Atas Undangundang Nomor 11 Tahun 2008 Tentang Informasi Dan Transaksi Elektronik [Comparison Matrix of Amendments to Law of the Republic of Indonesia Number 11 of 2008 Concerning Electronic Information and Transactions with Law of the Republic of Indonesia Number 19 of 2016 Concerning Amendments to Law Number 11 of 2008 Concerning Electronic Information and Transactions], *jdih.kominfo.go.id* (April 24, 2024) https://jdih.kominfo.go.id/storage/files/mp-1491878641-matriks_perbandingan_perubahan_undang_undang_tentang_ite.pdf.

Kominfo, 2021, Sejak 2018 Kominfo Tangani 3640 Ujaran Kebencian Berbasis SARA di Ruang Digital [Since 2018, Kominfo Has Handled 3640 SARA-Based Hate Speeches in Digital Space], *kominfo.go.id* (April 28, 2022) https://www.kominfo.go.id/content/detail/34136/siaran-pers-no-143hmkominfo042021-tentang-sejak-2018-kominfo-tangani-3640-ujaran-kebencian-berbasis-sara-di-ruang-digital/0/siaran_pers.

Kontras, 2022, Putus Daftar Panjang Upaya Kriminalisasi terhadap Pejuang Lingkungan Hidup! [End the Long List of Criminalization Attempts against Environmental Activists!], *Kontras* (February 2, 2022) https://kontras.org/2022/02/02/putus-daftar-panjang-upaya-kriminalisasi-terhadap-pejuang-lingkungan-hidup/.

Manushya Foundation, 2023, The Defamation Trial Against Fatia Maulidiyanti and Haris Azhar is Ongoing!, *Manushya Foundation* (June 19, 2023) https://www.manushyafoundation.org/post/the-defamation-trial-against-fatia-maulidiyanti-and-haris-azhar-is-ongoing.

Matthew Lower, 2013, Can and Should Human Rights be Universal?, *International Relations Info* (Jan 4, 2022) https://www.e-ir.info/pdf/44590.

Mochamad Januar Rizki, 2024, Pasal Karet dalam UU ITE Terbaru Masih Mengancam Masyarakat yang Kritis [Rubber Articles in the Latest ITE Law Still Threaten Critical Society], *hukumonline.com* (April 3, 2024) https://www.hukumonline.com/berita/a/pasal-karet-dalam-uu-ite-terbaru-masih-mengancam-masyarakat-yang-kritis-lt6597e40be9b8c.

Moh Afaf El Kurniawan, 2023, Sejarah UU ITE di Indonesia: Perkembangan Regulasi dan Kontroversi di Dunia Digital [History of ITE Law in Indonesia: Regulatory Developments and Controversies in the Digital World], *Narasi TV* (September 14, 2023) https://narasi.tv/read/narasi-daily/sejarah-uu-ite.

Normand Edwin Elnizar, 2021, SKB UU ITE tak bisa Mengikat Penafsiran Hakim, Apakah Berfaedah? [Joint Decree on ITE Law Cannot Bind Judges' Interpretation, Is It Useful?], *hukumonline* (April 14, 2022), https://www.hukumonline.com/stories/article/lt60eeb6125ce8c/skb-uu-ite-tak-bisa-mengikat-penafsiran-hakim--apakah-berfaedah.

Oliver Holmes, 2016, Indonesia Accused of Arresting more than 1000 in West Papua, *the Guardian* (June 17, 2016) https://www.theguardian.com/world/2016/jun/17/indonesia-accused-of-arresting-more-than-1000-in-west-papua.

Pusat Studi Hukum Dan Kebijakan, 2021, 5 Alasan Menolak Pasal Penghinaan Presiden dimasukkan Kembali ke dalam RKUHP [5 Reasons to Reject the Article on Insulting the President from Being Reinserted into the RKUHP], *pshk.or.id*, https://pshk.or.id/publikasi/siaran-pers/5-alasan-menolak-pasal-penghinaan-presiden-dimasukkan-kembali-ke-dalam-rkuhp/ (July 17, 2021).

Rahmat Nur Hakim, 2021, Revisi UU ITE: Berawal dari Keresahan Jokowi namun Batal Masuk Prolegnas Nasional 2021 [Revision of ITE Law: Starting from Jokowi's Concerns but Not Included in 2021 National Legislation Program], *Kompas.com* (September 9, 2023) https://nasional.kompas.com/read/2021/03/12/20521121/revisi-uu-ite-berawal-dari-keresahan-jokowi-namun-batal-masuk-prolegnas?page=all.

Rebecca Henschke and Ayomi Amindo, 2019, Papua Protest: Racist Taunts Open Deep Wounds, *BBC.com* (Aug. 23, 2021), https://www.bbc.com/news/world-asia-49434277.

Rofiq Hidayat, 2022, Alasan Pemerintah Pertahankan Pasal Penghinaan Kepala Negara dalam RKUHP [The Government's Reason for Maintaining the Article on Insulting the Head of State in the RKUHP], *hukumonline.com*, https://www.hukumonline.com/berita/a/alasan-pemerintah-pertahankan-pasal-penghinaan-kepala-negara-dalam-rkuhp-lt62a17f49e4d5a/ (June 29, 2022).

SNO Staff, 2018, Surprise? It's A Crime To Insult, Mock Or Call A Person Names Anywhere In Saint Lucia Criminal Code, *St. Lucia News Online*, (Oct 8, 2021) https://www.stlucianewsonline.com/surprise-its-a-crime-to-insult-mock-or-call-a-person-names-anywhere-in-saint-lucia-criminal-code/.

Supriyadi Widodo Eddyono, Fajrimei A. Gofar, and Adiani A. Viviana, 2020, Tindak Pidana terhadap Pemerintah yang Sah dalam RKUHP [Criminal Acts against Legitimate Government in the Draft Criminal Code], *icjr.or.id* (Oct. 15, 2022) https://icjr.or.id/wp-content/uploads/2016/12/TINDAK-PIDANA-PENGHINAAN-Pemerintah.pdf.

Tempo.Co, 2014, Wartawan Jawa Post Group Divonis Sembilan Bulan Penjara [Jawa Post Group Journalist Sentenced to Nine Months in Prison], *Tempo.co* (Dec. 22, 2022), https://nasional.tempo.co/read/53509/wartawan-jawa-post-grup-divonis-sembilan-bulan-penjara.

Tri Indah Oktavianti, 2020, Prosecutors Seek up to 17 Years for Papuan Protesters Accused of Treason, *The Jakarta Post* (Jun. 7, 2020) https://www.thejakartapost.com/news/2020/06/07/prosecutors-seek-up-to-17-years-for-papuan-protesters-accused-of-treason.html.

United Nations, (n.d.) Understanding Hate Speech, *un.org* (Jan. 30, 2024) https://www.un.org/en/hate-speech/understanding-hate-speech/what-is-hate-speech#:~:text=To%20provide%20a%20unified%20framework,person%20or%20a%20group%20on.

Virginia Gorlinski, 2023, Minangkabau, *britannica.com* (March 12, 2024) https://www.britannica.com/topic/Minangkabau.

VOI, 2021, SKB Guidelines for the ITE Law are not Legal Products, their Application is not Retroactive, *Voi.id* (April 14, 2022), https://voi.id/en/news/61698/skb-guidelines-for-the-ite-law-are-not-legal-products-their-application-is-not-retroactive.

4 Limitations on Freedom of Speech in Indonesia

4.1 Implementation of Defamation Laws

Defamation has been a long debate in Indonesian law. Interestingly, the discussion on defamation, especially criminal defamation, has become one of the main topics in the Indonesian criminal justice system, especially since the ITE Law was passed in 2008. This is due to the significant number of criminal prosecutions and trials related to expressions. The ITE Law was later amended in 2016 and 2024; however, as discussed in the previous chapter, it still stipulates criminal punishment for expressions, including defamation. Through the recent constitutional changes, the ITE Law governs criminal online defamation, while the Criminal Code Act addresses criminal offline defamation.

Since the ITE Law was passed, defamation cases have risen significantly. Data show that from 2001 until 2021, 985 offline defamation cases were processed under the Current Criminal Code; meanwhile, from 2008 to 2021, when the ITE Law was passed, there were 996 online defamation cases processed under the ITE Law[1]. In total, 1,981 defamation cases were on trial and resulted in verdicts in the First Degree Court[2].

The data indicates that, in just 13 years, the number of criminal defamation cases based on the ITE Law has surpassed the number of cases based on the Criminal Code. Despite the controversies it raises, the ITE Law has facilitated unnecessary criminal prosecutions and, in many cases, punishments for so-called defamation.

The term "unnecessary" here is used to highlight that many criminal defamation cases in Indonesia were not evidently actionable as defamation; instead, the verdicts were against the freedom of expression. The following list of cases will be analyzed for the element of criminal defamation. These case studies are taken from cases that have been decided in the First Degree Court. In each section, it will be indicated whether the Court's decisions found the defendant guilty or not guilty.

Although the Current Criminal Code has been in effect since 1946, the use of its defamation provisions is very rare. A search of the Indonesian Supreme Court's repository (*Mahkamah Agung*) shows that, before the Reformation Order in 1998, the criminal defamation provisions in the Current Criminal

DOI: 10.4324/9781032661544-4

Code were rarely, if ever, enforced. One notable case was noted in 1970[3], but the link led to an appeal decision from 2013, which is irrelevant to the discussion in this section. However, some cases discussed here were found in the repository, while others became subjects of public discussion and scrutiny due to their controversial elements and/or the profile of the defendants.

4.1.1 Defamation Cases under the Current Criminal Code

4.1.1.1 Bambang Harymurti Case

Bambang was a journalist and editor-in-chief of *Tempo*, one of the prominent magazines in Indonesia. In 2003, the magazine published an investigative story about a fire in Tanah Abang (Tenabang) market in Jakarta[4].

Tempo's investigation found that Tomy Winata, a businessperson, would receive 53 million Rupiahs for the renovation of the market. Soon after the investigative story-titled "*Ada Tomy di Tenabang*" (There is Tomy in Tenabang) – was published, Tomy called *Tempo*'s office, demanded that the magazine retract the story, and claimed it was character assassination[5]. However, *Tempo* refused to retract the story, which then led to a lawsuit against Bambang for criminal defamation and against *Tempo* for civil defamation. The civil defamation lawsuit was filed against *Tempo Inti Media* LLC, the owner of *Tempo* magazine, along with Zulkifli Lubis (*Tempo Inti Media*'s CEO), Bambang Harymurti (Editor-in-chief), Fikri Jufri (General Manager), Toriq Hadad (Vice Editor), Ahmad Taufik (writer of the article *Ada Tomy di Tenabang*?), Bernarda Rurit, and Cahyo Junaedy (reporters).

Unfortunately, in Decision 223/PDT.G/2003/PN.JKT.PST, the Central Jakarta District Court ruled that *Tempo* was guilty of defamation. In addition, Tempo was required to pay 500 million Rupiahs for the immaterial loss of Tomy Winata, along with 300,000 Rupiahs per day as *dwangsom*[6] (an additional penalty in a civil lawsuit) and to publish an apology in printed advertisements in national news media for three consecutive days.

Tempo appealed the decision to the Jakarta Appellate Court, which overturned the ruling of the Central Jakarta First Degree Court in September 2004. The Appellate Court emphasized that the 1999 Press Law should have been prioritized in handling such a case[7].

In the criminal defamation case against Bambang Harymurti, the Court found him guilty of defamation as his actions were considered to have violated Article XIV of Law Number 1 of 1946 and Article 311 of the Current Criminal Code. Ironically, the Court failed to explain the element of "with intention" in these provisions, as the judges merely explained the types of intention in criminal law without referencing any specific theory or explaining why that theory was used as the basis for the verdict[8]. The theories of intention in criminal law are used to determine whether a crime is committed deliberately or due to negligence, which leads to different punishments.

The common theories of intention in criminal acts are[9] *Intentional purposefulness, intentional conviction certainty, and intentional conversion of possibility*. The first theory, intentional purposefulness, means that before or during the commission of a crime, the offender is aware that his or her actions constitute a criminal offense and understands the impact of those actions on the victims. The second theory, intentional conviction certainty, explains that the offender may not have intentionally committed a crime due to anger or rage, but he or she is still aware of the impact of his or her actions The third theory, *intentional conversion of possibility*, occurs when the perpetrator has an idea of offense that only carries a slight possibility of happening, yet the potential consequences concerned may still occur without being addressed. Therefore, it is important to determine whether there is potential certainty – not only possibility – that the offender would still commit the act.

Of all the three theories explained above, the Court in Bambang Harymurti's verdict did not clarify whether Bambang's role as editor-in-chief of *Tempo* fell into the category of intention. In fact, given that Bambang is a journalist and his role involves publishing news in the area of public interest, such as conflicts of interest and bribery, the *Tempo* news story should not have been treated as a criminal case at all.

In addition, another criminal defamation lawsuit was filed against Ahmad Taufik (the writer of the article *Ada Tomy di Tenabang*?) and Teuku Iskandar Ali (the Deputy Editor) both of whom were acquitted of the defamation charges. the Appellate Court' verdict stated that Ahmad Taufik and Teuku Iskandar Ali were not guilty, citing that editor-in-chief was the responsible party for news publication according to the Press Law[10].

Similar to the civil defamation lawsuit against the magazine, Bambang also attempted to appeal the First Degree Court's decision. Unfortunately. the Appellate Court upheld the conviction, citing the dissemination of a hoax by Bambang as the editor-in-chief of *Tempo*. Interestingly, although the Court did not reference the right to reply as the proper mechanism under the 1999 Press Law, it still upheld Bambang's conviction, resulting in a one-year prison sentence.

The true justice, however, emerged in 2007, when the Indonesian Supreme Court decided the cassation process. The Supreme Court argued that an important element of Bambang Harymurti's case was that it was not a criminal offense from the beginning[11], and it emphasized the mechanisms of the Press Law, including the right to reply and dispute settlement arbitrated by the Indonesian Press Council.

4.1.2 Defamation Cases Under the ITE Law

4.1.2.1 The Prita Mulyasari Case

One of the first significant cases in Indonesia was Prita Mulyasari's case in 2009. The case started when Prita shared her story with a mailing list of close friends about her awful experience after undergoing a medical checkup at Omni International Hospital. One of Prita's friends posted the story on a blog, and it subsequently went viral. Prita faced criminal prosecution and a civil lawsuit from the hospital for alleged online defamation, although she was not the one who posted the story outside the mailing list. In the end, Prita was found not guilty by the Indonesian Supreme Court, but only after she appealed the First-Degree Court's verdict, which had found her guilty and imprisoned her for 20 days[12].

The whole legal process, based on an obscure provision of the ITE Law, lasted for nearly two years. The legal problem arose from the Indonesian legal system's classification of an e-mail intended as a consumer complaint as online defamation. Prita's case was the first to be processed under the ITE Law. Prita's expression. which was a consumer complaint about inadequate medical treatment, was unnecessarily investigated as criminal conduct. This highlights one of the problems with the ITE Law since the Act, despite its unclear legal ground in Prita's case, is still enforced as the primary legislation for criminalizing online expression.

In 2008, when the ITE Law was passed, online defamation began to be regulated under this statute. Article 27 Section 3 is the provision for online defamation, while the criminal punishment is specified under Article 45. According to the ITE Law, defamatory expressions are considered online when they are disseminated through electronic formats, such as e-mails, social media posts, text messages, or any other electronic means that use electronic systems.

These distinctions between offline and online defamation, along with their respective criminal provisions, were further emphasized after several judicial review processes for the ITE Law were denied by the Indonesian Constitutional Court (*Mahkamah Konstitusi*-MK). One of the Constitutional Court's judicial decisions was a verdict issued in 2008, just a few months after the ITE Law was officially passed. In this ruling, the Court stated that the ITE Law did not violate the 1945 Indonesian Constitution. The distinction between online and offline defamation is necessary, as the Court noted differences in how defamatory content is published in each format.[13]

According to the Indonesian Constitutional Court, one reason for the distinction between offline and online defamation laws is the difference in how certain acts are defined in the Criminal Code Act and the ITE Law. The terms "to distribute," "to transmit," and "causes to be accessible" in Article 27 Section 3 of the ITE Law, were not initially defined when the law was first enacted in 2008. After its partial amendment in 2016, which allowed both the ITE Law 2008 and ITE Law 2016 to coexist in internet law in Indonesia, definitions for these terms were provided in the Explanation Section of the Act. "To distribute" means sending electronic information to a group of people, while "to transmit" means sending electronic information to individuals. Last, "causes to be accessible" is defined as "any other acts besides distribution and transmission through an electronic system that can disclose electronic information to a third party or the public[14]."

4.1.2.2 Florence Sihombing Case

This 2014 case was ironic for two reasons: The offender was a law graduate student at the time, and her alleged hate expression was directed at people in a city rather than a particular group of people.

Florence was originally from Medan but was studying for her Master's degree in Notarial Law at Universitas Gajahmada, Yogyakarta. On 27 August 2014, Florence went to a gas station to refill her motorcycle's fuel. However, she mistakenly lined up in the car lane, and the gas station clerk refused to serve her, instructing her to go to the motorcycle line instead. Upset, Florence decided to go home and post about her bad experience on the then-popular social media platform, Path. In her post, Florence wrote (not official translation):

> *Jogja*[15] *is poor, stupid and uncultured. Friends from Jakarta-Bandung don't stay in Jogja. Jogja people are bastards. I wanted to buy Pertamax 95*[16] *but was rejected because I was using a motorbike in the car lane and was not served. They even told me to queue in the motorcycle lane, which already had a long line. This is discrimination, as if I can't pay anything. huh. KZL*[17].

Her post went viral, angering many people in Yogyakarta. Florence was reported to the police by a non-governmental organization named Jatisura and was arrested for a few weeks. Before the trial, Florence made a statement expressing her regret about her post and even met with the Governor of Yogyakarta, Sultan Hamengkubuwono X. The Governor stated there was no problem between himself and Florence, but he hoped for a solution to Florence's case and reminded her to act properly[18]. The Governor also asked the people of Yogyakarta to forgive her and let go of their anger toward her[19].

Unfortunately, the trial continued despite Florence's apologetic statements. The prosecutors indicted Florence with an alternative indictment that included provisions from the ITE Law, which were Article 27 Section 3 (online defamation) and Article 28 Section 2 (Online Hate Speech). Eventually, in Decision No. 382/Pid.Sus/2014/PN.Yyk from the Yogyakarta First Degree Court, Florence was found guilty of online defamation, while the hate speech charge was not proven. She was sentenced to two months of probation for a criminal offense. Florence later filed an appeal and a cessation against the lower Court's decision, but the Appellate Court upheld the conviction, even though it revoked the penalty imposed by the lower Court[20]. The Indonesian Supreme Court also rejected Florence's cessation and upheld the lower Court's decision, confirming her guilt for defaming Yogyakarta[21].

Even though the Court's decision stated that Florence was guilty of online defamation, some of the scrutiny of this case was about hate speech[22]. One of the indictments also included provisions for online hate speech, which is why this case is discussed in this section.

Florence's post may have been offensive, but offensive expressions do not necessarily violate any laws. Prosecuting Florence for online hate speech, as indicated in the indictment, is already questionable. Furthermore, the Court's decision to find her guilty of online defamation is even more problematic because the Court treated Yogyakarta as if it were a human being or an individual capable of being offended.

In the Yogyakarta First Degree Court, the Court did not address the elements of online hate speech, as it was listed as the second charge in the alternative indictment. Since the Court found that all elements of the first indictment of online defamation were satisfied, there was no need to prove the second indictment of online hate speech.

The Court even cited the expert witness' statement that Florence's post, which insulted Yogyakarta, actually implied an expanded meaning by also referring to its people. While the statement from the expert may have been valid in a linguistic context – reflecting the expert's area of expertise – it does not necessarily apply in a legal context. Insulting a city does not satisfy the elements of defamation, which, as mentioned earlier, cannot be offended, may not qualify as hate speech either, because the term "Yogyakarta" in the context of this case is too broad. However, the Court's analysis narrowed it down by interpreting Florence's alleged expression as specifically targeting the Javanese ethnic group, the majority group who domicile in Yogyakarta.

Furthermore, despite the fact that Florence's statement was offensive, freedom of expression is not only for the protection of inoffensive expressions but also for those that offend, shock, and disturb[23]. While this principle was established by the European Court of Human Rights in *Handyside v. United Kingdom*[24], it also aligns with the three-step test of the ICCPR, particularly the second threshold of "legitimate aim." The conviction does not serve the legitimate aim of protecting the rights and reputation of others, as Yogyakarta's reputation was not evidently tainted, and the people of Yogyakarta did not feel defamed because the individuals involved in the trial could not represent the whole of Yogyakarta city. Furthermore, the Governor actually forgave Florence. The case did not aim to protect public order, public health, or national security, as the chaos occurred online and did not incite any physical riots. Unfortunately, the trial represented another excessive implementation of the ITE Law to defuse public anger over some insults that could have been settled through mediation or civil law mechanisms.

4.1.2.3 Muhammad Asrul Case

In 2021, another defamation case involving journalists occurred. Muhammad Asrul, a reporter for *berita.news* at Paolopo, Makassar, South Sulawesi province,, covered an alleged corruption case that involved Farid Judas Karim, the son of the Palopo Mayor.

Asrul wrote three news articles in May 2019 with the following titles:

> *Crown Prince Palopo Allegedly "Mastermind" of PLTMH*[25] *Corruption and IDR 11 Billion Zaro Chips*[26]*, The Scent of Corruption from the Revitalization of the Palopo Pancasila Field Allegedly Drags Farid Judas*[27]*, and "Volume II" West Ring Road Corruption IDR 5 Billion, Investigator's Signal for Farid Judas?*[28].

After the news were published, through his lawyer, Farid filed a subpoena, which was responded to by *berita.news*. Furthermore, the dispute was submitted to the Indonesian Press Council, which stated in its announcement that the three news stories by Asrul are considered journalistic work[29]. Therefore, the dispute should be settled under the Press Law; the Press Council even initiated its expertise in the case. Not only is the Press Law the basis for the case settlement, but the Press Council and the Indonesian Police have also signed Memorandum of Understanding No.2/DP/MoU/II/2017 on Coordination in Protecting Press Freedom and Law Enforcement against Abuse of the Journalist Profession[30].

The MoU between the Press Council and the Indonesian Police covers data and information exchange, coordination on press freedom, legal enforcement related to the journalism profession, and human resource development between the two institutions[31].

Although the initial process was correctly conducted through mediation by the Press Council, the investigation proceeded to trial, where the Court eventually found Asrul guilty of online defamation for violating Article 27 Section 3 of the 2016 ITE Law.

In the trial, it was revealed that *berita.news* was registered as corporation on 13 May 2019, and received verification from the Press Council on 21 November 2019. In addition, Asrul had not yet passed the qualifications to be considered a journalist[32]. Meanwhile, the three news stories were published on the *berita.news*'s website on 10 May 2019, 24 May 2019, and 25 May 2019.

However, despite the fact that neither the media nor Asrul qualified as a press entity, making the dispute not a press dispute under the Press Council, this should not justify a criminal defamation trial for Asrul.

There were at least two important points in Asrul's case. The first was the implementation of criminal defamation as a penalty for alleged private reputational harm. The second was the sharp rise in the number of press companies not verified by the Press Council, which poses challenges to the protection of press freedom. These two issues are closely connected to press freedom. Following the 1998 political reforms, it became easier for Indonesian to establish media companies. One report even indicated that the 1999 Press Law – revoking the 1982 Press Law, which had regulated permit applications for establishing press companies – led to the creation of 1,600 new print media outlets, although most of them closed after the 1999 Election[33].

On the one hand, the significant increase in new media indicates a positive trend in freedom of the press and freedom of expression, providing numerous platforms for people to channel their expressions. This trend has been particularly notable with the rise of the internet, which offers additional options in digital media.

However, the large number of media outlets comes with consequences, such as content that may go against public norms and collaborations between major media companies and political or business actors, which can lead to media distortion[34]. Therefore, the Press Council's verification aims to ensure quality journalism and the credibility of media companies. As stipulated in the 1999

Press Law[35], this verification is not a permit application like it was under the previous law; instead, it serves to provide a comprehensive database for all media in Indonesia.

The more media outlets that can be verified in the database, the more the Press Council can advocate for their professionalism and credibility. Unfortunately, as of March 2024, only 1,700 media outlets have been verified in the Press Council's database[36], out of about 47,000 in total[37]. Therefore, these unverified media not only result in questionable journalism but also lead to news stories that do not meet the standards for non-defamatory content.

Reflecting on Asrul's trial, Herlambang Perdana Wiratraman's statement, a law professor at Universitas Gadjah Mada in Yogyakarta and an expert witness in the case, stated that the lack of verification for a press company does not mean that the press is not protected under the Press Law. He emphasized that the press serves as a social institution and a communication platform, regardless of the status of the company as a legal entity[38].

However, the Court ultimately decided that Asrul was guilty. In its argument, the Court cited Chairul Huda's work on "Trial by the Press and its Practice in Press," which states that the Press Law should not be considered as *lex specialis* because there is no defamation provision in the Press Law. Nevertheless, law enforcers should still prioritize the Press Law and the Journalistic Ethics Code when proving the element of "against the law" to determine whether a news story contains elements of a crime[39].

Considering that the plaintiff intended to exercise the right to reply as stipulated in the Press Law. However, since there was no clear address registered due to the status of *berita.news* as a legal entity, the criminal defamation investigation continued. Therefore, despite the political will of the Press Council officials to consider verification as a simple database, the provisions of the Press Law still normatively require that all press companies be registered as legal entities, as stated in Article 9 Section 2, which mandates registration with the Indonesian Minister of Law and Human Rights. This procedure resembles a simpler version of self-censorship that should ideally be revoked through an amendment to the Press Law[40].

4.1.2.4 Haris Azhar and Fatia Maulidiyanti

Considering the new passage of the 2024 ITE Law, one notable case involves two Indonesian human rights activists, Haris Azhar and Fatia Mauilidiyanti, who were charged with online criminal defamation in 2021 for a YouTube video that discusses the socioeconomic implications of the military operation in Papua[41]. The plaintiff, Luhut Binsar Panjaitan, Indonesia's Coordinating Minister of Maritime and Investment, was mentioned in the video, which discussed research findings alleging Luhut's involvement through his stock ownership in a company that was influential in the Papua military operation[42]. Luhut stated that he filed the lawsuit to protect his family's reputation. However, while the video criticized his abuse of power as a public official for personal interest, Luhut's claim to protect his family's reputation is not comparable because the video did not cause harm to his family's reputation in any way.

The Court addressed the cases in two separate trials: The Decision of the East Jakarta Court No. 202/Pid.Sus/2023/PN Jkt.Tim for Haris and No. 203/Pid.Sus/2023/PN Jkt.Tim for Fatia. During the trials, prosecutors claimed that the activists' statements violated Article 27 Section 3 of the 2016 ITE Law[43]. In a podcast that was uploaded to Haris Azhar's YouTube channel, Haris and Fatia discussed research findings on military operations that affected the society in Papua, which were profitable for several individuals, including Luhut Binsar Panjaitan.

In the video titled "There is Lord Luhut Behind Intan Jaya's Military Ops Intan Jaya-Economic Relations!!BIN[44] General is also there!!NgeHAMtam[45]" (*Ada Lord Luhut Dibalik Relasi Ekonomi-Ops Militer Intan Jaya!! Jenderal BIN Juga Ada!!NgeHAMtam*), both Haris and Fatia mentioned Luhut's name and his alleged involvement in the military operation. However, despite grounding their discussion in research, one focus of the trial was whether Haris and Fatia were disrespectful for using the title "Lord. The trial transcript cited "Lord, "Lord Luhut" and "Luhut Binsar Pandjaitan" at least six times throughout the 26-minute video[46].

In the prosecutor's indictment[47], three laws were cited by the prosecutor for Haris and Fathia's alleged defamatory expressions: Article 27 Section 3 of the 2016 ITE Law, Article 14 (subsidiary[48] to Article 15) of Law Number 1 of 1946, Article 310 of the Current Criminal Code. The indictment suggests that the prosecutor was either uncertain about the specific law violations, and hence included several criminal provisions, or was more focused on justifying the indictment rather than looking for the truth[49].

While a combined indictment, such as the one submitted by the prosecutor in this case, is permissible under the Indonesian criminal procedural legal system, including the offline criminal defamation provision (Article 310 of the Current Criminal Code) in the final indictment was clearly inconsistent with the circumstances, as the alleged defamatory expressions by Haris and Fatia were recorded and distributed through online media (YouTube). Furthermore, the provisions on hoaxes in Law Number 1 of 1946 are questionable, as the law was never truly intended to address hoaxes in the context of the digital era. This law is a product of colonial legislation and, in most cases where it is cited, it is used in conjunction with other laws. Even before Articles 14 and 15 of the Law were eventually declared unconstitutional by the Constitutional Court in early 2024[50], it was already considered problematic due to its unclear validity status within Indonesian criminal law[51].

The debate over the use of the term "Lord Luhut" and the accusation that Luhut benefited financially from the Intan Jaya Operation was not thoroughly examined. One of the prosecutor's arguments was not even aligned with the basic defamation law, which requires the existence of reputational harm. The prosecutor claimed that Fathia's statement at minute 14 of the video was not true and constituted a lie, thus qualifying as defamation. However, this argument can be countered by examining the basis of the case, which combines the elements of spreading false news and defamation into a single criminal offense[52].

The fundamental theory of defamation law is that a statement must not only be false but also harm the reputation of the victim. While these basic elements are unfortunately not properly stipulated in Indonesian law, such a formulation has been acknowledged in international human rights treaties. Article 19 Section 3 of the International Covenant on Civil and Political Rights (ICCPR) states that restrictions imposed by countries should serve to protect the rights and reputation of others as part of the three-step test: Legality, Legitimacy, and Necessity. Therefore, legitimate criticism directed at a public official, in this case, Luhut Binsar Pandjaitan, should not be restricted[53]. Moreover, the element of spreading lies, as cited by the prosecutor as satisfying defamation law, is inconsistent with the prosecutor's indictment, which differentiates between online defamation, spreading false news, and offline defamation, as discussed previously.

The Court ultimately found both Haris and Fatia not guilty of any charges. It determined that their discussion on the podcast did not violate Article 27 Section 3 of the ITE Law, as it falls into the category of Article 315 of the Current Criminal Code concerning simple defamation. This category is not referenced by the ITE Law, according to the 2008 constitutional change by the Constitutional Court. While this is a valid argument by the Court, it is still concerning that the Court equated Haris and Fathia's expression with name-calling and insults, which should not be considered defamation since the expression did not harm one's reputation. However, this may have been considered by the Court because the law stipulates it, as outlined in Article 315 of the Current Criminal Code.

Another interesting argument made by the Court is that the usage of the term "Lord Luhut," which was repeatedly used by Haris and Fatia, is not considered defamation. Not only is the term "Lord" used to address someone with respect and honor, but the prosecutor also considered only the meaning of the title, rather than the whole conversation in the podcast[54].

The Court's decision was not only a significant milestone for the protection of freedom of expression in Indonesia but also an important advancement in recognizing the significance of public interest defense in defamation cases[55]. This is particularly relevant given that Haris and Fathia's discussion about Luhut's involvement is an inevitable fact, considering that Luhut evidently had[56] a 99% stock in one of the companies engaged in business collaboration with another company in Papua's mining industry.

The case of Haris and Fatia also highlights that Anti Strategic Litigation Against Public Participation (Anti-SLAPP) remains a challenge for human rights defenders[57]. Although Article 66 of the Law No. 32 of 2009 on Environmental Protection and Management, along with Indonesian Supreme Court Regulation No. 36 of 2013 on Implementation of Guidelines for Handling Environmental Cases, regulates protections for those who advocate for environmental rights, including Haris and Fatia, these protections remain difficult to enforce, as the mining and military operations have affected environmental aspects in Papua.

While defamation cases are indeed concerning for the protection of freedom of expression in Indonesia due to unclear laws and instances of malicious implementation, hate speech presents another challenge to these protections. The following section will also discuss several judicial decisions on hate speech in detail.

4.2 Implementation of Hate Speech Laws

Hate speech has long been a debated issue in Indonesian criminal law. As discussed in Chapter 3, several provisions in the Current Criminal Code were drafted in response to socio-political circumstances. Unfortunately, Indonesia has historically experienced mass atrocities and numerous discrimination cases based on identity factors such as race, ethnicity, and religion[58].

Given that the definition of hate speech is still disputed in international law, the implementation of hate speech laws in both the Current Criminal Code and the ITE Law varies. This section discusses cases of hate speech based on the Current Criminal Code and ITE Law by analyzing the implementation of these laws, which, to some extent, serve as a test of balancing public interest against the risk of public disorder caused by hateful expression.

Unfortunately, there is no proper official record of hate speech cases that were investigated under the Current Criminal Code. A search in the Indonesian Supreme Court's repository using the keywords "*permusuhan*" and "*kebencian*" ("hostility" and "hatred"), which are the most common elements in hate speech provisions of the Current Criminal Code, resulted in online hate speech cases processed under the ITE Law. Furthermore, some judicial decisions categorized under hate speech were actually related to other cases[59].

Another limitation is that hate speech and blasphemy sometimes overlap. In the Current Criminal Code, hate speech and blasphemy provisions are found in the same chapter, "Crimes Against Public Order." Therefore, the discussion of offline hate speech cases does not include the variety of online cases presented in the following section. Unfortunately, most of the hate speech cases discussed here do not contribute positively to the limitation of hate speech in Indonesian law. By the time of this book writing, only one case did contribute positively, but that was after an appeal to the Appellate Court.

4.2.1 Hate Speech Case under the Current Criminal Code

4.2.1.1 Pandapotan Lubis and Joki Simbolon Case

There has been a significant increase in hate speech cases in Indonesia, especially since the ITE Law was passed in 2008[60]. Most of these cases typically involve an overlap between offline hate speech and its legal provisions. Such overlaps can be found in the indictments discussed in the next section on online hate speech.

This overlap highlights the limitations in identifying particular cases of offline hate speech that have been investigated solely under the relevant provisions of the Current Criminal Code. The case presented in this section is one of the very few that fit this criterion, although the repository of the Indonesian Supreme Court does not provide the full version of the case file on its website[61].

Another challenge in finding valid data on offline hate speech is the classification of the cases. According to the Indonesian Supreme Court, the case is considered a crime against state security, but on the East Jakarta Court's website, the case is listed as a labor dispute settled through criminal law.

While there is not much information available, the case seems to have started as a protest by Pandapotan Lubis and Joki Simbolon, who worked at a company. They protested using materials that included several posters containing allegedly offensive expressions. The posters featured text such as "People are Protesting" and "Statement of the Voice of Conscience of the People on the Periphery of the Capital."

In April 2013, the Court issued Decision No. 1453/Pid.B/2012/Pn.Jkt.Tim, which found both Pandapotan and Simbolon guilty of hate speech as stipulated in Article 157 of the Current Criminal Code. The prosecutor had indicted them under Article 160 of the Criminal Code, which reads:

> *Whoever in public orally or in writing incites to do criminal acts, committing violence against the general authorities or disobeying Both statutory provisions and incumbent orders of office are based on provisions of the law, punishable by imprisonment for a maximum of six years or criminal fines of up to four thousand five hundred Rupiahs.*

However, the Court decided that the defendants were convicted under Article 157 Section 1 of the Current Criminal Code, which read as follows:

> *Anyone who broadcasts, displays or displays writings or paintings in public, the contents of which contain statements of feelings of hostility, hatred or insults between or against groups of the Indonesian people, with the intention that its contents become known or better known to the public, is threatened with a maximum prison sentence of two years and six months or a maximum fine four rupiah five hundred rupiahs.*

Despite the limited information available about the case, both the prosecutor's indictment and the court's verdict show that a simple protest by Pandapotan and Joki was viewed as banned expression. It is also unclear whether the posters that were distributed at the Matraman traffic light in Jakarta in September 2011 were considered to incite hostility[62].

The main question raised by the judicial decision is whether the protest by Pandapotan and Joki intentionally expressed hostility or even enmity. While the protest took place in a public space, the issue of normative regulations, such as obtaining proper permits to hold the protest, should also be considered as part of the overall determination of the case.

As mentioned earlier, offline hate speech cases are very few, and offline hate speech provisions in the Current Criminal Code often fall under other specific criminal offenses, such as Article 156a, which is considered blasphemy. Hence, public discourse rarely addresses offline hate speech. However, this changed after the ITE Law passed, as indicated by the first case discussed in the next section.

4.2.2 Hate Speech Cases Under the ITE Law

4.2.2.1 Mangasa Situmorang Case

The case that occurred in 2020 involved an alleged expression of defamation of religions. Mangasa watched a YouTube video that contained a scene of a possessed woman. He shared the video on his Facebook page and wrote "*God's*[63] *work is to lead humans astray.*" Moreover, Mangasa was further involved in a conversation with other Facebook users, making insulting remarks about religion. At one point, he stated, "*I was born in Tapian Nauli village and do not believe in God,*" and "*Where is your God, your God is powerless. During the Corona pandemic, experts do not rely on God. Eat your God!*"

Mangasa's statement about not believing in God sparked controversy and led to him being reported to the police. In the trial, the court eventually ruled that Mangasa was guilty of online hate speech, as stipulated in Article 28 Section 2 of the ITE Law.

Mangasa's case is an example of the overlapping prosecution of hate speech in Indonesia. Not only was the alleged hate speech in this case alternatively indicted under Article 28 Section 2 of the ITE Law and Article 167 of the Current Criminal Code, but defaming religion was also considered hate speech, rather than blasphemy.

As discussed in other cases in this chapter, expressions that often offend, shock, or disturb are prosecuted because they do not align with the common moral standards of society. However, particular standards, such as the Rabat Plan of Action on Hate Speech, which is based on 6 thresholds – Context, Speaker, Intent, Content, Extent of the Speech Act, and Likelihood – should also be considered in the trial of hate speech cases. Unfortunately, these standards were not applied in the evaluation of Mangasa's expression.

With regard to inciting hatred and enmity as stipulated in the provisions of the ITE Law, the court found that some people in Mangasa's neighborhood reacted by holding a meeting and inviting him, but he did not attend, which led the residents to report him to the police. While their reaction was valid, it is not sufficient to determine that hatred and enmity had occurred, the residents' disagreement.

On a related note, the court did analyze the phrase "without right" in Article 28 Section 2 of the ITE Law. The full text of the provision states "*Any person intentionally and without right disseminates information aimed at creating feelings of hatred or enmity towards certain individuals and/or groups of people based on ethnicity, religion, race and inter-group.*" However, there was not enough discussion on whether Mangasa's statements about his disbelief in any religion and God constituted a valid expression, as long as it was not proven to influence others to become atheist. Even though this expression reflects atheism, it should be protected under international law[64].

4.2.2.2 *Wilfred Hendrik Nawipa Case*

In 2019, Wilfred Hendrik Nawipa, a citizen of Timika in Papua province, posted on his Facebook page named "PERE," about an incident of food poisoning. At the time, there were indeed several incidents of food poisoning, not only in Timika[65] but also in other areas of Papua, such as Merauke[66]. While the causes of food poisoning differed in each incident, these occurrences became the subject of criminal investigations.

In October 2019, Wilfred posted a long message on his Facebook page as follows (not an official translation):

> *FOOD POISONING.*
>
> *Food poisoning that eventually attacked Hadelina Hagabal and Gerentasia Hagabal. Below is a chronological version from the victim's family, T. Hagabal (son of the victim) …!!!*
>
> *On Saturday, 05-10-2019, I arrived at Kwamki's house around 02:50 (half past three) after coming from Tembagapura. In the house, I saw four people (his mother, his wife, and his two younger siblings) lying helplessly in the living room. I then gave them Aqua*[67] *mineral water that my mother and I had brought. She woke up and said, "Our child is sick because in the morning we bought food at the sewer stall and then ate it, which made our bodies hurt." Then I took the initiative to call my friends to bring them to Rumah Sakit Mitra Masyarakat (RSMM) SP 5.*
>
> *When we got there (RSMM), the lights were off, so we went home. I immediately arrived at my wife's house, where Gerentasia Hagabal (24 years old) looked very helpless that night (Saturday night) and she also died at home. However, because my mother's condition was burdensome when attending my wife's funeral, On Monda,y 10-07-2019, I took her back to RSMM SP 5. After a while, my mom also died that night.*
>
> *While my mother was at home, she vomited continuously until I vomited blood. My two younger siblings, Fery Hagabal (10 years old) and Fredy Hagaba (12 years old) were doing well because they received treatment for two days at RSMM and were sent home on Thursday morning. When I regained consciousness, I asked my younger sister* if she knew where Mommy bought the food, *and she replied that she didn't know and was too young to remember.*

> *Suggestion ...!!*
> *To all brothers and sisters with black and curly hair, please be careful when consuming*
> *ready-made or instant food sold by irresponsible and unclear parties.*
> *Greetings sober...!!!*

In addition to his long post, Wilfred also posted four photos depicting the condition of the food poisoning victims. The Timika Court, through its Decision No. 206/Pid.Sus/2019/PN Tim, determined that Wilfred was guilty of hate speech.

Unfortunately, while the elements of hate speech include incitement of hatred, hostility, and enmity based on race, religion, tribe, and intergroup relations, the verdict part of the ruling did not provide details about which specific part of Wilfred's post led to his conviction.

The prosecutor's indictment argued that there was a provocation directed at the people in Papua. However, it was unclear whether the lack of verification by Wilfred before he made the post about the food poisoning. Wilfred's statement "*So to the brothers and sisters who have black and curly hair, be careful when consuming ready-made or instant food sold by other parties who are responsible and unclear*", was considered a provocation.

In addition, there is an inconsistency in the indictment. The prosecutor's first argument falls into the category of disseminating hoaxes or false news, which does not fulfill the criteria for an online hate speech offense, while the second argument potentially constitutes online hate speech. However, the prosecutor submitted only a single indictment based on online hate speech, as outlined in Article 28 Section 2 of the ITE Law.

Given that cases of food poisoning occurred, the Court failed to determine the truth of Wilfred's post and did not specify what kind of potential provocation might arise from it. Despite the discussion in Chapter 3 regarding whether online hate speech provision can be classified as a *materiil* offense or a *formil* offense – where the former pertains to the consequences of the act and the latter refers simply to the execution of the deed – the Court should have determined which offense Wilfred's expression fell under. Moreover, the fact that Wilfred's post was about the concern of public health is another example of how greater interests can, unfortunately be hindered by harsh criminal punishments.

4.2.2.3 I Gede Aryastina (Jerinx) Case

During the COVID-19 pandemic, the prosecution of hate speech shockingly increased; this problem emerged from the Indonesian government's response through various legislations and policies aimed at combating a large number of hoaxes that spread during the pandemic[68].

This case happened in the early stages of the pandemic in 2020 and involved an unnecessary implementation of online hate speech laws that imposed disinformation. I Gede Aryastina, also known by his nickname Jerinx, a musician who is famous for being the drummer of the band Superman is Dead (SID). In addition to his music career, Jerinx actively advocated for social and environmental issues, such as rejecting the reclamation plan for Benoa Gulf in Bali, his home region[69].

When the pandemic hit the world, Jerinx was also one of those who advocated on the COVID-19 issue. However, he simultaneously believed in the conspiracy that COVID-19 was a fabricated virus created by parties that took advantage of the pandemic[70].

Jerinx consistently campaigned for this conspiracy theory about the virus, especially through his social media. On 13 June 13 2020, in his Instagram post, Jerinx claimed that the Indonesian Medical Association (*Ikatan Dokter Indonesia-IDI*) was acting as a lackey for the World Health Organization (WHO) in spreading news about the dangers of the COVID-19 virus. His full post on Instagram was the following (not the official translation):

> *Proud to be a lackey of the WHO*[71]*, IDI*[72]*, and RS,*[73] *requiring everyone who is in labor to be tested for CV19. There's a lot of evidence that if test results are often inconsequential, why are they being forced? If the test results make you stressed and cause death to the baby/mother, who is going to be responsible?*

In the comment section of the same post, Jerinx also added:

> *"DISMISS IDI! I will not stop attacking you, @ikatandokterindonesia, until there is an explanation regarding this! (pig emoticon) Are the people being pitted against IDI/RS? NO. IDI & RS are pitting themselves against the rights of the people.*

Given his status as a public figure, Jerinx's post gained a lot of attention, including from IDI itself. IDI reported Jerinx to the police, and after a series of trials, he was found guilty of online hate speech toward IDI and convicted to 14 months in prison[74]. Jerinx filed an appeal and got his punishment reduced to 10 months[75]. In 2021, the prosecutor in his case filed a cessation as they disagreed with the reduced punishment by the Appellate Court. However, the Indonesian Supreme Court rejected the cessation[76].

In the trial, the Court determined that Jerinx's post was considered hate speech against IDI. However, the case should have focused on the dissemination of false news, as in disinformation, because the element of what Jerinx did fulfilled the intention of spreading false news that may affect public health. The Court's decision regarding online hate speech highlights the lack of specific regulation on misinformation and disinformation[77].

Unfortunately, the Court found that the alleged harmful expression toward IDI falls into the category of intergroup[78]. The Court opined that, according to the Indonesian Constitutional Court No. 76/PUU/XV/2017, any particular group not defined by race, ethnicity, and religion should fall in the category of intergroup. However, the Court failed to recognize that being a medical doctor is a different identity factor compared to race, ethnicity, and religion. A job or profession, such as a medical doctor, is not something inherently attached to an individual's identity from birth; rather, it is an identity or occupation that one can change at any time in life. Meanwhile, race, ethnicity, and religion are closely attached to a person's identity and can be used to identify him or her, which, in the context of hate speech, makes individuals from these groups vulnerable.

On a related note, the term "offended" was discussed several times in the trial, particularly in relation to the "pig emoticon" that was used in the comment on Jerinx's "WHO Lackey" post. Meanwhile, the Court simplified Jerinx's expression as a personal dislike for medical doctors and IDI, whereas the expression should have been evaluated to determine whether it constituted a valid criticism or a hoax[79].

The Court's decision represented not only an unnecessary prosecution for online hate speech but also a wrong implementation of the law due to a lack of clear regulations. Jerinx's conviction illustrates how the Indonesian legal system attempted to justify the prosecution of offensive expressions using any applicable laws, thereby expanding the definition of "rubber provision" associated with the ITE Law through the judicial decision on Jerinx's case.

4.2.2.4 Daniel Tangkilisan Case

While two human rights activists, Haris Azhar and Fatia Maulidiyanti, were acquitted of online defamation charges in January 2024, another activist was unfortunately found guilty of online hate speech a few months later. Daniel is an environmental activist who advocates for KarimunJawa, an archipelago of 27 islands in Central Java province, as a tourist destination. Since 2017, Daniel has been leading his advocacy efforts to protect the region's natural beauty and ecosystem. However, despite Karimunjawa's popularity among tourists, illegal shrimp farming has been harming the marine environment by polluting the ocean and damaging the fishers' boats[80].

In 2022, Daniel and his friends launched an online campaign #SAVEKARIMUNJAWA to protest the illegal shrimp farms. However, it was not the online campaign itself that led to his prosecution, but a comment Daniel made on one of the campaign videos on Facebook (not an official translation):

> *The shrimp-brain (otak udang)*[81] *community enjoys eating free shrimp while being exploited by the (illegal) farmers. The point is that* shrimp-brain *society is like the (illegal) shrimp farming itself-receiving regular, delicious, and plentiful food.*

Although Daniel's post was a sarcastic critique of those benefiting from the illegal shrimp farms, he was reported to the police for online hate speech. In December 2023, Daniel was arrested[82], and his case proceeded to trial.

Similar to other cases discussed earlier in this chapter, Daniel was also charged with an alternative indictment containing two different provisions under the ITE Law, which were online defamation (Article 27 Section 3) and online hate speech (Article 28 Section 2). The Court found Daniel guilty of online hate speech and sentenced him to seven months in prison[83].

Daniel's activism should be protected by law, as stipulated in Article 66 of the Law No. 32 of 2009 on Protection and Management of Environment and Indonesian Supreme Court Regulation No. 36 of 2013 on Implementation of Guidelines for Handling Environmental Cases. Additionally, Daniel's post did not refer to any particular group (tribe, ethnicity, religion, or intergroups-SARA) as defined by the Court.

Daniel's case was another example of SLAPP, especially since the lawsuit focused on the insult using the phrase "shrimp farm," which was intended as a sarcastic expression. During the trial, despite the fact that Daniel's comment referred to the general public who did not understand the harm of illegal farming, the Court found that his expression stemmed from a quick conversation. In this conversation, Daniel and another Facebook user discussed how not everyone on the islands agreed to oppose the illegal shrimp farms, which led to his expression being interpreted as alleged hate speech[84].

Unfortunately, while the element of hate speech involves inciting hatred and enmity, the court failed to properly assess the extent and imminence of the hatred and enmity in Daniel's expression. Ironically, the Court found that only 75 people felt offended and reported Daniel to the police. Furthermore, the Court even used the phrase "some of the people of Karimun Jawa" in the minutes of the trial, which implied that the hatred and enmity were evident in how this group of people attended the trial and demanded Daniel's conviction[85].

Such analysis should be examined more deeply, as these factors are part of the six-part threshold test of the Rabat Plan of Action, which serves as a legal interpretation of international law. The threshold test consists of Context, Speaker, Intent, Content and Form, Extent of the Speech Act, and Likelihood, including Imminence[86]. As mentioned before, the Extent of Speech Act and Imminence were not even addressed, and these are the last two parts of the threshold that should be assessed after the previous parts of the test have been satisfied.

None of the elements of the threshold are satisfied in Daniel's case. Context and Speaker were explained, noting that Daniel is an environmental activist discussing the potential harm of the illegal shrimp farm in the area. The Intent element was also addressed during the trial, indicating that it referred to people who do not realize the harm caused by the illegal activity. While the Content and Form elements were provocative and direct, they did not satisfy the Intent. Moreover, the element of the Extent of the Speech Act, as stipulated in the Rabat Plan of Action, includes the magnitude of the speech, including the size of the audience. Although Daniel's comment may be ubiquitously found on the internet, the level of offense felt was not significant compared to the total population of 5,003 people in Karimunjawa[87]. Finally, the Likelihood element was also not fulfilled, especially considering that the Court only found disagreement and scrutiny during the trial, with some people requesting that Daniel be criminally charged.

In May 2024, it seemed that the saga of Daniel had ended well because his appeal was accepted by the Appellate Court[88]. However, while the Appellate Court's decision represented good practice against SLAPP[89], the case should have been resolved before the trial started, which means the public prosecutor could have halted the trial process, considering they have Anti-SLAPP guidelines[90]. Moreover, the fact that the Appellate Court accepted Daniel's appeal based solely on his identity as an environmental activist, while still upholding the finding of online hate speech, is still concerning[91]. Such a decision by The Appellate Court indicates a continued chilling effect on freedom of expression in Indonesia. Another concern is that, at the time of this writing, the prosecutor has submitted a cassation to the Indonesian Supreme Court. Although the prosecutor has refused to state the reason for the cassation submission[92], it indicates that Daniel's legal battle is not over yet. Despite the judicial decision in the lower court that cleared Daniel of criminal defamation charges and the fact that he fought for the right to a healthy environment, the state, as represented by the prosecutor, chose to use its resources against him for lesser damage compared to the illegal farming in Karimunjawa.

With all the weaknesses in the current laws, Indonesian legislation should be revised to prevent abusive situations from continuing to arise under the criminal defamation provisions. Considering that judicial reviews have been rejected, the only feasible course of action is to revise the laws.

The controversial ITE Law has already been excluded from the National Legislation Program by the Indonesian Representative Council. This means the representatives will not draft the bill's amendment as one of their legislation priorities, despite the criticisms[93]. Instead, to address the amendment, the government is planning to draft guidelines for the problematic provisions[94], while awaiting the limited revisions to Articles 27, 28, 29, and 36 and adding one more section under Article 45, resulting in Article 45B.

The guideline is being written under the Joint Decree of the Ministry of Communication and Information, the National Police Chief, and the Attorney General[95], signed on 23 June 2021[96]. The decree has been drafted to address several legal issues in Indonesia. However, in terms of the legal hierarchy in Indonesia, the Form of Legislation Act of 2011 is not recognized in the joint decree as one of the formal pieces of legislations in Indonesia. Hence, it is still under dispute whether the norms outlined in the decree can constitute binding law, while the guidelines themselves serve as directions for legal enforcers in processing cases under the ITE Law, specifically Articles 27, 28, and 29.

This chapter discusses in detail several key cases of defamation and hate speech, both offline and online. From the aforementioned examples, it is evident that some concerning facts about the case rulings stem from the weak implementation of the laws, which are draconian in nature. The public interest defense in the cases discussed above is rarely considered because the lawsuits usually arise from angry reactions from the public or the alleged victims of defamation and hate speech. This often depicts the cases as retaliation rather than a pursuit of true justice, particularly through criminal law. In the stipulated punishments within the provisions, prison terms are viewed as a state resource, while fines contribute to state income. This means that the criminal laws concerning both defamation and hate speech in Indonesia are normatively not focused on repairing the reputation of the victims in such cases.

Therefore, imposing a stronger public interest defense in freedom of expression cases could contribute to more robust protection for freedom of expression in Indonesia. While there is still no uniform definition, the next chapter of this book will discuss "public interest" and how it contributes to the fulfilment of the right to free expression.

Notes

1 The data gathered from the search of judicial decisions in the repository of the Indonesian Supreme Court: https://putusan3.mahkamahagung.go.id, the data was analyzed and reorganized in my dissertation entitled "Criminal Defamation and Freedom of Speech in Internet Age: A Study for Indonesian Democratic Value." See more at Eka Nugraha Putra, 2022, https://www.repository.law.indiana.edu/etd/113/.

2 See more Eka Nugrah a Putra, 2022, Criminal Defamation and Freedom of Speech in Internet Age: A Study for Indonesian Democratic Value," https://www.repository.law.indiana.edu/etd/113/.

3 The 2013 Decision in question is The Surabaya Appellate Court Decision No. 190/PID/2013/PT.SBY.

4 Tempo, 2003, *Ada Tomy di 'Tenabang'? [Is Tommy in 'Tenabang'?]* (March 1, 2024), tempo.co https://majalah.tempo.co/read/nasional/85648/tomy-winata-pasar-tanah-abang.

5 Ady Anugrahadi, 2021, *18 Tahun Lalu, Berita Tempo Berujung Gugatan Tomy Winata [18 Years Ago, Tempo News Leads to Tomy Winata's Lawsuit]*, liputan6.com (March 3, 2024) https://www.liputan6.com/news/read/4578638/18-tahun-lalu-berita-tempo-berujung-gugatan-tomy-winata.

6 Muhammad Yasin, 2019, *Mengenal Dwangsom dan Jejaknya dalam Hukum Indonesia [Getting to Know Dwangsom and Its Footprint in Indonesian Law]*, hukumonline.com (March 14, 2024) https://www.hukumonline.com/berita/a/mengenal-dwangsom-dan-jejaknya-dalam-hukum-indonesia-lt5dccbb0753910.

7 Ady Anugrahadi, *18 Tahun Lalu, Berita Tempo Berujung Gugatan Tomy Winata [18 Years Ago, Tempo News Leads to Tomy Winata's Lawsuit]*.

8 Mys, 2005, *Eksaminasi Putusan Pidana Tempo, Pertimbangan Hakim tidak Mendalam [Examination of Tempo's Criminal Decision, Judge's Consideration Not Deep]*, hukumonline.com (April 14, 2024) Eksaminasi Putusan Pidana Tempo, Pertimbangan Hakim tidak Mendalam (hukumonline.com).

9 Wirjono Projodikoro, Asas-Asas Hukum Pidana Indonesia [Principles of Indonesian Criminal Law], 80, (2003).

10 Sukma, 2006, *Pengadilan Banding Kuatkan Vonis Bambang Harymurti [Appeals Court Upholds Bambang Harymurti's Verdict]*, tempo.co (March 29, 2024). https://nasional.tempo.co

11 Liputan 6, 2006, *Bambang Harymurti Menang di Mahkamah Agung [Bambang Harymurti Wins at Supreme Court]*, liputan6.com (April 2, 2024) Bambang Harymurti Menang di Mahkamah Agung - News Liputan6.com.
12 Tangerang First Degree Court, 2009, 1269/PID.B/2009/PN.TNG (Indon).
13 Mahkamah Konstitusi [MK] [The Indonesian Constitutional Court] 2008, Putusan Mahkamah Konstitusi Nomor 50/PUU-VI/2008 (Indon.).
14 Indonesian Act, 2016, Explanation Section of art. 27 (Indonesia), Information and Electronic Transaction Act (Indon.).
15 Jogja or Yogya is shortened version of Yogyakarta.
16 Type of the gasoline that Florence want to bought at the time.
17 A slang expression as a shortened version of "Kesel" which means upset.
18 Widiarsi Agustina, 2014, *Apa Tanggapan Sultan Yogya Soal Florence?[What is the Sultan of Yogya's Response to Florence?]*, tempo.co (March 31, 2024) Apa Tanggapan Sultan Yogya Soal Florence? - Nasional Tempo.co.
19 Detiknews, 2014, *Beri Maaf, Sultan Minta Agar Florence Tetap Selesaikan S2 di UGM [Forgiveness, Sultan Asks Florence to Complete Her Masters at UGM]*, detik.com (March 31, 2024), Beri Maaf, Sultan Minta Agar Florence Tetap Selesaikan S2 di UGM (detik.com).
20 Yogyakarta Appellate Court, 2015, Decision No. 26/Pid.Sus/2015/PT.YYK (Indon).
21 Mahkamah Agung [MA] [The Indonesian Supreme Court] 2015, Decision No. 2580 K/Pid.Sus/2015 (Indon).
22 The Jakarta Post, 2014, *Activist Condemn Arrest of Student who Insulted Yogyakarta*, The Jakarta Post (March 5, 2024) Activists condemn arrest of student who insulted Yogyakarta - National - The Jakarta Post .
23 See Nani Jansen Revenlow, "The Right to Offend, Shock, or Disturb," or the Importance of Protecting Unpleasant Speech, in Perspectives on Harmful Speech Online (2017).
24 See more at Handyside v. United Kingdom, 1 Eur. Ct. H.R. 737 (1976).
25 *Pembangkit Listrik Tenaga Mikro Hidro* - Micro Hydro Power Plant.
26 Muhammad Asrul, 2019, *Putra Mahkota Palopo Diduga "Dalang" Korupsi PLTMH dan Keripik Zaro Rp11 M [Crown Prince of Palopo Allegedly "Mastermind" of Rp11 Billion PLTMH and Zaro Chips Corruption]*, berita.news, (April 1, 2024) https://berita.news/2019/05/10/putra-mahkota-palopo-diduga-dalang-korupsi-pltmh-dan-keripik-zaro-rp11-m/.
27 Muhammad Asrul, 2019, *Aroma Korupsi Revitalisasi Lapangan Pancasila Palopo Diduga Seret Farid Judas [The Aroma of Corruption in the Revitalization of Pancasila Field in Palopo Allegedly Drags Farid Judas Into It]*, berita.news, (April 1, 2024) https://berita.news/2019/05/24/aroma-korupsi-revitalisasi-lapangan-pancasila-palopo-diduga-seret-farid-judas/.
28 Muhammad Asrul, 2019, *"Jilid II" Korupsi Jalan Lingkar Barat Rp5M, Sinyal Penyidik untuk Farid Judas? ["Volume II" of Rp5 billion West Ring Road Corruption, Investigator's Signal for Farid Judas?]*, berita.news, (April, 1 2024) https://berita.news/2019/05/25/jilid-ii-korupsi-jalan-lingkar-barat-rp5-m-sinyal-penyidik-untuk-farid-judas/.
29 Indonesian Press Council, Statement No. 03/P-DP/XI/2021, On the Press Council's Concern Regarding the Criminalization of Journalist Muhammad Asrul at the Palopo District Court (2021).
30 Memorandum of Understanding between the Press Council No. 2/DP/MoU/II/2017 and No. B/15/II/2017 on Coordination in the Protection of Press Freedom and Law Enforcement Related to Abuse of the Journalism Profession. Indonesian Press Council, Memorandum of Understanding, No. 2, No. B/15/II/2017 (2017).
31 Memorandum of Understanding between the Press Council No. 2/DP/MoU/II/2017 and No. B/15/II/2017 on Coordination in the Protection of Press Freedom and Law Enforcement Related to Abuse of the Journalism Profession. Indonesian Press Council, Memorandum of Understanding, No. 2, No. B/15/II/2017 (2017).

32 Palopo First Degree Court, 2021, No. 46/Pid.Sus/2021/PN Plp (Indon).
33 The Indonesian Press Council, 2016, *Pengantar [Introduction]*, Jurnal Dewan Pers Edisi 13 Desember 2016, 6.
34 Afdal Makkuraga, 2013, *Ekonomi Politik Kebebasan Pers di Indonesia Pasca Reformasi: Kritik atas Praktek Neoliberalisme pada Industri Media [Political Economy of Press Freedom in Post-Reformation Indonesia: A Critique of Neoliberal Practices in the Media Industry]*, Jurnal Visi Komunikasi Volume XII, No. 01, Mei 2013, 2.
35 Indonesian Act, 1999, Art 9 Section 2 and Article 15 Section 2 (Indonesia), Press act (Indon.).
36 Binti Mufarida, 2024, *Dewan Pers: Baru 1700 Media yang Sudah Terverifikasi [Press Council: Only 1700 Media Have Been Verified]*, sindonews.com (April 3, 2024) https://nasional.sindonews.com/read/1331869/15/dewan-pers-baru-1700-media-yang-sudah-terverifikasi-1709283799.
37 Sidra, 2023, *Dewan Pers Sebut Jumlah Media Massa Terbanyak bukan di Pulai Jawa, Tapi Ada Di Sumatera [Press Council Says Largest Number of Mass Media is Not in Java, But in Sumatra]*, inews Palembang (April 15, 2024) https://palembang.inews.id/read/252404/dewan-pers-sebut-jumlah-media-massa-terbanyak-bukan-di-pulau-jawa-tapi-ada-di-sumatera.
38 Palopo First Degree Court No. 46/Pid.Sus/2021/PN Plp (2021).
39 *Id.*
40 M. Iqbal Al Machmudi, 2021, *UU Pers Perlu Dimutakhirkan untuk Lindungi Pers [Press Law Needs to be Updated to Protect the Press]*, mediaindonesia.com (March 30, 2024) https://mediaindonesia.com/politik-dan-hukum/436523/uu-pers-perlu-dimutakhirkan-untuk-lindungi-pers.
41 Nur Janti, 2022, *Activists Face "Danger" Amid Shrinking Civic Space*, The Jakarta Post (April 12, 2022) https://www.thejakartapost.com/indonesia/2022/03/21/activists-face-danger-amid-shrinking-civic-space.html.
42 Asfinawati, et al., 2021, *Ekonomi Politik Penempatan Militer di Papua [Political Economy of Military Deployment in Papua]*, Walhi (April 12, 2022) https://www.walhi.or.id/uploads/blogs/Kajian/2021%2008%2012.%20FA%20LAPORAN%20PAPEDA%20SINGLE%20PAGE.pdf, 17.
43 When the trial was started, it was in 2021, which the ITE Law 2024 has not been passed yet.
44 BIN is the abbreviation for *Badan Intelijen Negara* (National Intelligence Agency).
45 NgeHAMtam is the name of the podcast, a pun from "Ngehantam" which mean "To Punch," HAM (in capital letters) stands for Hak Asasi Manusia (Human Rights).
46 East Jakarta First Degree Court Decision, 2023, No. 202/Pid.Sus/2023/PN.Jkt Tim (Indon).
47 The form of the indictment in the trial was a combination indictment, which imposed three different alleged criminal law violations, but in the second alternative indictment, the prosecutor added a subsidiary (*subsider*) indictment where the primary indictment of the second alternative indictment (Article 14 of Law No.1 of 1946) has subsidiary indictment (Article 15 of Law No.1 of 1946) in which the primary indictment could not be proven during the trial. See Law Number 8 of 1981 on the Indonesian Criminal Law Procedure (*Kitab Undang-Undang Hukum Acara Pidana*).
48 As mentioned above, a subsidiary indictment could be imposed by the prosecutor if there are layers of alleged criminal offences that should be proven before the court. The Court should determine the offences based on the order arranged by the prosecutor of each criminal act. See Afina Akmalia and Arsyad Aldan, "Analisis Penggunaan Dakwaan Alternatif Subsidair Oleh Penuntut Umum dalam Perkara Perlindungan Anak" (2023) Verstek Vol. 11 Issue 3.

49 Ady Thea Da, 2023, *Jaksa Tuntut Hari Azhar 4 Tahun dan Fatia 3 Tahun 6 Bulan Penjara [Prosecutors Order Hari Azhar 4 Years and Fatia 3 Years and 6 Months in Prison]*, hukumonline.com (April 14, 2024) https://www.hukumonline.com/berita/a/jaksa-tuntut-haris-azhar-4-tahun-dan-fatia-3-tahun-6-bulan-penjara-lt65522c5898670/.

50 Agus Sahbani, 2024, *Alasan MK Batalkan Pasal Penyebaran Berita Bohong dalam KUHP [Reasons for the Constitutional Court to Cancel the Article on Spreading Fake News in the Criminal Code]*, hukumonline.com (April 14, 2024) https://www.hukumonline.com/berita/a/alasan-mk-batalkan-pasal-penyebaran-berita-bohong-dalam-kuhp-lt65fc5895ba9d1/.

51 See Fatih Al Rosyid, 2018, *Menjerat Hoaks: Tentang Berlakunya Pasal 14 dan Pasal 15 UU 1 tahun 1946 tentang Peraturan Hukum Pidana [Trapping Hoaxes: Regarding the Applicability of Article 14 and Article 15 of Law 1 of 1946 concerning Criminal Law Regulations]*, 2018, Viva Justicia (https://vivajusticia.law.ugm.ac.id/2018/11/29/menjerat-hoaks-tentang-berlakunya-pasal-14-dan-pasal-15-uu-1-tahun-1946-tentang-peraturan-hukum-pidana/.

52 East Jakarta District Court No. 202/Pid.Sus/2023/PN.Jkt Tim (2023), Id.

53 Defamation laws can not be justified if there is no merit in protecting individuals against harm to a reputation. See more Article 19, Defining Defamation: Principles on Freedom of Expression and Protection of Reputation, 2000 https://www.article19.org/wp-content/uploads/2018/02/defining-defamation.pdf.

54 East Jakarta District Court No. 202/Pid.Sus/2023/PN.Jkt Tim (2023), Id.

55 In addition, although not specifically cited in the Court's decision, there were four important pieces of evident presented before the Court to support the public interest defense, Exhibit 14: Research titled "*Ekonomi-Politik Penempatan Militer di Papua, Kasus Intan Jaya*"; Exhibit 15: Article by Greenpeace International entitled "*Stop Baku Tipu: Sisi Gelap Perizinan di Tanah Papua*"; Exhibit 16: Letter No. 01/TAUD/III/2011 dated 23 March 2022 on Report of Alleged Bribery Stock Giving of 30% By West Wits Mining to Luhut Binsar Pandjaitan; and Exhibit 17: Letter dated 4 July 2022 on Report of Alleged Bribery of Foreign Officials which addressed to Australian Federal Police.

56 East Jakarta District Court No. 202/Pid.Sus/2023/PN.Jkt Tim (2023), Id.

57 See Aju Putrijanti and Sekar Anggun Gading Pinilih, *Strenghtening Anti-Eco-SLAPP Regulations in Indonesia*, Proceeding of the 1st International Workshop on Law, Economic, and Governance, 27 July 2022, Semarang, Indonesia.

58 See Lina A. Alexandra and Alif Satria, 2023, *Identifying Hate Speech Trends and Prevention in Indonesia: a Cross-Case Comparison in: Global Responsibility to Protect*, Volume 15, Issue 2-3.

59 One example is that the Indonesian Supreme Court No. 1381K/PID/2007 state that the case is about hate speech, but when the PDF file of the Court's Decision is clicked, it displays another case, cessation of the Supreme Court No. 456K/AG/2007.

60 During the first 10 years of the ITE Law, online defamation and online hate speech are two most common cases that reported to the police and then under investigation, particularly by public officials at the plaintiff, see more at Scholastice Gerintya, Tirto.id, 2018. Another data was from 2020 until 2021, where there were 473 online hate speech reported and investigated, the highest statistic compared to 259 cases of online fraud and 82 cases of online pornography. See more at kumparanews, kumparan.com, 2021.

61 The discussion of this case is based on the excerpt in the Indonesian Supreme Court's repository and the East Jakarta Court's websites.

62 East Jakarta First Degree Court, 2012, Decision No. 1453/PID.B/2012/PN.JKT.TIM (Indon.).

63 The original post in Bahasa Indonesia state "*Kerjaannya allah itu menyesatkan manusia*," "Allah" here is refer to God which worshipped by Muslims and Christian. However, in the ruling, "Allah" is written as "allah" with small "a," this note is to indicate the difference that taken from the original judicial decision. See Rengat Court Decision No. 293/Pid.Sus/2020/PN Rgt.

64 See more at Rapporteur's Digest on Freedom of Religion or Belief Second Edition (2023).

65 Robert Isidorus, 2019, *37 Orang Keracunan Makanan di Timika [37 People Suffer Food Poisoning in Timika]*, beritasatu.com (April 11, 2024) https://www.beritasatu.com/news/579835/37-orang-keracunan-makanan-di-timika.

66 Evarukdijati, 2019, *60 Warga Merauke Keracunan Makanan [60 Merauke Residents Suffer Food Poisoning]*, antaranews.com (April 11, 2024) https://papua.antaranews.com/berita/483101/60-warga-merauke-keracunan-makanan.

67 A brand of mineral water in Indonesia.

68 See Sastramdijaja, 2023, *Indonesia's COVID-19 Infodemic: A Battle for Truth or Trust?*, Trends in Southeast Asia Issue 12, 2023.

69 Sunu Dyantoro, 2014, *Jerinx SID dan Gerakan Tolak Reklamasi Teluk Benoa [Jerinx SID and the Movement to Reject Benoa Bay Reclamation]*, tempo.co (April 17, 2024) https://nasional.tempo.co/read/628392/jerinx-sid-dan-gerakan-tolak-reklamasi-teluk-benoa.

70 News Desk, 2020, *Conspiracy Theory-Endorsing Musician Jerinx Named Suspect for Allegedly Defaming IDI*, The Jakarta Post, (April 17, 2024) http://www.thejakartapost.com/news/2020/08/12/conspiracy-theory-endorsing-musician-jerinx-named-suspect-for-allegedly-defaming-idi.html.

71 World Health Organization.

72 *Ikatan Dokter Indonesia.*

73 Abbreviation for *Rumah Sakit* (Hospital).

74 Denpasar First Degree Court, 2020, Decision No. 828/Pid.Sus/2020/PN Dps (Indon.).

75 Denpasar Appellate Court, 2020, Decision No. 72/Pid.Sus/2020/PT.Dps (Indon.).

76 ICJR, 2021, *ICJR Hormati Putusan Kasasi Jerinx: Mahkamah Agung Harus Juga Ambil Peran Atasi Masalah Norma UU ITE [ICJR Respects Jerinx's Cassation Ruling: Supreme Court Must Also Take Role in Resolving ITE Law Norm Issues]*, icjr.or.id (April 1, 2024) https://icjr.or.id/icjr-hormati-putusan-kasasi-jerinx-mahkamah-agung-harus-juga-ambil-peran-atasi-masalah-norma-uu-ite/.

77 Eka Nugraha Putra, 2021, *Yang Luput Dibicarakan dari Kasus Jerinx: Kita Tak Punya Aturan Jelas Melawan Hoax, Misinformasi dan Disinformasi, The Conversation Indonesia [What's Missing from Jerinx's Case: We Don't Have Clear Rules Against Hoaxes, Misinformation and Disinformation, The Conversation Indonesia]* (April 9, 2024) https://theconversation.com/yang-luput-dibicarakan-dari-kasus-jerinx-kita-tak-punya-aturan-jelas-melawan-hoax-misinformasi-dan-disinformasi-145172.

78 First Degree of Denpasar Decision No. 828/Pid.Sus/2020/PN Dps (2020).

79 First Degree of Denpasar Decision No. 828/Pid.Sus/2020/PN Dps (2020).

80 Kristi Dwi Utami, 2024, *Beragam Masalah Akibat Limbah Tambak Udang di Karimunjawa [Various Problems Caused by Shrimp Pond Waste in Karimunjawa]*, kompas.id (May 22, 2024) https://www.kompas.id/baca/nusantara/2024/04/29/beragam-masalah-akibat-limbah-tambak-udang-di-karimunjawa.

81 "Otak Udang" or "Shrimp Brain" is an insult among Indonesians, which as equal as saying someone is "stupid.".

82 Beni Jo, 2024, *Siapa Daniel Tangkilisan dan Apa Kasusnya Hingga Dipenjara? [Who is Daniel Tangkilisan and what is his case that led to his imprisonment?]*, tirto.id (May 13, 2024) https://tirto.id/siapa-daniel-tangkilisan-dan-apa-kasusnya-hingga-dipenjara-gXBd.

83 Jepara First Degree Court, 2024, Decision No. 14/Pid.Sus/2024/PN Jpa (Indon.).
84 Jepara First Degree Court, 2024, Decision No. 14/Pid.Sus/2024/PN Jpa (Indon.)., Id.
85 Jepara First Degree Court, 2024, Decision No. 14/Pid.Sus/2024/PN Jpa (Indon.).
86 See Annual Report of the United Nations High Commissioner for Human Rights 11 January 2013.
87 Badan Pusat Statistik, 2021, *Penduduk Menurut Desa dan Jenis Kelamin di Kecamatan Karimunjawa [Population by Village and Gender in Karimunjawa District]*, bps.go.id (May 15, 2024) https://jeparakab.bps.go.id/id/statistics-table/2/Mjk2IzI=/penduduk-menurut-desa-dan-jenis-kelamin-di-kecamatan-karimunjawa.html.
88 Ikhsan Reliubun, 2024, *Daniel Frits Bebas, ICJR: Kita Belum Bebas dari Ancaman Kriminalisasi [Daniel Frits Free, ICJR: We Are Not Yet Free from the Threat of Criminalization]*, tempo.co (May 15, 2024) https://www.tempo.co/arsip/daniel-frits-bebas-icjr-kita-belum-bebas-dari-ancaman-kriminalisasi--56525.
89 By the time of this writing, the file of the Appellate Court's decision has not been uploaded in the Semarang's Appelate Court Website.
90 By the time of this writing, the file of the Appellate Court's decision has not been uploaded in the Semarang's Appelate Court Website.
91 The Indonesian Supreme Court, *Direktori Putusan [Judicial Decisions Repository]* https://putusan3.mahkamahagung.go.id/direktori/putusan/zaef171f9e707c849377313031303034.html.
92 Kristi Dwi Utami, 2024, *Daniel Tangkilisan Released, Prosecutor Files Cessation*, kompas.id (June 9, 2024) https://www.kompas.id/baca/english/2024/06/02/en-daniel-tangkilisan-dibebaskan-hakim-pengadilan-tinggi-semarang-jaksa-ajukan-kasasi.
93 VOI, *Still Hearing Public Input, Menkum HAM Has Not Sumitted the Revision of the ITE Law to the DPR*, VOI (September 4, 2021) https://voi.id/en/news/38068/still-hearing-public-input-menkum-ham-has-not-submitted-the-revision-of-the-ite-law-to-the-dpr.
94 Dio Suhenda, 2021 *New Guidelines No Substitute for ITE Law Revision, Activists Say*, The Jakarta Post (June 12, 2022) https://www.thejakartapost.com/paper/2021/06/24/new-guidelines-no-substitute-for-ite-law-revision-activists-say.html.
95 Joint Decree of Indonesian Ministry of Communication and Information, National Police Chief and Attorney General on Implementation Guidelines of Some Particular Articles on Information and Electronic Transaction Acts (Decree No. 229 of 2021, No. 154 of 2021, and No. KB/2/VI/2021) (Indon).
96 Under the Indonesian legal system, the joint decree is known as *Surat Keputusan Bersama*, a cross-institution legislation product in a form of decree from the cross-governmental agencies that governing a same issue.

Bibliography

Books

Adami Chazawi and Ardi Ferdian, *Tindak Pidana Informasi & Transaksi Elektronik [Information Crime & Electronic Transactions]* (2011).

Josua Sitompul, *Cyberspace, Cybercrimes, Cyberlaw: Tinjauan Aspek Hukum Pidana [Cyberspace, Cybercrimes, Cyberlaw: A Review of Criminal Law Aspects]* (2012).

Nani Jansen Revenlow, *"The Right to Offend, Shock, or Disturb," or the Importance of Protecting Unpleasant Speech, in Perspectives on Harmful Speech Online* (2017).

Wirjono Projodikoro, *Asas-Asas Hukum Pidana Indonesia [Principles of Indonesian Criminal Law]* (2003).

Journals

Afina Akmalia and Arsyad Aldan, Analisis Penggunaan Dakwaan Alternatif Subsidair Oleh Penuntut Umum dalam Perkara Perlindungan Anak [Analysis of the Use of Subsidiary Alternative Charges by Public Prosecutors in Child Protection Cases] (2023) *Verstek* Vol. 11 Issue 3, 492.

Afdal Makkuraga, 2013, Ekonomi Politik Kebebasan Pers di Indonesia Pasca Reformasi: Kritik atas Praktek Neoliberalisme pada Industri Media [Political Economy of Press Freedom in Post-Reformation Indonesia: A Critique of Neoliberal Practices in the Media Industry], *Jurnal Visi Komunikasi* Volume XII, No. 01, Mei 2013, 2.

The Indonesian Press Council, 2016, Pengantar [Introduction], *Jurnal Dewan Pers Edisi* 13 Desember 2016, 6.

Sastramdijaja, 2023, Indonesia's COVID-19 Infodemic: A Battle for Truth or Trust?, *Trends in Southeast Asia Issue* 12, 2023.

International Laws

Criminal Procedure Code Act [Crim. Pro. Code.], 1981, [Criminal Procedure Code Act] (Indon.).

International Cases

Handyside V. United Kingdom, 1 Eur. Ct. H.R. 737 (1976).

Indonesian Legislations

Indonesian Act, 1999, (Indonesia), Press Act (Indon.).

Indonesian Act, 2016, Information and Electronic Transaction Act (Indon.).

Joint Decree of Indonesian Ministry of Communication and Information, National Police Chief and Attorney General on Implementation Guidelines of Some Particular Articles on Information and Electronic Transaction Acts (Decree No. 229 of 2021, No. 154 of 2021, and No. KB/2/VI/2021) (Indon).

Indonesian Cases

Denpasar First Degree Court, 2020, Decision No. 828/Pid.Sus/2020/PN Dps (Indon.).

Denpasar Appellate Court, 2020, Decision No. 72/Pid.Sus/2020/PT.Dps (Indon.).

East Jakarta First Degree Court, 2012, Decision No. 1453/Pid.B/2012/Pn.Jkt Tim (Indon.).

East Jakarta First Degree Court Decision, 2023, No. 202/Pid.Sus/2023/PN.Jkt Tim (Indon).

Jepara First Degree Court, 2024, Decision No. 14/Pid.Sus/2024/PN Jpa (Indon).

Mahkamah Agung [MA] [The Indonesian Supreme Court] 2015, Decision No. 2580 K/Pid.Sus/2015 (Indon).

Mahkamah Konstitusi [MK] [The Indonesian Constitutional Court] 2008, Putusan Mahkamah Konstitusi Nomor 50/PUU-VI/2008 (Indon.).

Palopo First Degree Court, 2021, No. 46/Pid.Sus/2021/PN Plp (Indon).

Rengat First Degree Court, 2020, Decision No. 293/Pid.Sus/2020/PN Rgt (Indon.).

Surabaya Appellate Court, 2013, Decision No. 190/PID/2013/PT.SBY (Indon).

Tangerang First Degree Court, 2009, 1269/PID.B/2009/PN.TNG (Indon).

Yogyakarta Appellate Court, 2015, Decision No. 26/Pid.Sus/2015/PT.YYK (Indon).

Government Documents

Indonesian Press Council, Statement No. 03/P-DP/XI/2021, On the Press Council's Concern Regarding the Criminalization of Journalist Muhammad Asrul at the Palopo District Court (2021).

Memorandum of Understanding between the Press Council No. 2/DP/MoU/II/2017 and No. B/15/II/2017 on Coordination in the Protection of Press Freedom and Law Enforcement Related to Abuse of the Journalism Profession. Indonesian Press Council, Memorandum of Understanding, No. 2, No. B/15/II/2017 (2017).

Reports

Annual Report of the United Nations High Commissioner for Human Rights 11 January 2013.

Aju Putrijanti and Sekar Anggun Gading Pinilih, *Strenghtening Anti-Eco-SLAPP Regulations in Indonesia*, Proceeding of the 1st International Workshop on Law, Economic, and Governance, 27 July 2022, Semarang, Indonesia.

Rapporteur's Digest on Freedom of Religion or Belief Second Edition (2023).

Internet

Ady Anugrahadi, 2021, 18 Tahun Lalu, Berita Tempo Berujung Gugatan Tomy Winata [18 Years Ago, Tempo News Leads to Tomy Winata's Lawsuit], *liputan6.com* (March 3, 2024) https://www.liputan6.com/news/read/4578638/18-tahun-lalu-berita-tempo-berujung-gugatan-tomy-winata.

Ady Thea Da, 2023, Jaksa Tuntut Hari Azhar 4 Tahun dan Fatia 3 Tahun 6 Bulan Penjara [Prosecutors Order Hari Azhar 4 Years and Fatia 3 Years and 6 Months in Prison], *hukumonline.com* (April 14, 2024) https://www.hukumonline.com/berita/a/jaksa-tuntut-haris-azhar-4-tahun-dan-fatia-3-tahun-6-bulan-penjara-lt65522c5898670/.

Agus Sahbani, 2024, Alasan MK Batalkan Pasal Penyebaran Berita Bohong dalam KUHP [Reasons for the Constitutional Court to Cancel the Article on Spreading Fake News in the Criminal Code], *hukumonline.com* (April 14, 2024) https://www.hukumonline.com/berita/a/alasan-mk-batalkan-pasal-penyebaran-berita-bohong-dalam-kuhp-lt65fc5895ba9d1/.

Article 19, Defining Defamation: Principles on Freedom of Expression and Protection of Reputation, 2000 https://www.article19.org/wp-content/uploads/2018/02/defining-defamation.pdf.

Asfinawati, et al., 2021, Ekonomi Politik Penempatan Militer di Papua [Political Economy of Military Deployment in Papua], *Walhi* (April 12, 2022) https://www.walhi.or.id/uploads/blogs/Kajian/2021%2008%2012.%20FA%20LAPORAN%20PAPEDA%20SINGLE%20PAGE.pdf.

Badan Pusat Statistik, 2021, Penduduk Menurut Desa dan Jenis Kelamin di Kecamatan Karimunjawa [Population by Village and Gender in Karimunjawa District], *bps.go.id* (May 15, 2024) https://jeparakab.bps.go.id/id/statistics-table/2/Mjk2IzI=/penduduk-menurut-desa-dan-jenis-kelamin-di-kecamatan-karimunjawa.html.

Beni Jo, 2024, Siapa Daniel Tangkilisan dan Apa Kasusnya Hingga Dipenjara? [Who is Daniel Tangkilisan and what is his case that led to his imprisonment?], *tirto.id* (May 13, 2024) https://tirto.id/siapa-daniel-tangkilisan-dan-apa-kasusnya-hingga-dipenjara-gXBd.

Binti Mufarida, 2024, Dewan Pers: Baru 1700 Media yang Sudah Terverifikasi [Press Council: Only 1700 Media Have Been Verified], *sindonews.com* (April 3, 2024) https://nasional.sindonews.com/read/1331869/15/dewan-pers-baru-1700-media-yang-sudah-terverifikasi-1709283799.

Detiknews, 2014, Beri Maaf, Sultan Minta Agar Florence Tetap Selesaikan S2 di UGM [Forgiveness, Sultan Asks Florence to Complete Her Masters at UGM], *detik.com* (March 31, 2024), Beri Maaf, Sultan Minta Agar Florence Tetap Selesaikan S2 di UGM (detik.com).

Dio Suhenda, 2021 New Guidelines No Substitute for ITE Law Revision, Activists Say, *The Jakarta Post* (June 12, 2022) https://www.thejakartapost.com/paper/2021/06/24/new-guidelines-no-substitute-for-ite-law-revision-activists-say.html.

Eka Nugraha Putra, 2021, Yang Luput Dibicarakan dari Kasus Jerinx: Kita Tak Punya Aturan Jelas Melawan Hoax, Misinformasi dan Disinformasi, The Conversation Indonesia [What's Missing from Jerinx's Case: We Don't Have Clear Rules Against Hoaxes, Misinformation and Disinformation, The Conversation Indonesia] (April 9, 2024) https://theconversation.com/yang-luput-dibicarakan-dari-kasus-jerinx-kita-tak-punya-aturan-jelas-melawan-hoax-misinformasi-dan-disinformasi-145172.

Evarukdijati, 2019, 60 Warga Merauke Keracunan Makanan [60 Merauke Residents Suffer Food Poisoning], *antaranews.com* (April 11, 2024) https://papua.antaranews.com/berita/483101/60-warga-merauke-keracunan-makanan.

Fatih Al Rosyid, 2018, Menjerat Hoaks: Tentang Berlakunya Pasal 14 dan Pasal 15 UU 1 tahun 1946 tentang Peraturan Hukum Pidana [Trapping Hoaxes: Regarding the Applicability of Article 14 and Article 15 of Law 1 of 1946 concerning Criminal Law Regulations], *2018, Viva Justicia* (https://vivajusticia.law.ugm.ac.id/2018/11/29/menjerat-hoaks-tentang-berlakunya-pasal-14-dan-pasal-15-uu-1-tahun-1946-tentang-peraturan-hukum-pidana/.

ICJR, 2021, ICJR Hormati Putusan Kasasi Jerinx: Mahkamah Agung Harus Juga Ambil Peran Atasi Masalah Norma UU ITE [ICJR Respects Jerinx's Cassation Ruling: Supreme Court Must Also Take Role in Resolving ITE Law Norm Issues], *icjr.or.id* (April 1, 2024) https://icjr.or.id/icjr-hormati-putusan-kasasi-jerinx-mahkamah-agung-harus-juga-ambil-peran-atasi-masalah-norma-uu-ite/

Ikhsan Reliubun, 2024, Daniel Frits Bebas, ICJR: Kita Belum Bebas dari Ancaman Kriminalisasi [Daniel Frits Free, ICJR: We Are Not Yet Free from the Threat of Criminalization], *tempo.co* (May 15, 2024) https://www.tempo.co/arsip/daniel-frits-bebas-icjr-kita-belum-bebas-dari-ancaman-kriminalisasi--56525.

Kristi Dwi Utami, 2024a, Beragam Masalah Akibat Limbah Tambak Udang di Karimunjawa [Various Problems Caused by Shrimp Pond Waste in Karimunjawa], *kompas.id* (May 22, 2024) https://www.kompas.id/baca/nusantara/2024/04/29/beragam-masalah-akibat-limbah-tambak-udang-di-karimunjawa.

Kristi Dwi Utami, 2024b, Daniel Tangkilisan Released, Prosecutor Files Cessation, *kompas.id* (June 9, 2024) https://www.kompas.id/baca/english/2024/06/02/en-daniel-tangkilisan-dibebaskan-hakim-pengadilan-tinggi-semarang-jaksa-ajukan-kasasi.

Liputan 6, 2006, Bambang Harymurti Menang di Mahkamah Agung [Bambang Harymurti Wins at Supreme Court], *liputan6.com* (April 2, 2024) Bambang Harymurti Menang di Mahkamah Agung - News Liputan6.com.

M. Iqbal Al Machmudi, 2021, UU Pers Perlu Dimutakhirkan untuk Lindungi Pers [Press Law Needs to be Updated to Protect the Press], *mediaindonesia.com* (March 30, 2024) https://mediaindonesia.com/politik-dan-hukum/436523/uu-pers-perlu-dimutakhirkan-untuk-lindungi-pers.

Muhammad Asrul, 2019a, "Jilid II" Korupsi Jalan Lingkar Barat Rp5M, Sinyal Penyidik untuk Farid Judas? ["Volume II" of Rp5 billion West Ring Road Corruption, Investigator's

Signal for Farid Judas?], *berita.news*, (April, 1 2024) https://berita.news/2019/05/25/jilid-ii-korupsi-jalan-lingkar-barat-rp5-m-sinyal-penyidik-untuk-farid-judas/.

Muhammad Asrul, 2019b, Aroma Korupsi Revitalisasi Lapangan Pancasila Palopo Diduga Seret Farid Judas [The Aroma of Corruption in the Revitalization of Pancasila Field in Palopo Allegedly Drags Farid Judas Into It], *berita.news*, (April 1, 2024) https://berita.news/2019/05/24/aroma-korupsi-revitalisasi-lapangan-pancasila-palopo-diduga-seret-farid-judas/.

Muhammad Asrul, 2019c, Putra Mahkota Palopo Diduga "Dalang" Korupsi PLTMH dan Keripik Zaro Rp11 M [Crown Prince of Palopo Allegedly "Mastermind" of Rp11 Billion PLTMH and Zaro Chips Corruption], *berita.news*, (April 1, 2024) https://berita.news/2019/05/10/putra-mahkota-palopo-diduga-dalang-korupsi-pltmh-dan-keripik-zaro-rp11-m/.

Muhammad Yasin, 2019, Mengenal Dwangsom dan Jejaknya dalam Hukum Indonesia [Getting to Know Dwangsom and Its Footprint in Indonesian Law], *hukumonline.com* (March 14, 2024) https://www.hukumonline.com/berita/a/mengenal-dwangsom-dan-jejaknya-dalam-hukum-indonesia-lt5dccbb0753910.

Mys, 2005, Eksaminasi Putusan Pidana Tempo, Pertimbangan Hakim tidak Mendalam [Examination of Tempo's Criminal Decision, Judge's Consideration Not Deep], *hukumonline.com* (April 14, 2024) Eksaminasi Putusan Pidana Tempo, Pertimbangan Hakim tidak Mendalam (hukumonline.com).

News Desk, 2020, Conspiracy Theory-Endorsing Musician Jerinx Named Suspect for Allegedly Defaming IDI, *The Jakarta Post*, (April 17, 2024) http://www.thejakartapost.com/news/2020/08/12/conspiracy-theory-endorsing-musician-jerinx-named-suspect-for-allegedly-defaming-idi.html.

Nur Janti, 2022, Activists Face "Danger" Amid Shrinking Civic Space, *The Jakarta Post* (April 12, 2022) https://www.thejakartapost.com/indonesia/2022/03/21/activists-face-danger-amid-shrinking-civic-space.html.

Robert Isidorus, 2019, 37 Orang Keracunan Makanan di Timika [37 People Suffer Food Poisoning in Timika], *beritasatu.com* (April 11, 2024) https://www.beritasatu.com/news/579835/37-orang-keracunan-makanan-di-timika.

Sidra, 2023, Dewan Pers Sebut Jumlah Media Massa Terbanyak bukan di Pulai Jawa, Tapi Ada Di Sumatera [Press Council Says Largest Number of Mass Media is Not in Java, But in Sumatra], *inews Palembang* (April 15, 2024) https://palembang.inews.id/read/252404/dewan-pers-sebut-jumlah-media-massa-terbanyak-bukan-di-pulau-jawa-tapi-ada-di-sumatera.

Sukma, 2006, Pengadilan Banding Kuatkan Vonis Bambang Harymurti [Appeals Court Upholds Bambang Harymurti's Verdict], *tempo.co* (March 29, 2024). https://nasional.tempo.co

Sunu Dyantoro, 2014, Jerinx SID dan Gerakan Tolak Reklamasi Teluk Benoa [Jerinx SID and the Movement to Reject Benoa Bay Reclamation], *tempo.co* (April 17, 2024) https://nasional.tempo.co/read/628392/jerinx-sid-dan-gerakan-tolak-reklamasi-teluk-benoa.

Tempo, 2003, Ada Tomy di 'Tenabang'? [Is Tommy in 'Tenabang'?] (March 1, 2024), *tempo.co* https://majalah.tempo.co/read/nasional/85648/tomy-winata-pasar-tanah-abang.

The Indonesian Supreme Court, Direktori Putusan [Judicial Decisions Repository] https://putusan3.mahkamahagung.go.id/direktori/putusan/zaef171f9e707c8493773 13031303034.html.

The Jakarta Post, 2014, Activist Condemn Arrest of Student who Insulted Yogyakarta, *The Jakarta Post* (March 5, 2024) Activists condemn arrest of student who insulted Yogyakarta - National - The Jakarta Post.

VOI, Still Hearing Public Input, Menkum HAM Has Not Sumitted the Revision of the ITE Law to the DPR, *VOI* (September 4, 2021) https://voi.id/en/news/38068/still-hearing-public-input-menkum-ham-has-not-submitted-the-revision-of-the-ite-law-to-the-dpr.

Widiarsi Agustina, 2014, Apa Tanggapan Sultan Yogya Soal Florence?[What is the Sultan of Yogya's Response to Florence?], *tempo.co* (March 31, 2024) Apa Tanggapan Sultan Yogya Soal Florence? - Nasional Tempo.co.

5 Public Interest Defense and Free Speech in Indonesia

5.1 Definition of Public Interest Defense

In law, public interest is commonly understood as a legal practice that advocates for the rights of marginalized or underrepresented groups, such as the poor and disabled. The term "public interest" stems from the Latin term "*pro bono publico*," which means "for the public good." For lawyers who are handling public interest cases, popularly known as pro bono cases, the service is typically voluntary and free of charge.

Pro bono cases, with their voluntary and free services, are based on the understanding that access to justice is a human right[1]. Furthermore, they ensure equality of rights and access to justice. Therefore, public interest litigation is an attempt to serve human rights by addressing the needs of society.

There is no uniformity in defining "public interest" in the international law treaty or customary international law[2], given that "public interest" is originally a practice in domestic law. Hence, its definition and practice can vary in each country, such as class action or pro bono. In international litigation, "public interest" has been used in various cases, and "public interest" despite the practice in various areas of law such as international investment law[3]. Another form that is also known as "public interest" is a class action, which stemmed from the importance of rights to education that was violated in the alleged segregation in the US case *Brown v. Board of Education*[4]. The case introduced the significance of public interest and how it bridges public law litigation[5].

In relation to the topic in this section, there are two terms "public interest" and "public interest litigation." While the former is defined as the potential common or benefit that draws individuals or broader groups to the issue[6], the latter is the litigation process that determines the issue of public interest, such as in the class action mentioned earlier.

Particularly in international human rights law, the public interest is discussed in Article 19 Section 3 of the ICCPR. The provision read as follows:

> The exercise of the rights provided for in paragraph 2 of this article carries with it special duties and responsibilities. It may therefore be subject to certain restrictions, but these shall only be such as are provided by law and are necessary:

DOI: 10.4324/9781032661544-5

a For respect of the rights or reputations of others;
b For the protection of national security or of public order (ordre public), or of public health or morals.

In the three-step test for limiting freedom of expression, public interest encompasses various interests, such as the public, public order, public health, and public morals, which should serve as legitimate aims for any human rights limitations imposed by the ICCPR state parties. This approach ensures that such limitations do not violate the treaty[7].

The provisions of ICCPR are imposed as obligations on state parties. However, differences in the interpretation of public interest across jurisdictions of state parties continue to spark debate among scholars and the international community.

While the European Court of Human Rights (ECHR) coined the legal doctrine of the "margin of appreciation," it was originally intended as a different implementation allowed by the ECHR within national legislative, executive, administrative, and judicial state agencies. However, as noted in *Ahmed and Others v. United Kingdom*, a state's implementation of the margin of appreciation should be clearly identified and addressed, although there are no clear principles governing its application[8]. For example, in the 1976 case of *Handyside v. United Kingdom*, the Court argued that the prohibition of *The Little Red Schoolbook*, deemed obscene, violated freedom of expression. The Court stated that "State authorities are in principle in a better position than the international judge to give an opinion on the exact content of these requirements." In addition, there was no standard for the protection of public morals, especially regarding children, at the European level.

The application of public interest is not exclusively for freedom of expression cases. In the Inter-American Court of Human Rights case of *Claude Reyes et. al v. Chile*, public interest was also recognized as an element to be respected regarding access to the public information about an environmental project determined during the trial[9].

While the implementation of public interest under international law varies, the examples provided above demonstrate that the legal context of public interest holds greater importance for the public, particularly when tested against issues in a legal trial. In the Indonesian legal system, the term "public interest" is recognized, primarily using the phrase "*kepentingan umum*." Article 33 Section 3 of the Indonesian Constitution stipulates that the management of natural resources should be for the greatest benefit of the people of Indonesia. In particular, regarding land management as part of the country's resources, the Indonesian government regulates this in Presidential Regulation Number 36 of 2005 on Land Acquisition for the Implementation of Development in the Public Interest. In addition to property law, the term "public interest" is also central to constitutional law, particularly concerning the protection of civil and political rights. Such protections are also stipulated in the Indonesian Constitution, notably in Article 28, which is considered a key distinction in recognizing human rights in Indonesia compared to other countries[10]. This Article regulates the obligation of citizens to respect the human rights of others. Importantly, while exercising their rights and freedoms, limitations must be in accordance with various considerations, including public order.

In the lower legislation than the Constitution, Law Number 9 of 1998 on the Freedom to Expressing Opinion in Public Area states in Article 6 that expressing an opinion should respect public safety and order. This law was drafted and passed after the fall of the authoritarian regime of Suharto, initiated by President Habibie, who succeeded Suharto after the reformation in May 1998. In September 1998, President Habibie issued Presidential Mandate No. R.14/PU/IX/1998, which includes the President's reasoning for drafting the Law on Expressing Opinion and is in accordance with the Declaration of Human Rights and the Indonesian Constitution. Therefore, protests and any form of expression should be protected under the law while ensuring public order[11].

Moreover, Law Number 40 of 1999 on the Press states that the press has a role in monitoring, criticizing, correcting, and suggesting solutions to issues related to the public interest. The Press Law is another piece of legislation that was passed after the reformation, along with several other legislations, such as the Law on Regional Autonomy and the Law on Human Rights, which were also passed in the same year. This indicates that the government is committed to respecting public interest and effectively protecting human rights. The former law was passed as an attempt to redefine the Indonesian governmental system, which emphasizes self-government, self-sufficiency, self-authority, and self-regulation,[12] principles that are important for citizens in the region. Meanwhile, the latter law indicates that the Indonesian government initiated its human rights obligations by incorporating civil rights (e.g., Article 9), political rights (e.g., Article 23), economic rights (e.g., Article 38), social rights (e.g., Article 41), and cultural rights (e.g., Article 71) into the legislation, years before the country ratified the ICCPR (International Covenant on Civil and Political Rights) and ICESCR (International Covenant on Economic, Social and Cultural Rights).

However, as discussed in Chapter 4, the implementation of the protection of the right to expression is currently facing challenges, particularly regarding the lack of effort to determine whether the public interest is an important element to be considered in cases of free expression limitations. Particularly in cases of censorship, government-imposed restrictions can be considered unnecessary if the censored information is important to the public. Therefore, in many instances of government-initiated internet shutdowns, human rights issues frequently emerge because the government argues that such measures are necessary for protecting public order and national security[13]. However, shutting down the internet obstructs individuals' rights to access and spread information, especially accurate and urgent information.

Such an issue was evident in Indonesia when the government shut down the internet for a week in several cities in the Papua and West Papua provinces. This occurred during a mass riot among Papuans in response to the racist conduct they experienced. They were angered by the situation, particularly because of the hoax that one of their fellow Papuans had died. The government then took action by shutting down the internet in Manokwari, Jayapura, Sorong, and Fakfak. Initially, the government only slowed down the internet connection, allowing for limited access, but then it was completely shut down. According to Rudiantara, the Indonesian Minister of Communication and Information, the shutdown was implemented for reasons of national security, but this action was legally baseless, particularly when considering the three-step test.

According to Article 40 of the 2016 ITE Law, the Indonesian government has the authority to limit internet access. The provisions read as follows:

> *Section 1*:
>
> *The government is obliged to prevent the dissemination of electronic information that contains prohibited content.*
>
> *Section 2*:
>
> *The government has the authority to terminate access and/or order Electronic System Operators to terminate access to Electronic Information that has content that violates the law.*

However, the internet shutdown was unlawful because, according to the legality test, the government should take action based on the enforcement of legislation. While Article 40 of the 2016 ITE Law allows for such authority, the action should also be based on an emergency situation officially declared by the government, which was not declared at that time. Therefore, when civil society organizations filed a lawsuit with the Jakarta Administrative Court regarding the unlawfulness of the internet shutdown in Papua and West Papua, the Court considered that the government's action was against Regulation in Lieu of Law Number 23 of 1959 on the Revocation of Law Number 74 of 1957, which indicates that the policy to shut down the internet was procedurally defective[14].

Furthermore, the shutdown was also in violation of Article 4 of the ICCPR, which states that any limitations on human rights may only be imposed by the state if a public emergency threatening the life and existence of the nation has been proclaimed. In other words, the Indonesian government imposed baseless action to cope with the riots in Papua and West Papua, which did not protect the public interest because the shutdown hindered the dissemination of important information during the riot.

The internet outage imposed by the government in 2019 was unfortunately not the last occurrence, as it happened 11 more times throughout 2021[15]. Despite the Administrative Court ruling that internet shutdowns are against the law, the Indonesian government continued to restrict public access to information. Moreover, such actions by the government have been evident in other instances, which will be discussed in the following chapter.

5.2 Case Studies of Public Interest Defense in Indonesia

In Chapter 4, several cases are discussed regarding defamation and hate speech limitations under Indonesian law. Some of these cases involve significant issues of public interest, such as the Haris and Fatia case, which is also discussed in Chapter 4. This case highlighted the importance of informing the public about a conflict of interest involving a public official in the mining industry, which constitutes a violation of the law. However, there are also other examples where the Indonesian trial system failed to determine the pertinence of public interest in such cases, which enables rulings that further harm freedom of expression.

Given that Chapter 4 provides a list of cases and detailed analyses of defamation and hate speech limitations, this section will only briefly discuss the cases, focusing on why the following cases are considered to have failed in determining the element of public interest.

5.2.1 Risang Bima Wijaya Case

The first case was the 2004 Risang Bima Wijaya case, which occurred a couple of years before the ITE Law was passed. Risang Bima Wijaya was a journalist and the General Manager of a newspaper called *Radar Jogja*. He was under investigation for defamation due to a series of news stories reported by *Radar Jogja* about the sexual harassment of a female employee at another newspaper called *Kedaulatan Rakyat*, allegedly committed by Soemadi M Wonohito, the founder and editor-in-chief of *Kedaulatan Rakyat*. In addition to the continuous reporting, *Radar Jogja* also published two cartoons, one of which depicted a man resembling Soemadi chasing a woman with her pants down, while the other showed a man sitting and imagining a naked woman. All of the news series and cartoons were published in 2002.

The victim went public and made a statement before the press, and *Radar Jogja* was one of the media outlets that attended and reported on the victim's statement regarding sexual harassment. Ironically, the continuous news coverage by *Radar Jogja* prompted Soemadi to report Risang Bima Wijaya to the police for defamation. In 2004, the defamation trial in the First Degree Court of Sleman resulted in Risang being convicted of criminal defamation and sentenced to nine months in prison. Risang filed an appeal with the Sleman Court in 2005, which was sent to the Appellate Court of Yogyakarta. However, the Appellate Court, through Decision No. 21/Pid/2005/PTY, only reduced Risang's penalty to six months. Risang's final attempt to seek justice was through cassation to the Indonesian Supreme Court, which unfortunately upheld the Appellate Court's Decision affirming Risang's guilt of criminal defamation (written defamation) and convicting him to six months based on Article 310 Section 2 in conjunction with Article 64 Section 2 of the Current Criminal Code.

While the defamation case was an attempt to harm the freedom of the press, the trial of Risang shows the lack of determination of the public interest.

Radar Jogja has published a story about the alleged sexual harassment of an influential person in the local media industry, which means that the defamation investigation is not necessary in the first place, given the urgency of the public to know whether the sexual harassment is true or not.

Both *Radar Jogja* and *Kedaulatan Rakyat* are based in Jogjakarta, and they have similar markets and readerships, which sparked concerns about competition between the newspapers in the case trial. However, several controversies arose during the case investigation and trial, particularly because it involved a criminal case related to journalistic work that, according to the 1999 Press Law, should be processed through mediation rather than a criminal case investigation. Unfortunately, no ethics hearing was held, nor was the news reported by Radar Jogja submitted to the Indonesian Press Council (*Dewan Pers*).

Another mechanism that was not attempted and used as a direct report to the police is the right-to-reply mechanism provided by the Press Law. According to the Press Law, the right to reply is the right to provide a response or refutation to news stories that contain facts that may harm individuals' reputations.

The publication was processed based on the victim's report to the police, but the investigation was eventually halted after the police issued a letter of cessation for the investigation and prosecution (*Surat Pemberhentian, Penyelidikan, Penyidikan dan Penuntutan-SP3*)[16]. The more alarming fact in Risang's case is that Soemadi was the owner of another local newspaper. The case trial did not rely on the Press Law 1999, and the judges ignored the Act's civil dispute mechanism. The sole reason the trial voided the Press Law was that one of the expert witnesses, who was ironically from the Council Press, argued that the Press Law is not *lex specialis*[17]. The verdict was a nine-month prison term for Risang, marking yet another example of press freedom being undermined.

Although Risang and the Radar Jogja team gathered valid sources and conducted several interviews, he was still convicted under Article 310 Section 2. The police's priority to use the Current Criminal Code instead of the Press Law as the *lex specialis* is concerning because the proper mechanism is available but not utilized. This raises the assumption that Risang was investigated based on retaliation rather than the significance of public interest regarding the alleged sexual harassment, which a criminal act that was committed by Soemadi.

5.2.2 Muhadkly Acho Case

Another example occurred in March 2015 when Muhadkly Acho, an Indonesian stand-up comedian, wrote on his blog about his complaints while living in the Green Pramuka City Apartment in Jakarta. Acho wrote that he had to pay an illegal levy to the apartment owner under the guise of supervision, in addition to being allegedly overcharged for the use of parking facilities and facing raised utility costs. The developer also failed to build a green area as promised[18].

Surprisingly, Duta Paramindo Sejahtera, the corporation that owns Green Pramuka City Apartment, reported Acho for criminal defamation in November 2015. However, it was not until June 2017 that Acho was officially named a suspect in the criminal defamation charge. Acho's blog post allegedly blocked Green Pramuka City Apartment's ability to promote itself to new consumers, especially the millennial generation, as they are typically the ones using the internet to find reviews of properties they are considering[19].

Despite the fact that Acho wrote the blog as one of the apartment's tenants at the time, a representative of Duta Paramindo Sejahtera believed that his post defamed the company's reputation. Regarding the alleged defamation, Acho had the right to complain about the facilities he gained as a tenant. Moreover, Acho was voicing not only his consumer rights but also the poor service given by the apartment, which had not been known to the public and could affect more consumers who were unaware of the issues with the apartment management. In other words, Acho's actions do not fall into the category of defamation, considering that he wrote something significant for potential consumers and the public at large, particularly regarding the property rental scheme. After years of investigation, the police decided to drop the charges and asked Acho to proceed with the mediation process, a method that he had requested twice but which had initially been rejected by the police[20].

5.2.3 The Saiful Mahdi Case

Another example of the test of freedom of expression against public interest happened in 2020. This case, which also demonstrates how Article 27 Section 3 of the ITE can be subject to multiple interpretations, involved Saiful Mahdi, a professor at the University of Syiah Kuala, Banda Aceh, Indonesia. In late 2018, in a WhatsApp group that consisted of 140 members, including professors and leadership of University Syiah Kuala (UNSYIAHKita), Saiful sent a message that criticized the results of a civil servant test for the engineering department. The following is the complete message that Saiful sent:

> *Innalillahiwainnailaihirajiun [We belong to Allah and to Allah we return]. I have received sad news about the death of common sense in the leadership ranks of [the university's] engineering school during the last civil servant test. [Is this] proof that the technological determinism of the engineering [school] is very easy to be corrupted?*
>
> ...
>
> *Why is a school that was once so glorious now so faint-hearted? Why do we take so much pride in a new faculty? Because meritocracy was applied, starting with recruitment. Only the mediocre or those entangled in "debt" are afraid of meritocracy.*

That message was then forwarded by one of the WhatsApp group members to Taufiq Saidi, Dean of the School of Engineering at Universitas Syiah Kuala, who was not part of the group chat. Taufiq felt defamed by the message and then forwarded it to the university's ethics court. Because there was no clear conclusion on the ethical sanction, Taufiq reported Saiful to the police for criminal defamation. Several unusual legal facts were revealed during Saiful's trial[21]. Even though the prosecutor charged Saiful with criminal defamation under Article 27 Section 3 of the ITE Law, the witnesses who testified in court frequently contradicted each other. Some testified that Saiful's message was a hoax, while others testified that the message was an accusation against the leadership of the Engineering Department.

Another fallacy in the court was how the message was interpreted as defamation of a person rather than criticism toward the institution. In the ITE Law, after the 2016 amendment, Article 27 Section 3 pointed to the defamation definition in Articles 310 and 311 of the Criminal Code Act, and this ruling was also emphasized by a Constitutional Court ruling in 2008. Based on the ITE Law, defamation can only be directed at individuals rather than organizations, institutions, universities, or companies. Yet, the judge ruled that Saiful's message intentionally attacked Taufiq's honor and reputation as the Dean of the School of Engineering. This ruling is strange, considering that Saiful's message did not mention any specific names or positions, only the leadership ranks of the engineering school at the Universitas Syiah Kuala.

Judges also ignored all the testimonies from Saiful's side, which supported his position in the case. However, this testimony clarifies why Saiful decided to send such a message in the WhatsApp group. He identified a fallacy in the results of the civil servant recruitment test based on his expertise in statistical science. Saiful also had the right to clarify that his statement aligned with the code of conduct set by the chat group administrator and was agreed upon by all the members. The messages above served as clarification and were part of Saiful's academic freedom. Whenever criticism like this arises, it should be counter-analyzed with data to uncover the truth. If the criticism is considered wrong or unethical, it should be addressed through the ethics process rather than the legal process.

Saiful's case finally ended when the Indonesian Supreme Court rejected the Banda Aceh Appeal Court's cassation. Saiful was sentenced to three months for criminal defamation. Currently, a total of 50 non-governmental organizations have sent letters to President Joko Widodo, urging him to grant Saiful a pardon through amnesty. One of the reasons is that the court's decision contradicted the ITE Law Joint Decree issued in June 2021. The Joint Decree provided clarity on how the scope of defamation should be applied. Specifically, it stated that criticisms based on facts and expression disseminated through closed groups like WhatsApp do not fall into the category of publicly disseminated expression. Those two circumstances were present in Saiful Mahdi's case. The amnesty was finally issued by the president in October 2021 through a presidential decree on Saiful Mahdi's amnesty.

Although the case was tested for the alleged harmed reputation of the university, the lawsuit against Saiful was a depiction of the overlook of the urgency of the public's need to be informed about potential scandals in a public university, which represents an educational service to the public. The cheating that occurred during the recruitment process affected equal employment opportunities in the public sector, particularly in higher education institutions.

5.2.4 The Mohammad Trijanto Case

This case serves as another important example of public interest, illustrating the failure of the Indonesian legal system to adequately assess the urgency of balancing individual rights with public interest. Unfortunately, despite the significance of this case for the topic of freedom of expression limitations and public interest, it is not recorded in the Indonesian Supreme Court's repository. A quick search for the number of the judicial decision from the Blitar First Degree Court No. 15/Pid.Sus/2019/PN Blt retrieved a page with case decision information, but as of this writing, there is no file of the actual judicial decision provided[22].

Mohammad Trijanto is an anti-corruption activist in Blitar, East Java Province. In October 2018, on his Facebook account, Trijanto posted information regarding the summons issued to the Blitar Regent, Rijanto, by the Indonesian Commission of Corruption Eradication (*Komisi Pemberantasan Korupsi-KPK*). The full post (with the attached image of the summons letter) by Trijanto reads as follows:

> *Sesuai informasi (hoax atau tidak ya??), Bupati Blitar akan dipanggil menghadap penyidik KPK (Komisi Pemberantasan Korupsi) pada hari Senin, 15 Oktober 2018 di gedung KPK Jakarta. Kira-kira Bupati Blitar dimintai keterangan terkait dugaan korupsi apa ya?? Tebak-tebakan yuk !!! Lawan korupsi!!! (((Makanya kalau jadi pejabat jangan sekali-kali melukai hati kaum petani, nelayan, honorer dan kaum marginal lainnya di Blitar Raya, bisa meyesal tujuh turunan deh hehehhehehe)))?*

which translated to as follow:

> *According to information (hoax or not??), the Regent of Blitar will be summoned to meet with KPK (Corruption Eradication Commission) investigators on Monday, October 15, 2018 at the KPK building in Jakarta. I wonder what information the Regent of Blitar will be asked regarding the alleged corruption? Let's guess!!! Fight corruption!!! (((So if you become an official, never hurt the feelings of farmers, fishermen, honorary workers and other marginalized groups in Greater Blitar, you could regret it for seven generations hehehhehehe)))?*

Due to this post, Trijanto faced an investigation for two potential crimes: Online defamation and hoax. However, the court found him guilty only of online defamation. Trijanto's statement on his Facebook account stemmed from his action of reporting to the Audit Board of the Republic of Indonesia (*Badan Pemeriksa Keuangan*-BPK) in Blitar regarding the suspected corruption case related to the 2018 Budget Drafting of Blitar Regency[23]. He reported the potential corruption on 5 October 2018. Five days later, he received a WhatsApp message from Yosi, a contractor, informing him that there was a summons letter from the KPK to Public Works and Public Housing Authority staff member Retiono Pratama and the Blitar Regent[24]. The next day, Yosi sent another message with a screenshot of the summons letter from the KPK, which was also confirmed by Pratama when Trijanto met him on 12 October 2018[25].

The KPK letter was eventually determined to be fake, and the person who spread it unfortunately could not be identified by the Police[26]. Rijanto, the Blitar Regent, also stated that the letter was a hoax[27] and that there was no indication of his involvement in corruption.

However, despite the harsh statements made in the post, the investigation and the trial were not necessary, especially considering the criminal provisions applied by the legal system. The plaintiff in this case was Agus Cunanto, who claimed to represent Rijanto. However, there is a discrepancy between the plaintiff and the individual whose reputation was allegedly harmed, which is inconsistent with the characteristics of criminal defamation in Indonesia. The law recognizes that it should be a complaint-based crime, given that feelings of offense are personal determination. In addition, Trijanto's expression should be further evaluated to determine whether it affects the reputation of the Blitar Regent, such as whether it could lead to Rijanto's occupation being revoked or him getting fired. The reporting to the police and the subsequent trial indicate that the entire litigation process seems abrupt. Furthermore, the prosecution of online expressions that criticize public officials has raised concerns among Indonesian citizens and civil society, as it has been inconsistently implemented across various cases. While there are court rulings that convict such expressions, there are also instances where expressions do not fall into the category of online defamation due to their valid criticism.

In a similar case to that of Mohammad Trijanto, another anti-corruption activist, Muhammad Arsyad faced an online defamation trial but was eventually found not guilty by the First Degree Court of Makassar in 2013. Arysad was held in custody for a period before his trial due to his Blackberry Messenger (BBM) status, which read: "*No fear Ancaman Nurdin Halid Koruptor!!! Jangan Pilih Adik Koruptor*" or "*No fear of Nurdin Halid's threat to Corruptors!!! Don't Choose Corrupt Brother*," referring to Kadir Halid, who was running for Makassar's mayoral election at the time. Nurdin Halid is the brother of Kadir Halid, who was convicted in a corruption case in 2007[28]. For Arsyad, his BBM status was an expression of his spirit as an activist and his criticism as a young member of Golkar (*Golongan Karya*), the political party to which Kadir and Nurdin Halid belonged and in which he was also involved[29].

Arsyad was detained by the police for 100 days due to a report made by Abdul Wahab Tahir, a member of the Regional Representative Council (*Dewan Perwakilan Rakyat Daerah*-DPRD) from Golkar. This report was incorrect as actionable defamation because Arsyad was not the one who felt defamed. At the time, the provision was still regulated as general defamation[30], which led to Arsyad being investigated and brought before the court.

The Makassar Court decided that, in the alternative indictment of Article 27 Section 3 of the ITE Law, Article 310 of the Current Criminal Code, and Article 315 of the Criminal Code, Arsyad was found not guilty on all charges[31]. The Court reasoned that the public prosecutor could not prove the truth of Arsyad's BBM status[32] and questioned the integrity of the evidence presented before the court, which relied on a printout of the BBM status[33].

In light of the few examples, such as the free ruling of Arsyad and the ruling of Iin Solihin, who was also found not guilty of defamation in 2021[34], the inconsistency of the Indonesian legal system becomes evident. It indicates that one expression could be protected because it is a valid and legal expression, while another could be prosecuted despite being a valid criticism. This inconsistency raises questions about the level of implementation, and the provisions of the ITE Law are currently considered draconian.

In the cases involving rich and powerful individuals or entities, such as those of Muhammad Trijanto, Muhammad Arsyad, Muhadkly Acho, and Saiful Mahdi discussed in this section, the retaliatory nuances by the plaintiffs are depicted by either a lack of evidence or the fact that the plaintiffs who reported to the police were not the ones directly offended by the expression. Therefore, there is a lack of careful examination regarding the scope of protected expressions that should be conducted when assessing such cases in trial[35].

The cases discussed above reflect that the lack of determination regarding public interest can lead to unnecessary lawsuits over alleged harmed reputations of individuals and institutions. However, such claims are not legally valid, given that the Current Criminal Code does not recognize legal entities as subjects in law, only individuals. The cases discussed in this section portray that not only has the area of public interest been overlooked, but also specific elements of the public interest, such as public health and public order, are rarely addressed in freedom of expression litigation. The next section will discuss the potential regulation and implementation of public interest defense, especially in cases related to freedom of expression.

5.3 Opportunity and Challenges in the Implementation of Public Interest Defense

Given the definition of public interest and how international law positions it, along with the related cases discussed, this section will analyze how Indonesian law should apply the public interest defense.

The significance of discussing the public interest defense in Indonesian law lies not only in its ability to define the scope of protected and unprotected expressions but also in its potential application during litigation to properly discontinue a case. In Indonesian trials, when proposing the indictment, the prosecutor should rely on the interests of the public and the state. As the state representative, the argument and attitude of the prosecutor during the trial should reflect those interests. The prosecutor should be objective in regard to posing the indictment and consider the interest of the public in the criminal case trial.

Among all the authorities of the public prosecutor in the criminal legal system, the power to discontinue a case in the public interest is one of the mandates stipulated by law, commonly referred to as the Opportunity Principle. According to the Opportunity Principle, a prosecutor in a criminal trial has the authority not only to pose an indictment against the defendant but also not to prosecute the defendant due to public or state interest.[36] The Principle is stated not only in the Criminal Procedure Code[37] but also in Law Number 16 of 2004 on the Prosecutor. In Article 35 Section C of the Prosecutor Law, the Opportunity Principle is applied in cases of discontinuation *(seponering)* as one of the authorities of the public prosecutor. In other words, *seponering* means that the Attorney General may dismiss the case in the public interest[38]. The Law was amended by Law Number 11 of 2021 on the Prosecutor, which also amended Article 35 and added Articles 35A and 35B that regulate the structure of the public prosecutor's office; however, the provisions regarding the authorities of the prosecutor were not affected by the amendment.

Wirjono Prodjodikoro, the former Chief Justice of the Indonesian Supreme Court, presents an interesting perspective on the Opportunity Principle. According to Justice Prodjodikoro, in practice, even if a criminal offense has occurred and all the required elements are proven, prosecuting the plaintiff may result in a loss for the state[39]. Prodjodikoro cited the example of a chemist working on a substance essential for state security. Due to his financial difficulties, he committed fraud. If he were prosecuted, there would be no one left to work on the essential substance because he is the only expert available[40]. In other words, his prosecution would lead to a loss for the state in regard to state security.

However, despite the authority mandated by the law to discontinue cases, especially those related to freedom of expression that often heavily rely on public interest, challenges arise in determining whether public and state interests are affected. In such cases, lower court prosecutors should consult with the Indonesian Attorney General before making a decision. In addition, this authority to dismiss cases can be contentious. One of the strong legal norms is equality before the law, which means everyone should be treated the same under the law. Case dismissal may potentially contradict this principle.

Additionally, Article 35 Section C of the Prosecutor Law itself does not specifically define "public interest." The Elucidation Section of the Prosecutor Law of 2004 and its amendment in 2021 only state that "public interest is the interest of nation or state and/or the interest of society," emphasizing the authority of the Attorney General while considering the input from relevant government agencies. There are two main problems with this explanation. First, it lacks a clear definition, as the formulation in the Elucidation Section still does not specify what falls into the categories of state, national, and societal interests, ultimately leaving the concept of public interest unspecified. Second, the government agencies from which the Attorney General can solicit input are also unclear, allowing decisions to be made without consultation.

The authority to either prosecute or not prosecute, as well as to discontinue the case, are not against each other; rather, they can be seen as options for the public prosecutor in handling a criminal case[41]. Although the laws state that case dismissal falls within the authority of the Attorney General, there has been debate about enforcing the Opportunity Principle. Chairul Huda, a criminal law professor at Universitas Muhammadiyah Jakarta, Indonesia, argues that the Opportunity Principle should not be the absolute authority of the Attorney General[42], as public interest can be defined as the interest of society, with the state represented by government agencies such as DPR[43] and KPK[44]. Additionally, the Opportunity Principle regulated in Indonesian criminal law is significantly different from the authority that is implemented globally, where any public prosecutor, not exclusively the Attorney General, can exercise this authority conditionally and unconditionally[45].

With regard to criminal defamation cases, the Opportunity Principle plays an important role. To prove that the allegedly defamatory expression contains the elements of a crime in the trial, the evidence process under the Indonesian criminal trial is based on the "*Negatief Wettelijk Bewijstheorie*." According to this theory, a criminal offense occurs whenever there is a congruence between the evidence presented in the trial and the judges' belief[46]. Under the Indonesian criminal legal system, criminal guilt is established with at least two valid pieces of evidence that support the judge's belief that a criminal act has occurred and that the defendant is the perpetrator of the crime[47]. The two valid pieces of evidence can be drawn from the five types of criminal evidence recognized under Indonesian criminal procedure: Witness testimony, expert testimony, letters, clues, and defendant's statements[48].

Even though witness testimony is the first item on the list of valid evidence according to Article 184 of the Indonesian Criminal Procedure Code, there are specific requirements for analyzing its validity. Judges should carefully assess the conformity of each testimony presented by witnesses, the consistency of the witnesses' testimony with other pieces of evidence presented, the background or motive of the witnesses for providing particular testimony, and the witnesses' way of living and decency, which can support the believability of their testimony[49].

Clues as valid evidence under Indonesian criminal law refers to behaviors, incidents, or circumstances that, due to the conformity with each other or with the alleged crime itself, strongly indicate that a crime occurred and identify the offender[50]. Clues are derived from other evidence, such as witness testimony, expert testimony, and letters. However, given that judges have the authority to use clues as valid evidence based on their own judgment[51], the use of clues as valid evidence has sparked debates. There has been a proposal, alongside the amendment of the Criminal Procedure Act, to replace clues as valid evidence with judges' observations during the trial. Judges' observations are considered more objective and appropriate for determining the nature of the crime during the trial. Scholars have also advocated for the replacement of clues as recognized evidence because one of the processes for determining clues involves judges' observations and defendants' confessions, even if those confessions are not presented before the court[52].

In the process of gathering evidence in a criminal trial, the evidence for criminal defamation should lead judges to believe that there is a valid defamatory expression that harms the plaintiff's reputation. Unfortunately, in many cases, the plaintiff's claim of defamatory expression is not properly cross-examined. Therefore, the case may not be discontinued, even though protecting free speech or civil society could be one of the reasons for the prosecutor to decline to impose an indictment.

While there are indeed opportunities and challenges in implementing the public interest defense, it should be feasible as long as Indonesian legislation adapts properly to the international human rights framework and implements it in the national legislation. However, its potential impact on the climate of free speech and the ideal conditions for the protection of such rights should also be considered in relation to human rights protection and democracy in Indonesia. The possible formulation of adequate protections for freedom of expression will be discussed in the next chapter. This next chapter, which is also the last chapter of this book, will conclude the findings that have been discussed throughout this book and propose recommendations for the protection of free speech in Indonesia.

Notes

1 See United Nations, Access to Justice, https://www.un.org/ruleoflaw/thematic-areas/access-to-justice-and-rule-of-law-institutions/access-to-justice/.

2 See Martinez-Fraga, P.J. and Reetz, R.C., 2015, *Public Purpose in International Law: Rethinking Regulatory Sovereignty in the Global Era.*

3 Alison Giest, 2017, *Interpreting Public Interest Provisions in International Investment Treaties*, Chicago Journal of International Law, Vol 18, No.1, 325.

4 Davids Marcus, 2015, *The Public Interest Class Action*, 104 Georgetown Law Journal, 6.

5 Davids Marcus, *The Public Interest Class Action, 7.*

6 Yusra Suedi & Justine Bendel, *Public Interest Litigation: A Pipe Dream or the Future of International Litigation*, in "*Public Interest Litigation in International Law*" 36 (Yusra Suedi & Justine Bendel eds., 2024).

7 For example, ICCPR stipulated that defamation laws should not stifle freedom of expression, in a matter of criticism of public interest should be viewed as a defense for defamation laws, which the laws should be in a reasonable limitation of rights, hence the encouragement of decriminalization of criminal defamation laws by the ICCPR. See more General Comment CCPR/C/GC/34 of Article 19 of the ICCPR.

8 Toby Mendel, 2010, *Restricting Freedom of Expression: Standards and Principles*, Centre for Law and Democracy (April 14, 2024) http://www.law-democracy.org/wp-content/uploads/2010/07/10.03.Paper-on-Restrictions-on-FOE.pdf.

9 Daniel Ospina Celis, 2023, *Transparency in the Spotlight: Global Case-law on Access to Public Information*, Global Freedom of Expression Columbia University, 8.

10 Pan Mohammad Faiz, 2016, *The Protection of Civil and Political Rights by The Constitutional Court of Indonesia*, Indonesian Law Review, Vol. 6, No. 2, 162.

11 Sayuti Una, *Freedom of Opinion Menurut Negara Hukum Indonesia [Freedom of Opinion According to Indonesian Legal System]*, 100 (2021).

12 Suparto, 2017, *Otonomi Daerah di Indonesia: Pengertian, Konsep, Tujuan, Prinsip dan Urgensinya [Regional Authonomy in Indonesia: Definition, Concept, Goal, Principle, and its Urgency]*, University Islam Riau, 7.
13 See Joan Barata and Andrei Richter, 2023, *Internet Shutdowns in International Law*, Global Freedom of Expression Columbia University.
14 Jakarta Administrative Court, 2019, Decision No. 230/G/TF/2019/PTUN.JKT (Indon.).
15 Engage Media, 2022, *How Internet Blackouts Violate the Digital Rights of Papuans*, Engage Media (July 5, 2024) https://engagemedia.org/2022/internet-blackouts-papua/.
16 SP3 is based on the Indonesian Criminal Procedure Act (KUHAP), Article 109 Section 2. The cessation of the legal process is due to several reasons: lack of evidence, the cases investigated was not a criminal case, for the sake of the law (loss of right to prosecute for instance). Another fact on SP3 is the letter consists of three processes (penyidikan, penyelidikan dan penuntutan). However, in several countries such as the US, "penyidikan" and "penyelidikan" is the same legal process called "investigation." These terms are distinguished in Indonesia as "penyidikan." It is a process to reveal that the case is criminal one and can be followed up into "penyelidikan" which is a process to gathering evidence and finding the suspect.
17 *Lex specialis* is a concept when there are two laws govern on the same factual situation, the law that governing specific subject matter overrides the general one.
18 Coconuts Jakarta, 2017, *#Achogaksalah: Indonesian Comedian named Defamation Suspect after Writing Complaint about Apartment Developers in Blog*, coconuts.id (November 30, 2021), https://coconuts.co/jakarta/lifestyle/achogaksalah-indonesian-comedian-named-defamation-suspect-writing-complaint-apartment-developers-blog/.
19 Jaring, 2021, *Perlindungan Konsumen Mentah di Jagat Maya [Raw Consumer Protection in Cyberspace]*, Jaring.id (November 30, 2021) https://semuabisakena.jaring.id/2021/06/11/perlindungan-konsumen-mentah-di-jagat-maya/.
20 Jaring, *Perlindungan Konsumen Mentah di Jagat Maya [Raw Consumer Protection in Cyberspace]*.
21 Banda Aceh First Degree Court, 2019, 432/Pid.Sus/2019/PN Bna (Indon).
22 By the time of this writing, only excerpt of this case, which will be discussed, in addition to some news stories covering the case. See more the Decision of Blitar Degree Court No. 15/PID.SUS/2019/PN BLT at the Indonesian Supreme Court Repository https://putusan3.mahkamahagung.go.id/direktori/putusan/zaed21f25b2b15528fcc313531333531.html.
23 Damar Juniarto, 2019, *Pemerintah Harus Lindungi Aktivis Anti Korupsi Mohammad Trijanto [Government Must Protect Anti-Corruption Activist Mohammad Trijanto]*, kumparan.com (August 6, 2024) https://kumparan.com/damar-juniarto/pemerintah-harus-lindungi-aktivis-antikorupsi-mohammad-trijanto-1qGtp0C4x0w/1.
24 Damar Juniarto, *Pemerintah Harus Lindungi Aktivis Anti Korupsi Mohammad Trijanto [Government Must Protect Anti-Corruption Activist Mohammad Trijanto]*.
25 Damar Juniarto, *Pemerintah Harus Lindungi Aktivis Anti Korupsi Mohammad Trijanto [Government Must Protect Anti-Corruption Activist Mohammad Trijanto]*.
26 Erliana Riady, 2019, *Penyebar Surat Palsu KPK Bebas, Polisi Kesulitan Ungkap Pelakunya [KPK Fake Letter Distributor Freed, Police Struggle to Identify Perpetrator]*, detik.com (August 6, 2024) https://news.detik.com/berita-jawa-timur/d-4629765/penyebar-surat-palsu-kpk-bebas-polisi-kesulitan-ungkap-pemalsunya.
27 Asmaul Chusna, 2018, *Bupati Blitar Rijanto Bantah Dipanggil KPK [Blitar Regent Rijanto Denies Being Summoned by KPK]*, antaranews.com (August 6, 2024) https://jatim.antaranews.com/berita/264812/bupati-blitar-rijanto-bantah-dipanggil-kpk.
28 Shinta Eka P, 2007, *Mahkamah Agung Hukum Nurdin Dua Tahun Penjara [Supreme Court Sentences Nurdin to Two Years in Prison]*, tempo.com (August 7, 2024) https://nasional.tempo.co/read/107594/mahkamah-agung-hukum-nurdin-halid-dua-tahun-penjara.

29 Zakki Amali, 2021, *Keputusan Bebas yang Menyisakan Takut [Free of Charge Decisions That Leave Fear]*, Jaring.ID (August 13, 2024) https://semuabisakena.jaring.id/2021/03/20/keputusan-bebas-yang-menyisakan-takut/.
30 Zakki Amali, *Keputusan Bebas yang Menyisakan Takut [Free of Charge Decisions That Leave Fear]*.
31 Makassar First Degree Court, 2014, Decision No. 390/PID.B/2014/PN.MKS (Indon.).
32 Anggara et.al, 2016, *Menimbang Ulang Pasal 27 Ayat (3) UU ITE dalam Putusan Pengadilan: Pertimbangan Putusan Pengadilan Terkait Penggunaan Pasal 27 (3) UU No. 11 Tahun 2008 tentang Informasi dan Transaksi Elektronik [Reconsidering Article 27 Paragraph (3) of the ITE Law in Court Decisions: Considerations of Court Decisions Regarding the Use of Article 27 (3) of Law No. 11 of 2008 concerning Electronic Information and Transactions]*, 20.
33 Zakki Amali, *Keputusan Bebas yang Menyisakan Takut [Free of Charge Decisions That Leave Fear]*.
34 See more First Degree Court of Cibinong No.139/Pid.B/2021/PN CBI.
35 Dian Rositawati et.al., *Protecting Expression: Criminal and Human Rights Law Analysis of Court Judgements in Indonesia*, 286 (2023).
36 Criminal Procedure Code Act [Crim. Pro. Code.], 1981, [Criminal Procedure Code Act] art. 14 (Indon.).
37 Kitab Undang-Undang Hukum Acara Pidana-KUHAP.
38 Criminal Procedure Code Act [Crim. Pro. Code.], 1981, [Criminal Procedure Code Act] art. 77 (Indon.).
39 WIRDJONO PRODJODIKORO, *HUKUM ATJARA PIDANA DI INDONESIA*, 17 (1962).
40 WIRDJONO PRODJODIKORO, *HUKUM ATJARA PIDANA DI INDONESIA*, 18.
41 Mahkamah Konstitusi [MK] [The Indonesian Constitutional Court] 2016, Decision No.29/PUU-XIV/2016 (Indon.).
42 ASH, 2016, *Begini Ahli KUHAP Maknai Seponering "Demi Kepentingan Umum [This is How Criminal Procedure Code Experts Interpret Seponering "For the Public Interest"]* HUKUMONLINE.COM (March 22, 2022) https://www.hukumonline.com/berita/a/begini-ahli-kuhap-maknai-iseponering-i-demi-kepentingan-umum-lt5731c8f006059.
43 The Indonesian Representatives Council.
44 The Indonesian Commision on Eradication Corruption.
45 Andi Hamzah, 28.
46 R. ATANG RANOEMIHARDJA, *HUKUM ACARA PIDANA: STUDI PERBANDINGAN ANTARA HUKUM ACARA PIDANA LAMA DENGAN HUKUM ACARA PIDANA BARU [CRIMINAL PROCEDURE LAW: A COMPARATIVE STUDY BETWEEN OLD CRIMINAL PROCEDURE LAW AND NEW CRIMINAL PROCEDURE LAW]*, 113 (1983).
47 CRIMINAL PROCEDURE CODE ACT [CRIM. PRO. CODE.], 1981, [CRIMINAL PROCEDURE CODE ACT] art. 183 (Indon.).
48 Criminal Procedure Code Act [Crim. Pro. Code.], 1981, [Criminal Procedure Code Act] art. 184 (Indon.).
49 Criminal Procedure Code Act [Crim. Pro. Code.], 1981, [Criminal Procedure Code Act] art. 185 sec. 6 (Indon.).
50 Criminal Procedure Code Act [Crim. Pro. Code.], 1981, [Criminal Procedure Code Act] art. 188 sec. 1 (Indon.).
51 Criminal Procedure Code Act [Crim. Pro. Code.], 1981, [Criminal Procedure Code Act] art. 188 sec. 3 (Indon.).
52 Rd. Achmad S. Soema Di Pradja, *Pokok-Pokok Hukum Acara Pidana Di Indonesia [Principles Of Criminal Procedure Law In Indonesia]*, 81 (1975).

Bibliography

Books

Anggara et.al, *Menimbang Ulang Pasal 27 Ayat (3) UU ITE dalam Putusan Pengadilan: Pertimbangan Putusan Pengadilan Terkait Penggunaan Pasal 27 (3) UU No. 11 Tahun 2008 tentang Informasi dan Transaksi Elektronik [Reconsidering Article 27 Paragraph (3) of the ITE Law in Court Decisions: Considerations of Court Decisions Regarding the Use of Article 27 (3) of Law No. 11 of 2008 concerning Electronic Information and Transactions]* (2016).

Martinez-Fraga, P.J. and Reetz, R.C., 2015, *Public Purpose in International Law: Rethinking Regulatory Sovereignty in the Global Era*, Cambridge University Press, Cambridge.

R. Atang Ranoemihardja, *Hukum Acara Pidana: Studi Perbandingan Antara Hukum Acara Pidana Lama Dengan Hukum Acara Pidana Baru [Criminal Procedure Law: A Comparative Study Between Old Criminal Procedure Law and New Criminal Procedure Law]* (1983).

RD. Achmad S. Soemadipradja, *Pokok-Pokok Hukum Acara Pidana Di Indonesia [Principles Of Criminal Procedure Law In Indonesia]* (1975).

Sayuti Una, *Freedom of Opinion Menurut Negara Hukum Indonesia [Freedom of Opinion According to Indonesian Legal System]* (2021)

Suparto, 2017, Otonomi Daerah di Indonesia: Pengertian, Konsep, Tujuan, Prinsip dan Urgensinya [Regional Authonomy in Indonesia: Definition, Concept, Goal, Principle, and its Urgency], University Islam Riau, 7.

Wirdjono Prodjodikoro, *Hukum Atjara Pidana Di Indonesia [Criminal Procedure in Indonesia]*, (1962).

Yusra Suedi & Justine Bendel, *Public Interest Litigation: A Pipe Dream or the Future of International Litigation, in "Public Interest Litigation in International Law"* (Yusra Suedi & Justine Bendel eds., 2024).

Journals

Alison Giest, 2017, *Interpreting Public Interest Provisions in International Investment Treaties, Chicago Journal of International Law*, Vol 18, No.1, 325.

Davids Marcus, 2015, The Public Interest Class Action, *104 Georgetown Law Journal*, 6.

Pan Mohammad Faiz, 2016, The Protection of Civil and Political Rights by The Constitutional Court of Indonesia, *Indonesian Law Review*, Vol. 6, No. 2, 162.

Indonesian Legislations

Criminal Procedure Code Act [Crim. Pro. Code.], 1981, [Criminal Procedure Code Act] (Indon.).

Indonesian Cases

Blitar First Degree Court, 2019, Decision No. 15/PID.SUS/2019/PN BLT (Indon.).

Banda Aceh First Degree Court, 2019, 432/Pid.Sus/2019/PN Bna (Indon).

Cibinong First Degree Court, 2021, No.139/Pid.B/2021/PN CBI (Indon.).

Jakarta Administrative Court, 2019, Decision No. 230/G/TF/2019/PTUN.JKT (Indon.).

Mahkamah Konstitusi [MK] [The Indonesian Constitutional Court] 2016, Decision No.29/PUU-XIV/2016 (Indon.).
Makassar First Degree Court, 2014, Decision No. 390/PID.B/2014/PN.MKS (Indon.).

Reports

Daniel Ospina Celis, 2023, *Transparency in the Spotlight: Global Case-law on Access to Public Information*, Global Freedom of Expression Columbia University.
Dian Rositawati et.al., *Protecting Expression: Criminal and Human Rights Law Analysis of Court Judgements in Indonesia* (2023).
Joan Barata and Andrei Richter, 2023, *Internet Shutdowns in International Law*, Global Freedom of Expression Columbia University.

Internet

ASH, 2016, Begini Ahli KUHAP Maknai Seponering "Demi Kepentingan Umum" [This is How Criminal Procedure Code Experts Interpret Seponering "For the Public Interest"] *hukumonline.com* (March 22, 2022) https://www.hukumonline.com/berita/a/begini-ahli-kuhap-maknai-iseponering-i-demi- kepentingan-umum-lt5731c8f006059.
Asmaul Chusna, 2018, Bupati Blitar Rijanto Bantah Dipanggil KPK [Blitar Regent Rijanto Denies Being Summoned by KPK], *antaranews.com* (August 6, 2024) https://jatim.antaranews.com/berita/264812/bupati-blitar-rijanto-bantah-dipanggil-kpk.
Coconuts Jakarta, 2017, #Achogaksalah: Indonesian Comedian named Defamation Suspect after Writing Complaint about Apartment Developers in Blog, *coconuts.id* (November 30, 2021), https://coconuts.co/jakarta/lifestyle/achogaksalah-indonesian-comedian-named-defamation-suspect-writing-complaint-apartment-developers-blog/.
Damar Juniarto, 2019, Pemerintah Harus Lindungi Aktivis Anti Korupsi Mohammad Trijanto [Government Must Protect Anti-Corruption Activist Mohammad Trijanto], *kumparan.com* (August 6, 2024) https://kumparan.com/damar-juniarto/pemerintah-harus-lindungi-aktivis-antikorupsi-mohammad-trijanto-1qGtp0C4x0w/1.
Engage Media, 2022, How Internet Blackouts Violate the Digital Rights of Papuans, *Engage Media* (July 5, 2024) https://engagemedia.org/2022/internet-blackouts-papua/.
Erliana Riady, 2019, Penyebar Surat Palsu KPK Bebas, Polisi Kesulitan Ungkap Pelakunya [KPK Fake Letter Distributor Freed, Police Struggle to Identify Perpetrator], *detik.com* (August 6, 2024) https://news.detik.com/berita-jawa-timur/d-4629765/penyebar-surat-palsu-kpk-bebas-polisi-kesulitan-ungkap-pemalsunya.
Jaring, 2021, Perlindungan Konsumen Mentah di Jagat Maya [Raw Consumer Protection in Cyberspace], *Jaring.id* (November 30, 2021) https://semuabisakena.jaring.id/2021/06/11/perlindungan-konsumen-mentah-di-jagat-maya/.
Shinta Eka P, 2007, Mahkamah Agung Hukum Nurdin Dua Tahun Penjara [Supreme Court Sentences Nurdin to Two Years in Prison], *tempo.com* (August 7, 2024) https://nasional.tempo.co/read/107594/mahkamah-agung-hukum-nurdin-halid-dua-tahun-penjara.
Toby Mendel, 2010, Restricting Freedom of Expression: Standards and Principles, *Centre for Law and Democracy* (April 14, 2024) http://www.law-democracy.org/wp-content/uploads/2010/07/10.03.Paper-on-Restrictions-on-FOE.pdf.
United Nations, (n.d.) Access to Justice, (August 1, 2024) https://www.un.org/ruleoflaw/thematic-areas/access-to-justice-and-rule-of-law-institutions/access-to-justice/.
Zakki Amali, 2021, Keputusan Bebas yang Menyisakan Takut [Free of Charge Decisions That Leave Fear], *Jaring.ID* (August 13, 2024) https://semuabisakena.jaring.id/2021/03/20/keputusan-bebas-yang-menyisakan-takut/.

6 Conclusion

6.1 Summary of Key Findings

6.1.1 The Laws

Despite the existence of various legislations protecting human rights in Indonesia, particularly the right to expression, such as the Indonesian Constitution of 1945, the Freedom of Expression in Public Law of 1998, the Human Rights Law of 1999, and the Press Law of 1999, there have been concerns about the implementation of these laws.

For example, the Freedom of Expression in Public Law of 1998 was indeed an "oasis" as a law that was passed after the 1998 political reformation. It not only guaranteed that public protests are a valid and legal form of expression but also encouraged the formation of political parties[1], resulting in 48 political parties that represented various spectra of political ideologies competing in the 1999 election, whereas for decades there had been only three political parties in the election: *Golongan Karya* (Golkar), *Partai Demokrasi Indonesia* (PDI), and *Partai Persatuan Pembangunan* (PPP).

However, after being in effect for more than 20 years, the law became "toothless" and backfired on the people, as it has not sufficiently protected the right to express and the right to assembly for Indonesians. Recently, the issues of strict limitations on freedom of expression and freedom of assembly were highlighted by the forced dissolution of Labour Day protests during the pandemic[2] and the forced dissolution of academic discussions[3]. In both instances, the authorities reasoned that the events were held without any prior permission. Moreover, the Indonesian National Human Rights Commission (*Komisi Nasional Hak Asasi Manusia*-KOMNAS HAM) reported that from 2020 to 2021, there was a 52% violation of the right to expression in digital space, which consisted of public online expression (17%), online academic discussions (10%), and witness processes before the court that were delivered online (2%)[4].

In addition to the "toothless" and backfire laws, such as the 1998 Law on Freedom of Expression in Public, violations of the right to expression have primarily occurred because the 1998 law, along with other laws mentioned

DOI: 10.4324/9781032661544-6

earlier, has not been properly considered in cases related to limitations on freedom of expression. The draconian laws of the Indonesian Criminal Code and the ITE Law have posed problems in implementing limitations on hate speech and defamation.

The discussion of hate speech and defamation cases in Chapter 3 also emphasizes that Indonesia lacks clear standards on several elements related to the limitation of free speech. Several elements of the provisions in the Criminal Code and the ITE Law are discussed in the following points.

First, the **plaintiff should not be a legal entity**, as under Indonesian law, only an individual can experience offensive feelings. However, legal entities, while incapable of such feelings, are still considered to have reputations that can be damaged. Cases such as Prita Mulyasari and Saiful Mahdi show how legal entities, like a hospital and a university, have been able to file reports as plaintiffs in defamation cases, despite the fact that legal entities, unlike individuals, cannot experience offensive feelings.

Second, there are **unclear elements in the acts defined under the laws**. Even though the Indonesian Constitutional Court has ruled that Article 27 Section 3 is the extensive ruling for online defamation based on the ITE Law's amendment in 2016, the actions "to distribute," "to transmit," and "cause to be accessible" should rely on the rulings for offline defamation found in Articles 310 and 311 of the Criminal Code. However, a weakness in this ruling is that if "to transmit" means sending electronic information from one party to another, it does not meet the element of "in the public eye" specified in Article 310[5]. Unless it refers to the transmission of electronic information in cyberspace, which is considered "in the public eye," the action "to transmit" remains misaligned with the rulings in the Criminal Code Act. Additionally, the latest amendment of the ITE Law in 2024 was not helpful, as it still contains criminal provisions and fails to provide a clear distinction between protected and unprotected expressions.

The provision regarding hate speech also has a similar problem as neither the Criminal Code nor the ITE Law clearly defines when hate speech constitutes an actionable crime. This ambiguity arises from the classification of hate speech as either a *materiil* criminal offense (where the effects of hate speech must occur) or a *formil* criminal offense (where the conduct has been committed, even if the effects of hate speech have not occurred).

Furthermore, criminal punishment is still regulated under both the Criminal Code and the ITE Law. Although the provisions of the ITE Law will be revoked in 2026, once the 2023 Criminal Code officially enters into force, it could lead to overcriminalization within the Criminal Code, given that its provisions have been criticized for potentially violating human rights.

Third, there is **a lack of definition and scope regarding the public interest in Indonesia**. Freedom of expression, like other human rights, has limitations. These limitations should respect the elements of legality, legitimacy, and necessity. In terms of the legitimacy test, it should be carefully examined with a significant focus on balancing the restriction against the public interest.

Unfortunately, public interest has not been properly defined in various pieces of legislation. This not only makes the scope of freedom of expression have no border, leading to unnecessary trials, but also creates problems during the investigation and prosecution process. This includes how public prosecutors interpret whether the expression under trial falls into the category of protected or unprotected expression.

Furthermore, unlike the framework of international human rights, there is a lack of limitations on freedom of expression, such as those concerning public health and public morals. This not only makes the boundaries of cases related to freedom of expression blurred and unclear but also, for some reason, enables improper prosecutions.

6.1.2 The Law Enforcers

First, **there is retaliation nuance in hate speech and defamation cases**. The long debate on whether the offense is taken or given still persists, especially in how plaintiffs report alleged hate speech and defamation to the police. However, examining many cases that have occurred in Indonesia, particularly those discussed throughout the book, it is ironic that hate speech and defamation are often regarded as offenses rather than given based on the defendant's intentions. Even though legal provisions state that the burden of proof for defamation lies with the plaintiff, this often overlooks the roles of the prosecutor and even the judges during the court trial.

Second, **there is an implementation problem with the Opportunity Principle**. Ideally, the Principle could help solve the problem of over-prosecution and overcriminalization in cases related to limitations on freedom of expression. However, current legislation regarding the Principle states that it can only be implemented by the Indonesian Attorney General after obtaining input from the relevant state agencies.

Regarding the implementation of the Opportunity Principle, the discontinuation of a case for public interest can only occur during the cassation legislation process, which is submitted by the Attorney General and ruled upon by the Supreme Court can occur. This makes the implementation of the Principle very complicated. In many countries, the Opportunity Principle has evolved to be based not only on public interest but also on discretion[6], allowing public prosecutors at lower levels of the Office of the Prosecutor to apply it. However, the Indonesian legal system has not enabled this, despite the fact that the basic principles of the litigation process should be simple, quick, and affordable under the Law on Judicial Power,[7] and that discretion is possible as stipulated by the Indonesian Criminal Procedure Code[8].

Third, **unnecessary prosecutions stem from the unclear public interest definition**. Building on the discussion in the previous section regarding the lack of a precise definition of public interest, improper and unnecessary prosecutions can occur because of the broad definitions of state, national, and societal interest, the specifics of which remain unclear. These unnecessary prosecutions are evident in various cases where law enforcers, such as the police and prosecutors, continue to pursue cases without assessing whether the alleged conduct constitutes an actionable crime.

Such cases are exemplified by the prosecution of Baiq Nuril, a female teacher who, in 2019, was prosecuted for sharing her employer's harassment call[9]. Although her case was eventually dismissed, she faced an online pornography charge under Article 27 Section 1. In 2016, Febi Nur Amelia was also subjected to a defamation trial under Article 27 Section 3 of the ITE Law[10] simply because she posted that a woman named Fitriani Manurung owed her 70 million Rupiahs[11]. Another example occurred in 2024 when Meila Nurul Fajriah, a public attorney in Yogyakarta, was charged with online defamation under the ITE Law for advocating on behalf of 30 victims of alleged sexual harassment by a student at Universitas Islam Indonesia[12]. In the last two cases, the individuals were eventually cleared of criminal charges, as the court ruled that Febi Nur Amelia was not guilty, and the Yogyakarta Police halted the investigation into Meila's case. However, the initiation of these litigation processes shows a lack of consideration for the greater interests at stake in such cases, especially regarding human rights and, in particular, freedom of expression.

6.2 Implications for the Future of Free Speech in Indonesia

Given the aforementioned problems related to law and legal enforcers, what does this mean for free speech in Indonesia? Several indexes on freedom of expression released in recent years depict a low rate of the right to express oneself in Indonesia. While the methodologies and the elements of these indexes vary, such as the Freedom House index, which uses political rights and civil liberties to rate the whole index of freedom of a country, and Reporters Without Borders, which assesses freedom of the press as one dimension of freedom of expression, all of these indexes agree that freedom of expression in Indonesia lacks of robust protection. Through its democratic system, Indonesia continues to hold elections for President and Representatives. However, there are growing concerns about the juxtaposition of citizens expressing their political views while being restricted by draconian government laws or facing abuse and harassment from opposing groups, which can lead to potential criminal conduct. Even more troubling is the rise of political dynasties, which, ironically, have emerged since the fall of Suharto's regime in 1998[13].

Against this backdrop, the protection of human rights and democracy in Indonesia continues to face challenges. The recent Presidential Election in 2024 resulted in the election of Prabowo Subianto, who has been criticized for human rights violations[14]. Additionally, his elected Vice President, Gibran Rakabuming Raka, has also come under criticism for his candidacy, which reflects the establishment of a political dynasty.

In particular, with regard to freedom of expression, the current draconian laws that have been attempted to amend but have failed make it difficult to foresee any significant changes. The elected President and Vice President have been voicing "continuity" during the campaign and after the 2024 Election, which suggests that the focus of the new administration may not be on human rights, as was the case during Jokowi's 10-year presidency[15]. In addition, the new President has a poor human rights record and may continue the authoritarian methods of governance[16].

It is not that citizens and civil society never fight back. Various studies referred to or cited throughout this book have also highlighted the problems with free speech, which emphasizes how the current legislation instills fear in people when expressing their opinions, especially those opposing government policies[17]. This is ironic, given that Indonesia is one of the largest democratic countries in the world[18].

The provisions of the ITE Law, particularly those related to defamation and hate speech, have been called draconian given their "rubber provisions," which are often flexible in protecting the interests of the rich and powerful. These provisions, according to the 2023 Criminal Code, will be revoked once the new Criminal Code comes into force. However, Article 622 Section 4 of the 2023 Criminal Code only refers to provisions in the 2008 and 2016 Laws, as the new Criminal Code was passed a year before the amendment of the 2024 ITE Law. Therefore, even though the 2024 ITE Law contains similar provisions and does not change the criminal provisions for the limitation of freedom of expression, it remains unclear how the 2024 ITE Law will coexist with the 2023 Criminal Code regarding these limitations.

Therefore, the potential overlap of laws would worsen and become an even greater challenge to the protection of free speech in Indonesia. The ITE Law remains a draconian law for online expression, but with the new Criminal Code, officially implemented in 2026, it could lead to a human rights catastrophe[19].

6.3 How Should Free Speech in Indonesia Go Forward?

Within its six chapters, the book explores the current state of free speech in Indonesia and its legislation, which, unfortunately, does not depict many positive examples of the implementation of free speech protection in practice. While Article 1 Section 2 of the Indonesian Constitution states that sovereignty rests with the people, which is the main element of democracy, the various discussions and case studies throughout this book demonstrate that the Indonesian government has failed to fulfil the mandate of the Constitution.

Contrary to the negative situation regarding free speech in Indonesia, there have been positive developments. For example, the Institute for Criminal Justice Reform (ICJR) recorded at least eight landmark cases of online defamation (up to 2016), which included sound reasoning by the courts[20]. In one case, the Bantul Court ruled that the defendant was not the direct party affected by defamation[21], while the Raba Bima Court reasoned that defamation claims should specifically mention the name of the person who feels defamed[22]. Furthermore, the Court's decisions declaring the defendants not guilty in the cases of Prita Mulyasari, Daniel Tangkilisan and Haris and Fatia are also encouraging signs for future implementation of the law, despite the uncessary long process that have been discussed in the previous chapters of this book.

However, the systemic problem requires a systemic solution. The law on free speech needs to be totally amended, given that the rulings mentioned above still involve a lengthy litigation process. Haris and Fatia were on trial for about two years before the Court decided they were not guilty, while Prita had to file a certiorari so that the Indonesian Supreme Court could review her case and ultimately ruled that she was not guilty. Therefore, given that the implementation is not robust and "negatively flexible" in favor of the interests of the rich and powerful, significant changes must be made to the legislation related to free speech limitations.

Revoking the criminal defamation provisions should be a main priority, but given that many attempts at judicial review through the Indonesian Constitutional Court have failed, another possible effort to amend the law may arise when the new Criminal Code Act, which consists of criminal provisions for both offline and online expressions, comes into force in 2026. Moreover, legislative changes remain a main priority in overcoming the challenges of declining free speech protections. In addition, despite a few positive rulings mentioned earlier, the implementation of the law still faces challenges, particularly regarding the advancement of the capability of law enforcers, especially judges, who need to refer to existing jurisprudence as one of the main sources of law in the Indonesian legal system.

Another necessary change is related to public interest litigation. Currently, the scope of public interest litigation is still too broad, covering state, national, and societal interests without any further explanation. Its definition remains overly broad and is not aligned with the international human rights framework. Changes should be made by amending the Prosecutor Law to extend the authority for case dismissal, as stipulated in the law and also known as the Opportunity Principle, not exclusively to the Attorney General but also to public prosecutors at lower levels. Additionally, given that the provision has already undergone juridical review and the Constitutional Court agreed that the criteria for case dismissal should be clearly defined[23], there is an opportunity to file another judicial review following the latest amendment in 2021 to the Prosecutor Law. Ideally, this would result in the mandate from the Constitutional Court to the government to establish a narrow and precise scope of public interest and to revise the authority over case dismissals held by public prosecutors.

More importantly, with any future political will from lawmakers, all proposed changes should carefully consider and assess the international human rights framework on freedom of expression. For example, these changes should refer to the ICCPR and its latest General Comment on Articles 19 and 20, as well as the Rabat Plan of Action, which ideally would contribute to more robust laws on free speech and the proper formulation of its limitations. Additionally, the Indonesian National Human Rights Commission has already issued Standard Norms and Regulation Number 5 on the Rights to Opinion and Expression, which also refer to international human rights laws. This standard could serve as a guideline for lawmakers when formulating laws and for law enforcers when implementing them, forming part of an advanced capacity-building effort for all stakeholders in the Indonesian legal system. By taking significant actions on both the substance of the law and the legal system, stronger protections for free speech in Indonesia can be attained, and a truly democratic Indonesia can finally be achieved.

Notes

1 M. Fazil Pamungkas, 2019, *Warisan Habibie untuk Indonesia [Habibie's Legacy for Indonesia]*, historia.or.id (August 14, 2024) https://historia.id/politik/articles/warisan-habibie-untuk-indonesia-vqmxr/page/5.

2 CNN Indonesia, 2021, *Penangkapan Massa Aksi, Arogansi Polisi Beralih Pandemi [Arrest of Protesters, Police Arrogance Turns to Pandemic]*, CNN Indonesia (August 14, 2024) https://www.cnnindonesia.com/nasional/20210505113833-12-638792/penangkapan-massa-aksi-arogansi-polisi-berdalih-pandemi.

3 Ayu Mumpuni, 2024, *Polisi: Diskusi People's Water Forum yang Dibubarkan tak Berizin [Police: Disbanded People's Water Forum Discussion Was Unauthorized]*, tirto.id (August 14, 2024) https://tirto.id/polisi-diskusi-peoples-water-forum-yang-dibubarkan-tak-berizin-gYRE.

4 Kabar Latuharhary, 2022, *KOMNAS HAM: Pelanggaran Bereskpresi dan Berpendapat Terjadi di Ruang Digital [KOMNAS HAM: Violations of Expression and Opinion Occur in Digital Space]*, komnasham.go.id (August 14, 2024) https://www.komnasham.go.id/index.php/news/2022/1/17/2065/komnas-ham-pelanggaran-kebebasan-berekspresi-dan-berpendapat-terjadi-di-ruang-digital.html..

5 Josua Sitompul, *Cyberspace*, 183.

6 Andi Hamzah, 17.

7 Indonesian Act, 2009, (Indonesia), Judicial Power Act, Art. 1 (Indon.).

8 Criminal Procedure Code Act [Crim. Pro. Code.], 1981, [Criminal Procedure Code Act] art. 139 sec. 1 (Indon.).

9 Silvano Hajid, Oki Budh, and Lara Owen, 2019, *Baiq Nuril: The Indonesian Woman Jailed for Sharing Boss's 'Harrasment' Calls*, BBC, (August 19, 2024) https://www.bbc.com/news/world-asia-pacific-48935981.

10 Apriadi Gunawan, 2020, *She Asked a Policeman's Wife to Repay is now Charged with Defamation*, The Jakarta Post (January 8, 2020), https://www.thejakartapost.com/news/2020/01/08/she-asked-a-policemans-wife-to-repay-debt-through-instagram-she-is-now-charged-with-defamation.html.

11 Equal to 4,793 U.S. dollars.

12 YLBHI, 2024, *Siaran Pers: Kriminalisasi Pendamping Korban Kekerasan Seksual, Meila (Pengacara YLBHI) "Serangan Serius terhadap Perempuan Pembela HAM serta Pendamping Korban dan upaya sistematis Polda DIY melindungi terduga Pelaku Kekerasan Seksual" [Press Release: Criminalization of Sexual Violence Victim Companions, Meila (YLBHI Lawyer) "Serious Attacks on Women Human Rights Defenders and Victim Companions and the Systematic Efforts of the DIY Regional Police to Protect Suspected Perpetrators of Sexual Violence"]*, ylbhi.or.id (August 19, 2024) https://ylbhi.or.id/informasi/siaran-pers/kriminalisasi-pendamping-korban-kasus-kekerasan-seksual-meila-pengacara-ylbhi/.

13 See more Yoes C Kenawas, 2023, *The Irony of Indonesia's Democracy: The Rise of Dynastic Politics in the Post-Suharto Era, Asian Journal of Comparative Politics*, Volume 8, Issue 3.

14 Victoria Milko, 2024, *Who is Prabowo Subianto, The Former General Who's Indonesia's Next President?*, AP News (August 19, 2024) https://apnews.com/article/prabowo-subianto-indonesia-election-general-dfd2cf2d8f25629d3f2dcb96fa7621a7.

15 Human Rights Watch, 2024, *Indonesia: Jokowi's Term Ends With A Whimper on Rights*, hrw.org (August 202, 2024) https://www.hrw.org/news/2024/01/11/indonesia-jokowis-term-ends-whimper-rights.
16 Hurriyah, 2024, *The Implications for Indonesian Democracy After Prabowo's 2024 Win*, Reset Doc (August 21, 2024) https://www.resetdoc.org/story/prabowos-victory-2024-elections-mean-indonesian-democracy/.
17 Rizki Fachriansyah, 2020, *Growing Fear of Speaking Out: Survey Finds Indonesia's Civil Liberties Under Threat*, the Jakarta Post (August 20, 2024) https://www.thejakartapost.com/news/2020/10/26/growing-fear-of-speaking-out-survey-finds-indonesias-civil-liberties-under-threat.html.
18 Tim Mann, 2024, *Indonesia is One of The World's Largest Democracies, but it's Weaponising Defamation Laws to Smother Dissent*, The Conversation (August 20, 2024) https://theconversation.com/indonesia-is-one-of-the-worlds-largest-democracies-but-its-weaponising-defamation-laws-to-smother-dissent-220651.
19 Human Rights Watch, 2022, *Indonesia: KUHP Baru Petaka Bagi Hak Asasi Manusia [Indonesia: New Criminal Code a Disaster for Human Rights]*, hrw.org (August 20, 2024) https://www.hrw.org/id/news/2022/12/08/indonesia-new-criminal-code-disastrous-rights.
20 NNP, 2016, *Putusan Pengadilan 'Landmark' Terkait Penggunaan Pasal 27 Ayat (3) UU ITE ['Landmark' Court Decision Regarding Use of Article 27 Paragraph (3) of the ITE Law]*, hukumonline.com (August 20, 2024) https://www.hukumonline.com/berita/a/putusan-pengadilan-landmark-terkait-penggunaan-pasal-27-ayat-3-uu-ite-lt56c0082ac70f1.
21 *See* the First Degree Court of Bantul Decision No. 196/Pid.Sus/2014/PN.BTL.
22 *See* the First Degree Court of Bima Decision No. 292/Pid.B/2014/PN.Rbi.
23 *See more* the Indonesian Constitutional Court Decision No. 29/PUU-XIV/2016. The Court partially granted the plaintiff's submission on the judicial review that the sole authority of the Indonesian Attorney General on case dismissal (*seponering*) was problematic, and the public interest definition is not defined in exact language.

Bibliography

Books

Josua Sitompul, *Cyberspace, Cybercrimes, Cyberlaw: Tinjauan Aspek Hukum Pidana [Cyberspace, Cybercrimes, Cyberlaw: A Review of Criminal Law Aspects]* (2012).

Journals

Yoes C Kenawas, 2023, The Irony of Indonesia's Democracy: The Rise of Dynastic Politics in the Post-Suharto Era, *Asian Journal of Comparative Politics*, Volume 8, Issue 3.

Indonesian Legislations

Criminal Procedure Code Act [Crim. Pro. Code.], 1981b, [Criminal Procedure Code Act] (Indon.).
Indonesian Act, 2009, (Indonesia), Judicial Power Act (Indon.).

Indonesian Cases

Bantul First Degree Court, 2014, Decision No. 196/Pid.Sus/2014/PN.BTL (Indon.).
Bima First Degree Court, 2014, Decision No. 292/Pid.B/2014/PN.Rbi (Indon.).

Reports

Freedom House, 2024, *Indonesia: Freedom in the World 2024 Country Report*, Freedom House (August 20, 2024) https://freedomhouse.org/country/indonesia/freedom-world/2024.

Reporters Without Borders, 2024, *Index 2024: Asia Pacific-Indonesia*, rsf.org (August 20, 2024) https://rsf.org/en/country/indonesia.

Svend-Erik Skaaning and Suthan Suthan Krishnarajan, 2021, *Who Cares About Free Speech*, futurefreespeech.org.

Internet

Apriadi Gunawan, 2020, She Asked a Policeman's Wife to Repay is now Charged with Defamation, *The Jakarta Post* (January 8, 2020), https://www.thejakartapost.com/news/2020/01/08/she-asked-a-policemans-wife-to-repay-debt-through-instagram-she-is-now-charged-with-defamation.html.

Ayu Mumpuni, 2024, Polisi: Diskusi People's Water Forum yang Dibubarkan tak Berizin [Police: Disbanded People's Water Forum Discussion Was Unauthorized], *tirto.id* (August 14, 2024) https://tirto.id/polisi-diskusi-peoples-water-forum-yang-dibubarkan-tak-berizin-gYRE.

CNN Indonesia, 2021, *Penangkapan Massa Aksi, Arogansi Polisi Beralih Pandemi [Arrest of Protesters, Police Arrogance Turns to Pandemic]*, CNN Indonesia (August 14, 2024) https://www.cnnindonesia.com/nasional/20210505113833-12-638792/penangkapan-massa-aksi-arogansi-polisi-berdalih-pandemi.

Human Rights Watch, 2022, Indonesia: KUHP Baru Petaka Bagi Hak Asasi Manusia [Indonesia: New Criminal Code a Disaster for Human Rights], *hrw.org* (August 20, 2024) https://www.hrw.org/id/news/2022/12/08/indonesia-new-criminal-code-disastrous-rights.

Human Rights Watch, 2024, Indonesia: Jokowi's Term Ends With A Whimper on Rights, *hrw.org* (August 202, 2024) https://www.hrw.org/news/2024/01/11/indonesia-jokowis-term-ends-whimper-rights.

Hurriyah, 2024, The Implications for Indonesian Democracy After Prabowo's 2024 Win, *Reset Doc* (August 21, 2024) https://www.resetdoc.org/story/prabowos-victory-2024-elections-mean-indonesian-democracy/.

Kabar Latuharhary, 2022, KOMNAS HAM: Pelanggaran Bereskpresi dan Berpendapat Terjadi di Ruang Digital [KOMNAS HAM: Violations of Expression and Opinion Occur in Digital Space], *komnasham.go.id* (August 14, 2024) https://www.komnasham.go.id/index.php/news/2022/1/17/2065/komnas-ham-pelanggaran-kebebasan-berekspresi-dan-berpendapat-terjadi-di-ruang-digital.html.

M. Fazil Pamungkas, 2019, Warisan Habibie untuk Indonesia [Habibie's Legacy for Indonesia], *historia.or.id* (August 14, 2024) https://historia.id/politik/articles/warisan-habibie-untuk-indonesia-vqmxr/page/5.

NNP, 2016, Putusan Pengadilan 'Landmark' Terkait Penggunaan Pasal 27 Ayat (3) UU ITE ['Landmark' Court Decision Regarding Use of Article 27 Paragraph (3) of the ITE Law], *hukumonline.com* (August 20, 2024) https://www.hukumonline.com/berita/a/putusan-pengadilan-landmark-terkait-penggunaan-pasal-27-ayat-3-uu-ite-lt56c0082ac70f1.

Rizki Fachriansyah, 2020, Growing Fear of Speaking Out: Survey Finds Indonesia's Civil Liberties Under Threat, *the Jakarta Post* (August 20, 2024) https://www.

thejakartapost.com/news/2020/10/26/growing-fear-of-speaking-out-survey-finds-indonesias-civil-liberties-under-threat.html.

Silvano Hajid, Oki Budh, and Lara Owen, 2019, Baiq Nuril: The Indonesian Woman Jailed for Sharing Boss's 'Harrasment' Calls, *BBC*, (August 19, 2024) https://www.bbc.com/news/world-asia-pacific-48935981.

Tim Mann, 2024, Indonesia is One of The World's Largest Democracies, but it's Weaponising Defamation Laws to Smother Dissent, *The Conversation* (August 20, 2024) https://theconversation.com/indonesia-is-one-of-the-worlds-largest-democracies-but-its-weaponising-defamation-laws-to-smother-dissent-220651.

Victoria Milko, 2024, Who is Prabowo Subianto, The Former General Who's Indonesia's Next President?, *AP News* (August 19, 2024) https://apnews.com/article/prabowo-subianto-indonesia-election-general-dfd2cf2d8f25629d3f2dcb96fa7621a7.

YLBHI, 2024, *Siaran Pers: Kriminalisasi Pendamping Korban Kekerasan Seksual, Meila (Pengacara YLBHI) "Serangan Serius terhadap Perempuan Pembela HAM serta Pendamping Korban dan upaya sistematis Polda DIY melindungi terduga Pelaku Kekerasan Seksual"[Press Release: Criminalization of Sexual Violence Victim Companions, Meila (YLBHI Lawyer) "Serious Attacks on Women Human Rights Defenders and Victim Companions and the Systematic Efforts of the DIY Regional Police to Protect Suspected Perpetrators of Sexual Violence"], ylbhi.or.id* (August 19, 2024) https://ylbhi.or.id/informasi/siaran-pers/kriminalisasi-pendamping-korban-kasus-kekerasan-seksual-meila-pengacara-ylbhi/.

Index

Pages in **bold** refer to tables

Kolibri 360 GmbH
Ferdinand-Jühlke-Straße 7
99095 Erfurt, Deutschland
produktsicherheit@kolibri360.de